STAYING SMALL
SUCCESSFULLY

STAYING SMALL SUCCESSFULLY

A Guide for Architects, Engineers, and Design Professionals

FRANK A. STASIOWSKI

A Wiley-Interscience Publication

JOHN WILEY & SONS, INC.

New York / Chichester / Brisbane / Toronto / Singapore

Copyright ©1991 by John Wiley & Sons, Inc.

All rights reserved. Published simultaneously in Canada.

Reproduction or translation of any part of this work
beyond that permitted by Section 107 or 108 of the
1976 United States Copyright Act without the permission
of the copyright owner is unlawful. Requests for
permission or further information should be addressed to
the Permissions Department, John Wiley & Sons, Inc.

Library of Congress Cataloging in Publication Data:

Stasiowski, Frank, 1948-
    Staying small successfully : a guide for architects, engineers, and other
design professionals / Frank A. Stasiowski.
        p.   cm.
    "A Wiley-Interscience publication."
    Includes index.
    1. Architectural services marketing—United States.
    2. Engineering services marketing—Untited States. 3. Design
services—United States—Marketing. I. Title.
    NA1996.S75   1991
    720' .68—dc20
    ISBN 0-471-50652-4   90-29887
                                                                      CIP

Printed in the United States of America

10 9 8 7 6 5 4 3 2

To all the entrepreneurs who have tried and failed:
Don't give up after one failure—read this book
then try again

CONTENTS

Foreword   **xi**
Acknowledgments   **xv**

Introduction   **1**

  Break from Tradition   1
  Control of Your Destiny   2
  Success is What You Want It To Be   2
  You Are Only As Small As You Think   3
  Being Different Means Being Visible   4

1. Planning and Strategy   **5**

  The Need For Vision   6
  Defining a Vision   8
  The Concise Written Vision   12
  Elements of a Plan   13
  Conducting a Planning Meeting   49
  Repeat the Process Periodically   53
  Success Challenges   54

2. Focusing Your Practice   **61**

  Advantages of Focusing the Practice   62
  Steps to Focusing   63
  Summary   99
  Success Challenges   99

3. Servicing the Client   **103**

  Service Versus Design   106
  Little Things That Count Big   106
  Responsiveness   110
  Quality Control   111
  Innovate Even Normal Activities   126
  Success Challenges   134

4. Personnel Hiring   137

Controlling Your Ego   139
How to Attract Top People   139
Develop Top Performers from Within   140
Announce Positions Within   143
Delegate   144
Probation Period   149
Fire Incompetents   149
Employee Contracts   150
Summary   151
Success Challenges   153

5. Compensation   157

Motivating Design Professionals   157
Benefits   160
Factors Affecting Employee Turnover   162
Timing Pay Raises   164
Incentive Compensation   166
Career Tracking   170
Create an Atmosphere of Achievement   171
Summary   174
Success Challenges   175

6. Managing the Bottom Line   177

Simplified Financial Planning   179
Budgeting   180
Key Financial Measures   185
Profit is Everything   197
No-paper Reporting   206
Sharing Financial Information   208
Summary   208
Success Challenges   209

7. Do's and Don'ts of Success   211

Do's   212
Don'ts   224
Summary   235
Success Challenges   236

8. Growth   239

Growing Too Fast   239
When To Grow   239
Ways To Grow   240
Growth Rate   240
Defining Your Growth   241

Stages of Growth 241

Benefits of Small Firms 243

Summary 244

Success Challenges 244

9. The Psychology of Winning 247

Ownership Transition 249

Competing with Your Peers 249

A Final Word 250

Success Challenges 251

**APPENDIX A. Management and Marketing
Consultant List** 253

APPENDIX B. Sample Marketing Plan 273

APPENDIX C. Seminar Attendee Statistics 279

Index 285

FOREWORD

The design profession is renowned for spawning entrepreneurs with visions of greatness. Of the hundreds of small design firms appearing each month, many are destined to flounder; the chances of overcoming all of the obstacles in the way of success are slim. The goal of today's young design professional is very often to open a small firm, or at least to become a partner in one. The question is how to do this profitably and provide excellent service to a wide array of client types.

This book provides a hands-on resource for setting up and/or improving a small business. It is a practical approach—not a theoretical one—to guiding the small firm to *success*. In Chapter 6, for example, a financial plan is presented to easily guide your firm and monitor its success. Key financial measures are given, by which you can manage your firm at a glance, on a one-page sheet. Easy market research is explained: How can you be successful unless you know you market? The author, Frank Stasiowski, uses his know-how and his contact with more than 5000 design professionals each year of his 20 years of consulting practice, to bring you an easy-to-use formula to get to know your market. Checklists, flow charts, and highly readable text give you easy access to Stasiowski's ideas.

Theories are presented in the context of real firm examples. Matarazzo Design (10 staff members), Meehan Architects (4 staff members), and Toby Nadel Architects (1 architect, 1 clerical person) are some outstanding examples of firms that have learned that success does not necessarily mean growth. But, in fact it is staying small that enables tight control over their firm's financial picture, their marketing efforts, and their staff needs. Even larger firms who practice in a small-firm (studio division) ethic maintain a small-firm benefit (closeness to the client).

Hiring smarter people than yourself, as suggested by billionaire Nelson D. Rockefeller, is perhaps the best advice you can take in hiring personnel for a small firm. Each person you hire must have something exceptional to offer—or don't hire them. Stasiowski echoes Rockefeller's great advice, and puts it into practical terms you can apply to your office activities. Stasiowski's endorsement of the focus on a niche theory gives reason to stop and think about how many hands you have in how many pots, and to consider whether you wouldn't do better to sell one or two items of service. Honing your work by doing the same kind of project over and over is the surest and easiest way to obtain higher and higher profit margins each year. You could then take on other markets or services if you decide growth or diversity is a factor of business.

Finally, it's all in the attitude toward your business, your clients, and your staff that will make or break your small firm, whether you have a fledgling firm or one that's been around for years, had a recent change of hands, or is floundering and blaming "the recession." There is always going to be some excuse for failure until you stop taking a look at what you shouldn't do and start taking action by cutting out the extras. Extra people, extra expenses can weigh you down and eat up profits. Chapter 7, "The Do's and Don'ts of Success" clearly draws the lines. The importance of making choices cannot be stressed enough. Above all, don't flounder in indecision. "The Psychology of Winning" in Chapter 9, has more to do with making choices as to what kind of firm you want to be, than it does with doing time on an analyst's, or an accountant's, couch.

In my years as a design professional:

I had to perform mainly a hands-on management and business degree because in my training as an architect, there was absolutely no training or testing ground. Consequently, I still go through a trial-and-error (learning experience) process, but the latter items are approaching a single digit number more and more as the years pass.

I also found it difficult to have fellow professionals share their experiences and secrets.

I had to practice for others. Even my first practice was a building experience with both a negative and a positive side. In my current practice, the positive experiences are such that our "service" philosophy has eliminated the negative experience.

I had to realize how I need people and am driven madly towards client satisfaction as well as an ecstatic staff.

In short, I had to struggle for years to learn what Stasiowski encapsulates in one book. There was no such resource when I finished my Bachelor of Architecture degree in 1973.

This book would have helped me to overcome such mistakes as:

1. Having three principals and 30 junior staff members which kept payroll low but the problems of well-conceived design and construction documents were nonexistent; not to mention all the problems in the field.

2. Basing a firm on a design philosophy, as I did in my first entrepreneurial effort, resulted in great commissions and one-time clients because projects were never done on-time or within budget. Also, after seven years, our value for three partners was $150,000 which equates to $50,000 after seven years of effort.

3. Finally, almost going bankrupt and firing my bookkeeper, I took hands-on control of financial management in my firm. With the premise of $100,000 in gross fees per year per person as a rule-of-thumb, we survived and I left that firm after seven years, where it never had grossed $1 million in one year. In my new practice, we did $1 million the first year and today do $4 million per year with a staff of 40. By watching overhead, collections, and billings on one side, and taking on aggressive marketing on the other, along with a great staff (attitude and intelligence), I have managed to strike a balance.

I recommend this book for any design professional—architect, engineer, interior designer, landscape designer—or anyone who proposes to become a principal or partner in a small design firm. It's not easy! This book highlights the necessary business functions—without attending business school yourself—that you need to not only survive, but to succeed!

RAYMOND L. SCOTT, A.I.A.

President
The Scott Companies

ACKNOWLEDGMENTS

While the essential ideas in this text were derived from my 20 years of consulting practice, certain individuals contributed significantly to developing these ideas into a unified and practical whole.

I would like to thank the following people without whom this book would not have been possible:

Wayne Schmidt, whose highly successful small firm and discussions during our Small Firm Roundtable in 1989 inspired me to think about finding more firms like his and discovering what made them successful.

Joshua Willard, who gave up his mother Julia to the work effort that went into this book, who will someday hopefully read it and understand that it might never have happened without his mother.

The staff at the *Professional Services Management Journal*, whose research and work over the past 15 years has uncovered the gems that fill these pages.

Steve Kliment whose patience over two years has made this a better book.

Anita, Kristin, Erik, and Justin, who have given up their time with me for five years out of the past 10, while I have pursued my search for success.

FRANK A. STASIOWSKI

Newton, Massachusetts
March 1991

STAYING SMALL SUCCESSFULLY

INTRODUCTION

Already in the 1980s we saw the proliferation of hundreds of thousands of small firms, just like the thousands more we will see spring up in the next decade. According to Tom Peters in *Organized Chaos,*[1] the business world of the 1990s will see increased numbers of small entrepreneurships and more people wanting to control their own destinies by working for themselves, some in small businesses, some even at home. Computer technology in the nineties will facilitate networking for these individualized workstyles—the hallmark of the small firm.

As the publisher of the *Professional Services Management Journal, A/E Marketing Journal,* and many other publications for design professionals, I've observed that the small business entrepreneur runs into scores of obstacles when trying to start and maintain a small business. In this book I review more than 40 successful small firms to bring you their solutions. You can choose your own blend of these original, practical ideas and develop a plan to make your design practice more profitable.

BREAK FROM TRADITION

Typical fast-paced, highly motivated entrepreneurs have so many ideas about how to succeed that they tend to outpace those around them—including staff. This is a problem when no one can keep up with you, and it is typical of every entrepreneur who accepts the challenge to start a small business, stay small, and succeed. Truly successful entrepreneurs recognize this problem and take action with a daring solution—they begin to hire people who outpace *them*. That is when a design firm becomes a truly successful enterprise.

Choosing people who outpace you is a nontraditional idea, and challenging the traditional way of thinking is a common characteristic of the most successful design firms today. Many of them proudly state that they "have never taken a seminar, never listened to other people's advice, and never read anything about management." Gifted with an intuitive confidence to follow their ideas, these entrepreneurs embrace change before it embraces them. Instead of accepting the traditional answer, they ask, "Why not?"

Restless, successful small firm owners are never satisfied with routine approaches. Perhaps this insatiable desire to do things better—whether a company's expertise is in design, marketing, financial management, human resource management, or profit planning—coupled with that elusive need to control one's own destiny is what fuels the fire inside the successful entrepreneurial firm.

CONTROL OF YOUR DESTINY

Many small design firm owners start their businesses out of crisis. Being fired, laid off, or quitting as a result of a conflict are three powerful reasons often mentioned as the motivation for starting one's own business. Control of one's own destiny is the real motivator behind all three, as well as a characteristic trait found in most entrepreneurs which gives them strength to persevere against all odds. If this sounds elusive, realize that one thing is certain. Unsuccessful, struggling, and mediocre firms don't have that entrepreneurial drive to reach their goals at all costs; successful firms do.

SUCCESS IS WHAT YOU WANT IT TO BE

Success is the reward for risking everything in order to reach your goal. The well-worn path of the innumerable traditional design professionals that came before you is not the one that will lead you to success. To go out on a limb, to strike out on your own path—despite your fears, however lonely the struggle, however unattainable the goal may seem—and to keep striving until you get there is the spirit that will bring you to your goal.

Some define success as being known for exceptional design, some want community recognition, others desire press coverage or personal glorification. In some cases these goals outweigh money, time, or growth as driving forces. Success is simply the ability to control your own destiny to reach whichever goal you wish to achieve.

Success is individual and only you know what you want and how to get it. There are so many different definitions of success, from doing what you *have* to do, to doing what you *want* to do, to reaching excellence. The only advice I can give you is this: Set your goals for you. Don't make the mistake many people do—setting unrealistic goals. There is only one U.S. president, only one Donald Trump, only one I. M. Pei. You can learn from these people if you can be realistic. Remember first and foremost to strive for a sense of balance—work, home, finances, health, love—in *your* life.

YOU ARE ONLY AS SMALL AS YOU THINK

Fifteen years ago, as co-chair of the Syracuse, New York, Chamber of Commerce Small Business Council, I struggled for a long time with the rest of the council trying to decide how to define "small." Should we use total number of staff? Should we use gross revenue? How about number of offices? Finally, after 18 months of haggling, we arrived at a definition that is still probably the best one I know—if you think you are small, you're probably right.

I've met principals in 600-person design firms who really believe that they are "small." I have also met partners from 5-person firms who believe 15-person firms are huge. Although there are cutoff points for statistics on small firms, large firms actually consist of groups of small teams that are really "firms within a firm." There are a few examples of large firms cited within this text, but within the largest firms there are small groups that operate as autonomous entities. Seldom do these groups grow larger than 15 to 20 people. Even the largest firms are just collections of very small operations. And all of the large firms were once small firms that used techniques found in this book to grow. You too can learn from their examples, and that is why I include a few significant ones in this book.

Management style is what marks a small business. One design professional running a drafting service could employ a hundred drafters all doing the same task. Such a firm is not large. It is small in management style. If everyone reports to you, you are really a small organization in management style or strategy. Similarly, if you manage a distinct group of 15 to 20 people within a large firm, this book is for you.

BEING DIFFERENT MEANS BEING VISIBLE

As the principal of a small firm, you have to be more than a technician: you enjoy people and truly enjoy your work. Long hours are the rule, not the exception. If you want to succeed, you must be an expert at networking—not in traditional professional circles, but in your community. You must be able to mingle with potential clients, not sit on a plateau above them. If you doubt this remember that Paul Revere is famed no less for his historic ride than for the quality of his copper and silver products.

Finally, never apologize for being a small practitioner. Small firms do not necessarily handle insignificant projects. The example of Paul Revere reminds us that small is not synonymous with second-rate. Be proud to put your hallmark on your work product. When you stamp your drawings, your clients know they are getting the very best. They deserve no less—you can give no more.

REFERENCES

1. Tom Peters, 1988. *Organized Chaos*. New York: Alfred A. Knopf.

1 PLANNING AND STRATEGY

Of the thousands of small firms that exist in the United States today, one common element appears to be prevalent in all firms that are not successful—the lack of planning. Harvard Business School recently performed a study of 1000 graduates.[1] Of the 1000, 80 percent had never written down any planned goals. Of the 20 percent who *had* written them down, 17 percent had only done so once. The remaining 3 percent, however, had written down their plan goals annually and then updated them monthly throughout the course of the year. The results were that the income of the 3 percent that wrote down their goals regularly superseded the income of the 80 percent that had no planned goals, by 400 percent. The results suggest that the physical act of writing down a plan is a powerful motivator toward achieving success.

You can trace most management problems directly to poor planning. Without planning, your organization moves slowly, awkwardly, and without direction. You will benefit from the tips, techniques, methods, and other materials in this book only if you recognize the importance of planning to your success.

One important characteristic of successful planning is flexibility. Successful firms plan regularly, then adjust, modify, update, criticize, mold, and work on variations of business plans.

Planning is

- participatory,
- ongoing, and
- critical to your success.

Planning is not

* one-time,
* a written text, and
* elaborate or involved.

Almost any business of any size periodically engages in planning. In many small firms, however, planning focuses heavily on numbers and doesn't include an assessment of the *strategic market position* of the business. The strategic market position is that market share that a company can obtain in selling its service or product. Within the total marketplace, how much business will your company obtain? This chapter shows you (1) how to assess your place in the market, (2) where to go, and (3) how to translate your vision of the future into an action-oriented strategic business plan. Many of the ideas presented in this chapter explaining the strategic plan are discussed in greater detail in later chapters. The concepts are introduced here within the framework of the strategic plan.

Most design professionals today conduct their practices using technologies and professional policies heavy with tradition. To succeed in 1990s, and if desired, to grow, a professional firm must be able to recognize and absorb the dynamic forces that shape its environment. This may mean laying aside the traditional lines of thought on running a design firm.

THE NEED FOR VISION

Before outlining your strategic plan, you must decide who you are, and where you want to be in 5, 10, even 15 years. Many companies operate without this type of clear vision. They just happen to be in business. But consider the individuals who have succeeded in recent years. Ted Turner persisted with his idea for cable news channel CNN, despite being turned down by dozens of banks, because he had a vision that it would work. He was $30 million in debt, but he succeeded and became one of the world's richest men. Turner's vision was clear, he stuck to it, and he did not give up when no one else believed in him.

Figure 1-1 contains a profile of a firm that began with no vision, floundered, and then adopted a simple goal, and earnings increased. Another architectural firm with a vision is Kohn Pedersen Fox (KPF). The principals' vision was to bring to commercial architecture the same quality and intellectual ap-

---

Profile of Firm Before and After Adoption of "Vision"

Firm: Meehan Architects
Staff: 4
Specialty: Commercial and residential design
Address: 764 Chestnut Street
            Manchester, N.H. 03104

Gary Meehan of Meehan Architects started his business six years ago with no real "plan," feeling that "you don't know where you are going to be in architecture or what areas will improve." Two years ago, Meehan and his associates were working 40 to 60 hours per week and his own salary was about $60,000. Assessing his work situation, he determined he would like to be making $75,000 a year, and, based on the size of his firm and the help of a consultant, determined that he should really be making $100,000 a year. "Much to my surprise, I far surpassed even that," Meehan says.

The changes he made included adopting a 9-hour workday for Monday through Thursday, and a 4-hour workday for Fridays to improve motivation and productivity; marking up reimbursables by 15%; refocusing from primarily residential work to unique commercial and residential work; and raising prices. These changes helped Meehan to reach his vision—that of making $100,000 a year.

Meehan Architects is a good example of how having a vision—even one that is relatively small—can improve your firm's success.

Figure 1-1

proach that many outstanding architects have brought to museums, houses, institutional projects, and to achieve this architecture with outstanding clients. In addition, the vision extended to being a national and eventually an international firm with an ever-expanding partnership level. Even though KPF became a very large firm indeed, the lesson it offers is the singlemindedness of its vision.

KPF started small and achieved tremendous growth in size and market penetration as a result of its undertaking strategic plans that were different, yet focused. American Institute of Architects' Firm of the Year 1990, Kohn Pedersen Fox Associates began in 1976 with three name partners. Success has come to this firm not just in terms of size, but also of quality. "Our intent was not just growth-oriented, but to attract and produce better work," says A. Eugene Kohn, one of the New York City-based firm's principals. For their first effort, KPF approached the American Broadcasting Company (ABC) for an opportunity to design the conversion of an armory on New York City's Upper West Side into daytime soap opera studios. This bold move gave KPF the opportunity to establish a long-term relationship (13 projects in 13 years) with ABC and a prominent position in the marketplace.

"Our vision (with a lot of good fortune) was to go down in history as a great architectural firm," Kohn maintains. Going after the best and at times the biggest was a career-launching start. To further that vision, KPF chose projects that would enhance the firm's reputation, ones that were "significant in moving the firm along."

Choosing such projects means turning away inappropriate ones. Kohn passes on some wisdom he learned as a young architect: "Your success will be greatly affected by the work you turn down." A design firm should admit what it can't do (or cannot grow into), because doing work that is second best will hurt your reputation. Kohn Pedersen Fox now works with the country's most prestigious developers and corporations, such as JMB/Urban, Lincoln Properties, Reliance, ABC, Rockefeller Center, Procter & Gamble, and IBM.

This firm is a good example of the impact of choosing a market, building a reputation in that niche, and always striving to achieve the firm's vision. A company that learns to be decisive has a greater probability for faster success, whereas one that is indecisive will suffer for it.

Figure 1-2 contains a profile of Pape-Dawson Consulting Engineering, another firm that overcame adversity.

These examples show that innovative persons who are leaders break with traditional ways of thinking. They act outside the mainstream, and eat, sleep, breathe their vision, sometimes to the point of obsession. Others say such individuals were clairvoyant, knowing of their success ahead of time. It was the energy, however, combined with passion, that drove these people to succeed. Moreover, you cannot have 15 visions—only one. Focus on your vision as you read the rest of this book to maximize its benefit to you.

A clear vision will allow you to stretch yourself, to succeed beyond your capacity, and to survive failure.

DEFINING A VISION

One method of developing a vision is to emulate a hero or champion. General George Patton emulated Napoleon. He had studied French and knew a scholar who compiled the

---

Profile of a Firm That Overcame Adversity

Firm: Pape–Dawson Consulting Engineers, Inc.
Staff: 70
Specialty: Civil engineering
Address: 9310 Broadway
             San Antonio, Tex. 78217

Although Pape–Dawson Consulting Engineers does not have a formal written vision, it lives out its vision every day in specializing in and producing top-quality civil engineering. "We are only civil engineering," according to Eugene Dawson, firm president. Specializing in land development and infrastructure development projects, the Texas-based firm also does municipal, wastewater treatment, school, hydraulics, and other large projects. Despite Texas's three years of economic depression in a market of 30 to 40 other engineering firms, some of which folded and others of which cut back employees by up to 80%, Pape–Dawson only cut employees by about 50% and continues to do $5,000,000 worth of fees per year (a little more than half of their previous fees of $9,000,000).

Why has Pape–Dawson succeeded despite the economic environment in Texas? Dawson says it's because the firm's vision to perform top-quality work has given them a venerable reputation. "Do a first-class engineering job and you'll get plenty of work from repeat clients," he says. Consistency and quality at Pape–Dawson are requisite. Dawson says he explains to clients that "you can never put price first. If someone else down the street is offering to cut corners and to do a job for less, I explain to them why you can't cut corners in civil engineering."

Dawson runs the firm with his two sons, who are major shareholders of the company. Together the Dawsons own 80% of the business.

Networking is part of the reason for the firm's success in carrying out its vision: "We've developed a list of blue-chip clients. And I have served on almost every political and civic council in town. I know everybody in town who's worth knowing," he says.

Not surprisingly, Pape–Dawson hasn't had to move into other parts of Texas or the national arena to get work. Its reputation for excellence keeps the Dawsons and their staff working right in their own Bexar (pronounced "bear") County.

Figure 1-2

memoirs of Napoleon. Patton carried these memoirs wherever he went. Despite the great differences in military technology, he would ask himself, before he made a move, how Napoleon would have acted in the situation. An example of an architect with a vision is Moritz Bergmeyer. While his firm never grew to more than 35 people, he was able to sell it a few years ago to buy a ski resort in Wyoming to fulfill his dream of building a community in the mountains. (See Fig. 1-3).

Developing a Vision By Emulating a Model

Firm: Bergmeyer Associates
Staff: 32 (when sold)
Specialty: Architecture, planning, and project development
Address: 134 Beach Street
            Boston, Mass. 02111

Bergmeyer Associates gained prominence after it redeveloped and converted over 60 warehouses on the historic Boston waterfront. Specializing in such projects, the firm gained experience in planning, design, and development of mixed-use (residential and commercial) waterfront projects, and marina facilities. According to Bergmeyer, the firm's success can be traced to a vision he had several years ago.

The firm began as a partnership in 1970. Bergmeyer split with the partner to form his own company in 1973. Growing steadily to 13 to 15 people, the size of the firm then hit a plateau for several years. Despite the steadiness of the company, Bergmeyer was analyzing a troublesome problem—"I was looking for a way to get away from being viewed as the boss and a pain to employees, being looked at negatively. A lot of architects are like martyrs, and if you're in the mode of being a martyr, it's not a good place. It's as bad as being an alcoholic or something because you feel sorry for yourself all the time, and you think everyone's going to take advantage of you," Bergmeyer says. "I spent a lot of time looking at this problem and hiring consultants, but I couldn't find any answers."

Suddenly an attitude change took place within Bergmeyer, inspired by a meeting with William Gore, founder of Goretex, at a leadership conference in Tarrytown, New York. Gore and several other high-tech executives were talking about solving the very problem Bergmeyer himself couldn't solve. They talked about creating profit centers, giving employees the room to make decisions, and profit sharing. The profit centers were fairly autonomous and were responsible for managing themselves—negotiating contracts, making a profit, hiring and firing personnel. The firm was simply there to provide overall goals, information, work environment, marketing, support, and other administrative functions.

The notion of giving autonomy to employees went against the traditional thinking in most design firms at the time, Bergmeyer says, mostly in the area of sharing financial information. However, once he developed a financial system to monitor each profit center on a monthly or sometimes even weekly basis (described later in this chapter and in Chapter 6, "Managing the Bottom Line"), the concept "took off."

"I got people to feel like they were owners, not employees, and because of all the information sharing, they saw why it was so important to meet budgets and deadlines."

Naturally, when Bergmeyer sold the firm, he sold it to the employees. There are now five principals, and the associates also own company stock.

"The person I really admired was Bill Gore of Goretex, because he solved the problem that I wasn't able to solve on my own. That was to deal fairly with people, share profits, giving people more accountability and respect."

Not surprisingly, the attitude change, information sharing, and profit centers launched the firm to success. "The firm made more money that year than it ever had. It grew 35 to 40% each year. That was the fun part of it."

Figure 1-3

ROLE OF THE CEO IN A SMALL BUSINESS FIRM

"How should we spend our time?"

PERSONNEL

Recruiting

Initial salary level

Employment letter

Position description

Annual evaluation

Technical development

Promotions

Daily greetings

Periodic lengthy chats

Reprimands

Dismissals

Exit interviews

Human resources committee

Respond to morale changes

Respond to walk-ins

FINANCE

Sign payroll checks

Expense logs/checks

Time report

—production ratios and trends

Accounts payable

Ageing report/collections

Project budget reports

Borrow/negotiate lending rate

Salary reviews/adjustments

Quarter review with accountant

Quarter review/financial statement to bank

Trends/statistics/ratios overall

Annual planning

—operating budget

—marketing goal

—major purchases

—building lease

—profit goal

—bonus goal

—accumulation goal

Bonus distribution

SPONTANEOUS OTHER
(marketing, administration, etc.)

Backlog

—contracted

—potential

—individual work load

Project problems/client sensitivities

Corporate programs/fringes

Policies/procedures

Project meetings

Long-range planning

Management committee

Proposals/fee development/negotiation

Contract review/signature

Services/diversification

Ownership transition

Marketing development

Technical development

—self

—managers

—staff

Corporate survey/evaluation/response

Corporate structure

Professional liability insurance

—review/application/renew

Maintenance marketing/feedback

Mail sort

Review/hire consultants

Acquisitions/mergers

Working conditions

Equipment/tools

Figure 1-4 Source: Michaels Engineering. Used with permission.

As you work to define your champion, run down this check-list:

1. What biographies have you read lately?
2. My vision is to be like _____.
3. Study this person: find out their traits, their methods, how they live or lived, how they were perceived prior to greatness.
4. How can you pattern your image after this person?
5. List tasks and thinking patterns that will allow you to act and think like your champion.

Take, for example, well-known architects such as Richard Meier, I. M. Pei, Philip Johnson, Helmut Jahn. Why do they receive so much publicity?

When you look at any of the great architects or engineers, notice that they break with tradition. They don't follow the norm. Consider: Who are their clients? How do they get to those clients? Then set up your personal and office image so your clients and prospects will see you as the kind of person they want to work with. It is good to follow norms, to stick with tradition, to read the textbooks on business management. But those who do are not always the ones who achieve great success. Sometimes individuals with less business knowledge take an idea to fruition with their unrivaled passion.

Study those who have passion, then develop your own un-written plan to be like the person or firm you envision. Figure 1-4 is a profile of the role of the CEO in a small business firm, courtesy of Michaels Engineering.

Success is relative. If you are an engineer with three employees, your vision of success may be to keep this staff profitably employed. You need not profess to become the richest or the most renowned architect in the world. Your vision can be much smaller—to stay small successfully.

THE CONCISE WRITTEN VISION

Partners of small firms often have difficulty in describing and writing down a vision because they think they are writing down "the answer." In fact, many successful firms have no written plans, but they have clear vision. They engage in a *planning process,* instead of a plan.

The planning process also involves your key people. Review with them what you want your firm to be; ask them how to get there. Get them to believe in you. Your ability to motivate others will establish whether or not you are a leader. If you are a leader, people will believe in your concept, and help you carry out your vision. Figure 1-5 is a profile of George Matarazzo, of Matarazzo Design (New Hampshire), a particularly motivational leader.

The next step is to convert your vision into a concise written statement. For a small firm that means one or two sentences. Then hone it. Every plan is written in pencil, to be erased, changed, and modified. Figure 1-6 contains some sample one-sentence visions. Write only enough so that you don't overwhelm your employees with paper. Eschew the 40-page plan.

ELEMENTS OF A PLAN

The strategic planning process is made up of six main elements. Coordinate these elements so there is no conflict among them. Follow the order below. If you don't, you will create conflict among the items. The six elements are

1. Mission and culture statements.
2. Marketing plan and direction.
3. Financial plan.
4. Organizational plan.
5. Human resources plan.
6. Leadership transition.

Mission and Culture Statements

A firm's vision must be translated into *mission statements* and *firm culture*.

MISSION STATEMENT

The mission statement should capture the essence of what you want your business to be. It should be unique, succinct, and tailored to the exact service your firm provides. It shouldn't be a middle-of-the-road, generic statement ("XYZ Associates is a unique architectural firm"). Instead, state specifically what the firm is trying to accomplish. For example, "We work only for

Profile of a Particularly Motivational Leader

Firm: Matarazzo Design
Staff: 10
Specialty: Landscape architecture, land planning
Address: 9 Hills Avenue
    Concord, N.H.

Matarazzo Design has expanded and contracted several times over its 15-year existence. Recently, the firm reduced its personnel from 50 to about 10, over a period of several years, and Matarazzo has been faced with a particularly difficult period with his staff. "If there's ever a time to motivate, it's when you reduce," he says, citing that growth has a built-in motivation and positive connotation. "In lean times there can be depression amongst the staff, and worry about the future. They need to be reassured that things are well, that their jobs are still there for today."

Matarazzo says he's learned over the years that there is no use in lying to an employee, and there is no way you can or should ever state that "your job is secure." Market size fluctuations control the size of his staff, he says, not his own whims. "The economic projections are what tell me to reduce."

Keep talking to the employees and reassuring them that they can speak with you any time. Open communication is most crucial in motivating your employees to carry out your goals, according to Matarazzo.

Matarazzo does not believe in employment contracts, and tells his employees they are free to go at any time. But he urges them to consider speaking with him about any move before deciding to go. He meets with people weekly or daily if necessary to keep ideas flowing.

Have a Champion

Like Mory Bergmeyer (Fig. 1-3), Matarazzo also has a vision and several champions. After graduating from the Harvard School of Design, he says, he set up specific benchmarks toward which he steers his course. The several champions include former teachers, a former employer, and his father.

"My former employer was the developer of New Seabury [a large New England resort area] and I worked with him for eight years. By the time I left I was president of his company, but the whole time I felt he was a great marketer. I was in awe of that and really listened to him and absorbed what I could.

"My Dad gave me a lot of sound business advice. He owned a landscaping company and he was a pusher. I didn't want to go to college but he pushed me to go to a technical school. In high school I was getting C's and D's and in the technical school I did the same. In about the second year, I was still moping around when one of the teachers took us outside to sketch a house and the surrounding landscaping. I had never drawn before but once I drew it I decided that's it. The teacher pointed me towards landscape architecture and I never got less than straight A's after that."

Matarazzo believes that if you have a passion and a vision for your work, that makes the difference between mediocrity and success. "You have to love it. You have to have a passion for what you do. You get into it with such enthusiasm and it flows over to the client. You get excited and you know the job so intimately that you can impress the clients by your mere interest, if it's great enough." When you have a passion and a vision, he says, you "don't have to turn cartwheels" to sell your work.

Figure 1-5

SAMPLE VISION STATEMENTS

To be the largest firm in the country.

To be the world's most noted expert in Victorian theater redesign.

To work in various corners of the world.

To have a firm culture that attracts the top engineering talent in the nation.

To be the wealthiest architect in the world.

To be known as the country's most successful small firm doing facilities management.

To emulate I. M. Pei.

Choose a single statement that crystallizes your focus and direction. This vision is, as it appears, a "massive wish." This statement is the impetus for the rest of your planning process.

Figure 1-6

hospital clients that are going to build major hospitals in the next 20 years." Figure 1-7 is a core mission worksheet, used by the Troyer Group. This worksheet has all the elements you will need to develop your own small firm mission statement. A finished mission statement appears in Figure 1-8, from the Scott Companies Architects, of Maitland, Florida. Figure 1-9 is another sample vision statement from the Cavendish Partnership.

CULTURE

A culture statement should answer questions such as

Is the firm a single corporate culture or is it multiple?

Do we believe in our people more than our clients or our clients more than our people?

How do we keep the team together?

How important is loyalty?

How important is hard work? Is it more important than performance? Or do we put performance first and hard work second?

How important are family, friends, and outside life to the interests of the firm?

Do we believe in hiring cheap labor or having a united, balanced family?

How will we serve our markets?	
What business are we in?	
What is our product or product mix?	
What is/are our market(s)?	
What is our competitive advantage?	
What is our strategic role?	

Figure 1-7 The Core Mission Worksheet. Used with permission.

Mission Statement for the Scott Companies Architects

The Scott Companies Architects Interiors Engineers, Inc.
35 Staff
601 S. Lake Destiny Road
Suite 400
Maitland, Fla. 32751

Mission Statement

To be the best is the mission of this firm: best in client satisfaction, best in diversity of services offered, and best in performance.

Client Satisfaction—Client satisfaction is defined in an architectural firm by the number of repeat clients; that is, clients for whom you continue to work on a project-to-project basis. The 100% repeat client base is a result of our client-first attitude expressed by members of our staff.

Diversity of Services—The "one-stop" service package we offer enables us to provide our clients with a diversity of services to fulfill their project needs such as architecture, planning, interior design, construction management, and public relations.

Performance—The stability of a 97% staff retention rate offers the continuity of an experienced team working together for the benefit of the client. Our specialty project teams offer the "hands-on" management style of a small firm backed by the stability, diversity of expertise, and staff capability of a large firm.

Figure 1-8

These will help define your firm's purpose, which all employees should understand and work toward. Figure 1-10 is a sample culture statement from an actual design firm. Another way to present the culture statement is in the form of tailored culture statements for each function, as shown in Figure 1-11. Although CH2M Hill is a large company, its culture statement appears here because it is one of the most well-defined culture statements the author has encountered. The statement clarifies each aspect of the business. Very few small firms take the time to define their culture statements so well. Although CH2M Hill is a massive firm, even the smallest firms can use its culture statement as a way to emulate CH2M Hill's success.

Mission Statement for the Cavendish Partnership

The Cavendish Partnership, Inc.
12 Staff
145 Main Street
Ludlow, Vt. 05149

Mission Statement

The Cavendish Partnership is a consulting company that assembles resources needed to solve problems in planning, architecture, landscape architecture, and communications for a diversified group of clients and consumers in an expanding geographic marketplace.

Our mission is to provide our clients with solutions to problems, which are socially acceptable, environmentally sound, economically feasible, profitable, and professional.

Eight Questions to Ask Before Taking on a New Assignment:

1. Is TCP the best organization to fulfill the needs of this client and the consumer?
2. Do all of the members of the problem-solving team believe that this assignment and the client have integrity?
3. Can TCP and the client expect to make a reasonable profit?
4. Can we expect to be proud of this assignment and the process once they are completed?
5. Can we learn from this assignment?
6. Will this assignment create a positive public awareness of the problem-solving process and of TCP?
7. Can we successfully complete this assignment with the available human and technical resources?
8. Will this assignment be fun? Will this client be fun to work with?

Figure 1-9 Source: The Cavendish Partnership. Used with permission.

Marketing Plan and Direction

Clear, concise, and *measurable* are the key goals of the marketing plan. Standard, normal marketing plans are well researched and give all the statistical data about clients in the market and dollar volume. As well as being measurable, large firm marketing plans target strategies and techniques for attacking the market, from call reporting to presentation strategies to proposal strategies. Well-researched plans contain detailed personnel plans, including who people are, what their roles should be, and how they should be involved in the entire marketing effort.

The smaller firm lacks the resources to do this research on the scale a large firm such as Skidmore Owings & Merrill or Black & Veetsch would, but you may compensate for this by means of elementary research. Consider calling 25 potential clients in the marketplace to find out how much they will spend in the next year, extrapolate from that data the number of clients in the market, then estimate a percentage of work that you could get out of it. (See Fig. 1-12.)

This next idea may seem impractical for small firms, but with one call you can get as many as 500 statistically accurate leads and estimates of what the client will spend in the marketplace. Objective market research can be purchased in several ways: by hiring a consultant to provide marketing research or by buying prepared marketing research. A management and marketing consultant list appears in Appendix A. Organizations that sell

---

Sample Culture Statement

Shared Values

The following are values that we share:

1. We serve with love.
2. Honesty and professionalism are fundamental to each of us.
3. Quality is the true criterion for our work.
4. Teamwork is the way we work.
5. The perception of our clients is reality to us.
6. Through generalized training and experience, we as individuals choose to become specialists.
7. We have fun.
8. We reward performance and correct nonperformance.
9. All that we do with and to the environment must contribute to its maintenance or improvement.
10. We support individuals and their families in their responsibility to achieve their fullest potential in a way that does not disable others.

Figure 1-10

A Well-Defined Tailored Culture Statement

CH2M Hill Inc.
P.O. Box 22508
Denver, Colo. 80222

Culture Statement:

" . . . We believe that each CH2M Hill employee must understand what the organization stands for. And so, presented in this publication are our beliefs and values. These ideas represent the collective thoughts of our founders and employees . . . "

Business:

CH2M Hill is a professional services firm focusing on engineering design and related services in water, wastewater, and hazardous waste management as its core business, while expanding its business in energy and transportation.

Ownership:

CH2M Hill is an employee-owned corporation with broad ownership existing throughout the organization. Employee ownership enhances the opportunities offered by the firm, and the employee's shared commitment to the firm's success. We believe our ownership program is a key element in sustaining our commitment to excellence.

Corporate Ethics:

We must be profitable, but we desire to make a profit by undertaking projects that are challenging and that contribute to the safety, health, and well-being of the public. The quality and integrity of our work is of overriding importance to us. We strive for technical excellence and innovative solutions.

Our clients are critical to our success, and our aim is for clients to receive full value for our services. We strive to be a good corporate citizen in those communities where we work.

Employee Philosophy:

We strive to recruit, develop, and retain outstanding people in our profession. We provide them with challenging assignments, a stable environment, and career opportunities, and we reward them with merit incentives and ownership.

We endeavor to maximize the strengths of our employees so that each is productive to the optimum extent of his or her abilities.

We recognize that family goals are as important as career goals and that the support of family members is integral to creating an atmosphere of productivity and contribution.

Management Philosophy:

Our management philosophy is based on participative decision-making and is supported by open, frequent, and nonhierarchical communications on all aspects of the firm's and the individual's performance.

We encourage informed decision-making at all levels in the organization, and we support individual market development initiatives or research interests at any level, provided these are aimed at improving the firm's long-term competitive position in markets we have identified as being of interest.

We promote leadership among our employees and we grant authority and responsibility to individuals and teams of individuals to achieve the goals of the firm.

Organization:

We are a matrix organization, balancing the maintenance of technical excellence and quality through our discipline structure with a decentralized, close-to-the-client, geographic structure. These strengths are embodied in our project teams, which combine technical and local knowledge in the unique blend required by each of our clients.

Growth:

Our growth resulted from continued high quality performance and client satisfaction, expansion in our major markets, increased market share in our core businesses, expanded geographic penetration, selected acquisitions, and new services to meet client needs.

Profit and Financial Condition:

We operate at a sufficient level of profit to provide for a reasonable net operating income relative to labor income, and manage operations to ensure a sound, long-term financial condition.

Figure 1-11 Source: CH2M Hill. Used with permission.

prepared research include the Economic Research Council, based in Bethesda, Maryland. The council monitors the activities of 2000 firms and publishes a list *(The Annual Analysis of Capital Spending Plans)* of 199 firms most likely to expand in the next two years. The council also publishes two other annuals, *The Fastest Growing Divisions of the Largest Companies* and *The Directory of Selected High Tech and Light Manufacturing Companies;* a quarterly, *Service Industry Analysis Reports;* and the monthly *Capital Investment Trends in Industry.*

Many firms make the mistake of writing elaborate, long, highly literate marketing plans. These are cumbersome and seldom followed. It is much better to have a one-to-two-page plan that is measurable and easily tracked by all in your firm.

Next make sure you share the plan not only with other principals, the marketing director, and other top people, but

---

Low-budget Market Research

1. Call 25 clients in your market area.
2. Those 25 people project a total of $4 million in fees in the next calendar year.
3. You have 10 people in your firm and there are three other firms in your marketplace serving the same clients. The total in all firms is 63 people.
4. Since you have 10 people in your firm, you represent roughly 1/6 of the total market.
5. Multiply 1/6 by the total fees for the next year:
   $1/6 \times \$4$ million $= \$666,666$
6. Your targeted market share for the next year should be $666,666.

Note: All of this information depends on the validity of the information you obtain in the telephone calls. If you get good information, you have valid market research. If the information is invalid, so is your research. To check the validity of your research or to obtain valid information, consult agencies such as the Economic Research Council, described in the text.

Figure 1-12

also with every employee in the company, from partner to receptionist and bookkeeper. If every secretary has a knowledge of how your vision translates into the marketing plan, then each will be able to correctly answer questions on first contacts from client prospects. This way everyone becomes a part of the marketing plan, thinking *sales* and *marketing* wherever they go. A successful firm will disseminate the marketing plan, and allow staff to share the information and the vision.

Make the marketing plan an integral part of the company, not something that sits on a shelf. This need not mean that you must hand every employee a physical copy of the plan. In some cases, a partner outlines the marketing plan in a semi-annual meeting. For such meetings, it is best to show the key targets and hand those out on a single piece of paper.

MEASURABLE GOALS

Saying "We want to be the biggest and best firm and do more hospitals" is not effective. A marketing plan should be specific;

for example, "We want to go after 75 university science buildings and libraries in the next nine months." This type of statement is measurable because it includes statistical information. For a more detailed sample marketing plan statement, or summary, see Appendix B.

FOCUS

Firms that solicit clients in a few distinct markets, as opposed to soliciting every project on the horizon, tend to be more lucrative. Thomas Wirth Landscape Architects, a six-person firm based in Sherborn, Massachusetts, successfully focuses on small, signatory gardens. Although Wirth has designed many large commercial landscape projects, focusing on the small projects he prefers has carried him to success—he is the landscape architect for public television's "The Victory Garden," and has written a book entitled *The Victory Garden Landscape Guide.* A description of this firm and further discussion of the importance of focusing your practice appear in Chapter 2.

COST AND ORGANIZATION

Include your marketing costs and an organizational chart in your marketing plan. By including costs, you are narrowing down your plan to *strict, measurable* goals. See Appendix B for a sample marketing plan.

Financial Plan

The next element of a strategic plan is a financial plan. Begin by targeting revenues and expense and keep it simple.

Moritz Bergmeyer, a successful Boston architect described earlier in this chapter (see Fig. 1-3), sold his design firm in 1988 to buy a ski resort in Wyoming. This individual emulated success from the very beginning. Bergmeyer never had a "financial management system," and instead decided to zero in on a few key elements of financial planning to measure his firm's success. Bergmeyer's key measures include utilization ratio and ratios of employee salary to overall revenue to measure productivity (explained in Chapter 6); return on equity; net profit before taxes; next year's target for gross and net revenue; percent of total revenue allocated to salaries; computer operations, and overhead. These key elements are presented in more detail in Chapter 6. The main point here is that Bergmeyer requested a one-sheet report from each profit center. By keeping it simple, he was able to identify problems quickly.

STANDARDIZATION

Successful firms have a clear financial direction. They standardize the terms and conditions of their financial system. The typical design firm draws up a contract any way the client wants it—lump sum, percentage of construction, hourly or unit-based, to name a few. You should aim for a narrower standard, perhaps one or two ways. With proper legal advice, develop your own consistent contracts, a standard approach to contracting, a consistent way of negotiating, a single invoice format. Avoid allowing clients to control you with their different ways of operating.

If a client refuses to use your contract, do you simply turn them away? In many cases, small firms have this as a "go, no go" criteria—they will not work with clients who will not do work their way. If you present a lump sum contract and the client says, "No, we want to pay you hourly," some design firms will say, "I'm sorry, we simply don't want to work with firms who won't do it our way." There is usually some negotiation, however, and the small firm should convince the client that their way is best. Still it may come down to saying "This is the way we want to do it, take it or leave it." Successful smaller firms must know when to walk away from clients who dig in their heels and detrimentally impact the company's business success. This is one of the toughest strategies that a small firm must employ, because it is incredibly hard to walk away from real work just because a client's contract procedures do not meet your standard.

EMPLOYEE INVOLVEMENT

Involve all employees in financial planning and its execution. Disseminate financial information within your firm. This way, the staff is motivated to compare budget versus actual costs on a routine basis. Involve project managers—from approval at the inception through fee collection.

You may look at this as a divulgence of private information. As Fran Tarkenton said, "People like to know the score," so that when they are carrying out their "plays," they know the impact on that score; namely, the budget.

If your players do not know the firm's finances, you are hurting your overall chance of success. Obviously you run the risk of some information being passed on to a competitor, but the benefits of an open culture that involves all people in the control of their destiny with the use of valid numbers far outweighs the risks involved.

PROFIT

The norm profit for design firms according to a recent *Professional Services Management Journal* survey is about 9 percent.[2] Typical firms with profits in this range start out the year saying, "We want to achieve 10 percent profit." Successful firms project much higher profits. This represents a philosophical difference in the financial planning effort. Such firms avoid mediocrity in their financial planning. For instance, they select utilization rate goals of 75 to 80 percent as opposed to the norm of 68 percent (see Chapter 6 for definitions). They target for return on equity in the 33 percent range compared to a norm of 8 percent. Net bottom-line profit before taxes is projected at 25 to 35 percent rather than the 5 to 10 percent typical to the industry.

Therefore, establish targets that are hard to reach and then stretch to get there. If you target at 30 percent net bottom-line profit and you achieve 22 percent, you are still ahead of the average firm. (See Chapter 6 for a section on profit and profit planning.) Figure 1-13 is a chart showing typical profit firms versus high-profit firms from the *PSMJ 1989 Financial Statistics Survey*.[3] Of the firms in the upper quartile of this chart, the top 25 had numbers that were double those shown.

Finally, do not tolerate staff who are skeptical of your goal to achieve high ratios and who aspire merely to a modest 5 percent project profit. Every member of the firm must believe in and work towards the profit goals you set for the firm.

Organizational Plan

Organizational makeup of a firm is a source of constant debate. In typical organizational charts, principals are at the top, project managers and staff below them.

Basic organizational types are market-focused teams, departmental, and matrix. Organization comes about because of a

KEY FINANCIAL PERFORMANCE RESULTS

	Lower Quartile	Median	Mean	Upper Quartile
Net Profit Before Profit Distribution and Income Taxes (Gross Revenues) *(%)*	2.9	7.6	8.0	13.0
Net Profit Before Profit Distribution and Income Taxes (Net Revenues) *(%)*	3.0	9.3	8.5	16.0
Net Profit Before Taxes (Gross Revenues) *(%)*	.8	3.0	4.1	7.1
Net Profit Before Taxes (Net Revenues) *(%)*	1.0	3.9	4.6	8.9
Net Profit (Gross Revenues) *(%)*	.5	2.2	2.6	5.2
Net Profit (Net Revenues) *(%)*	.6	2.6	2.9	6.1
Contribution (Gross Profit) Rate (Gross Revenues) *(%)*	43.2	50.3	48.9	56.1
Contribution (Gross Profit) Rate (Net Revenues) *(%)*	58.1	62.9	60.9	66.7
Overhead Rate (before Profit Distribution) *(%)*	171.3	149.7	146.3	121.5
Overhead Rate (after Profit Distribution) *(%)*	199.0	167.7	167.0	138.3
Net Multiplier Achieved *(x)*	2.44	2.74	2.76	3.09
Net Revenues per Total Staff *($)*	45,758	54,438	54,940	63,680
Net Revenues per Technical Staff *($)*	56,647	68,793	69,494	81,946
Net Revenues per Project Manager *($)*	226,000	341,000	423,000	541,000
Net Revenues per Partner/Principal *($)*	322,000	570,000	781,000	1,037,000
Net Revenues per Full Time Marketer *($)*	1,119,000	1,800,000	2,147,000	2,888,000
Net Revenues per Chargeable Hour *($)*	35.76	41.92	43.05	50.11
Direct Labor Cost per Chargeable Hour *($)*	13.10	15.23	15.56	17.79
Chargeable Ratio (Payroll Dollars) *(%)*	58.2	62.7	62.8	67.9
Marketing Costs (Gross Revenues) *(%)*	1.8	3.4	4.0	5.5
Marketing Costs (Net Revenues) *(%)*	2.3	4.2	5.2	7.4

OVERHEAD RATE (BEFORE PROFIT DISTRIBUTION)

The overhead rate is the ratio of all overhead (indirect) expenses to the total direct labor expended on projects. For each dollar of project (direct) labor spent, the median overhead expenditure was 149.7% and the mean 146.3%.

OVERHEAD RATE (AFTER PROFIT DISTRIBUTION)

The after profit distribution overhead rate includes expenditures for bonuses, profit sharing and incentive compensation in the overhead rate. For firms that normally fund such expenditures, this rate is considered more meaningful. The survey found the median to be 167.7% and the mean to be 167.0%.

Figure 1-13 Typical profit firms versus high-profit firms, from the *PSMJ 1989 Financial Statistics Survey*.[3]

common, basic conflict in architecture and engineering practice—that between quality control and client service. These two, often opposing issues are relevant even in a one-person firm. The person must decide whether or not to spend more time on a project or to stop the project. The frequently opposing forces of providing good client service versus higher and improved quality are what drive larger organizations to develop organizational plans as they move from 1 to 2 people to 5 to 10 people to 20 to 25 people. The earliest of these organizational plans is the development of teams to serve the client (market-focused). As teams grow, companies often move into matrix and departmental organizations, each of which is described below.

MARKET-FOCUSED TEAMS

To achieve a market-focused organization, define clearly the relationship between the client and your firm. Instead of dividing staff up by discipline (e.g., interior designers, landscape architects, mechanical engineers, electrical engineers), create separate teams, each serving a particular client. In this organization, project managers become the most important entities. (See Fig. 1-14.) A market-focused team approach will produce a more client-driven organization, better able to serve the client. An example of a 12-person firm, R. C. Byce & Associates, that uses market-focused teams, appears in Figure 1-15.

Market-focused teams are better for the small firm—other organizational types are better for larger firms. Another example of a firm's market-focused team approach appears in Figure 1-16.

DEPARTMENTAL ORGANIZATIONS

In a departmental structure, the whole staff focuses internally (as opposed to externally toward the client, like market-focused teams) on the quality of the department's work. This encourages competition with other departments, to the detriment of the project. For example, the mechanical engineers are departmentally focused on mechanical engineering, but they are not thinking about the client. See Figure 1-17 for an illustration of the departmental approach.

Another disadvantage of the departmental structure is that the project manager's authority is diminished by the role of department managers, who tend to be senior, more powerful

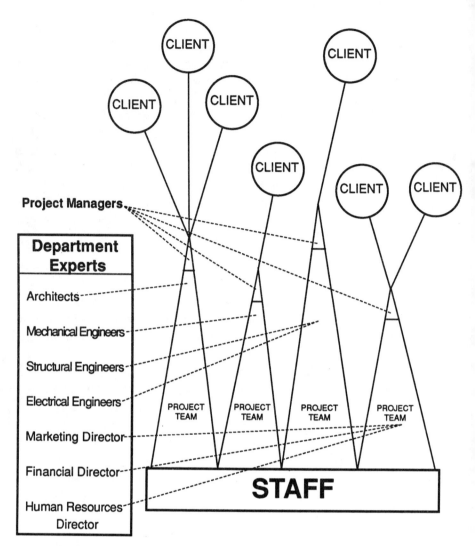

Figure 1-14 Market-focused team organization.

members of the firm. Where the project manager has less power, the client's budget and schedule suffer. So does quality control, because drawings go from one department to the next without continuity. Finally, the department becomes more important than the project, the firm, or the client.

Departmental organizations are successful when a project stays in one department. Obviously there are advantages to the departmental approach—it helps when working with clients that are massive departmental agencies such as the federal

Profile of R. C. Byce & Associates'
Market-focused Team Approach

Firm: R. C. Byce & Associates, Inc.
Staff: 14
Specialty: Heavy commercial/industrial engineering
            487 Portage Street
            Kalamazoo, Mich. 49007

The most difficult management problem, according to R. C. Byce, is that of providing a smooth, easy environment so the design team members can do their best work, maintain the required quality, and stay in touch with each other, the client, and the company president. To eliminate communications problems and facilitate office production, the firm operates department-free, with a minimal number of draftspersons, and allows no one a private clerk or secretary. Project managers are experienced, dominate in a team consensus way, and insist that communications flow. Therefore the only project managers are the executive vice president and the president of the firm. Although company capacity is limited because of this qualification, the organization usually works. Below is an organizational chart of R. C. Byce & Associates.

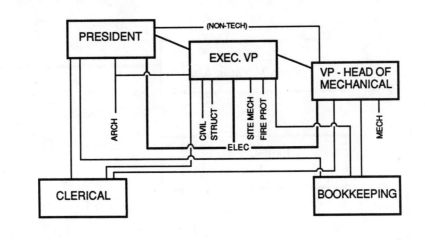

Figure 1-15   *Source:* R. C. Byce & Associates. Used with permission.

government or other large bureaucracies. Generally small firms shouldn't have departments. As a small firm, if you start growing, don't grow with departments, grow with teams. Smith, Seckman, and Reed is a mechanical, civil, and electrical engineering firm that became *un*profitable by growing as a departmentalized structure. It started as a small organization with a team approach, grew as a departmental structure, and then returned to the team approach to become more profitable. Thomas Seckman, of the Nashville-based engineering firm, says that as recently as three years ago his company was still using a departmental approach. After years of considering a change, he returned to the team-oriented approach. The firm is now significantly more successful—morale is higher and profits are up. Seckman says the team approach improves client relations. The client has someone with genuine authority to carry out its requests. The project manager writes bills, follows up, and thus has a better chance of collecting the fees, since the client has worked with him all along.

Small firms usually start out with one discipline and add more as they grow. Adding disciplines can undermine your success if the process destroys the focus of your vision and therefore of your strategic plan.

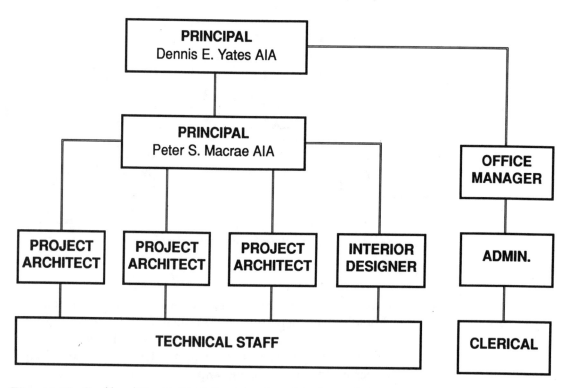

Figure 1-16 Profile of Dennis Yates Associates' market-focused team approach. Used with permission.

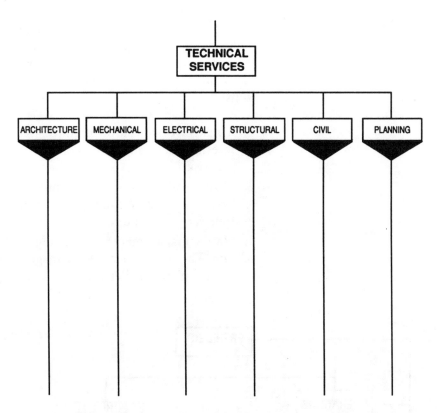

Figure 1-17   The departmental organization approach.

MATRIX ORGANIZATIONS

A matrix organizational structure seeks to balance power among the project leaders/managers and department managers. Both managers are equal, and each staff member has two bosses—the architectural or engineering department manager and the project manager. The staff's time is split 50–50 between the two bosses.

In a matrix organization the scales are usually tipped in favor of the person with the most power. If the department manager pays the staff, gives raises, and promotes, then the project manager has little control. The staff's allegiance is to the department. This is the case in the majority of design firms using a matrix approach, and they are really departmental organizations. On the other hand, if the project manager has more power, then the staff becomes more project-oriented, and hence client-oriented. Unfortunately, this is the exception, not the rule.

The only way a pure matrix can exist is if both the department heads and the project managers have equal power. Figure 1-18 shows the matrix-type organizational structure.

The matrix is not good for the small firm for the following reasons:

1. A matrix organization requires that energy be focused internally instead of on clients. Small firms cannot take this risk.
2. Most small firms offer only one service. Matrix works best in a multidisciplinary environment where three to four services are offered.
3. Matrix management requires higher overhead to maintain. The cost of increased management time is generally too great for smaller firms.

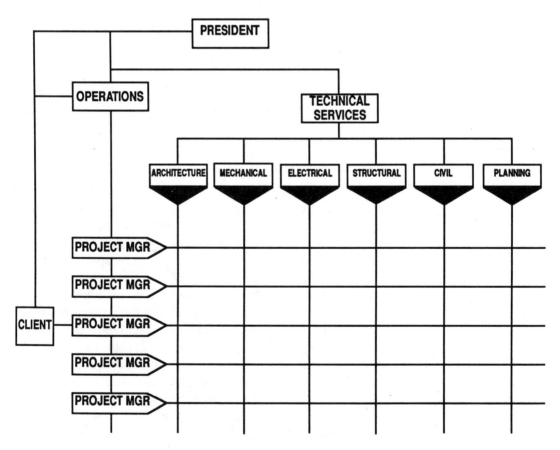

Figure 1-18 The matrix organizational structure.

The matrix structure generally first appears in firms of 40 to 50 people in a multidisciplinary environment. The exception may be a 30-person firm that provides architectural, mechanical, and civil engineering services. In such cases, the smaller organization moving toward a medium size may find this type of structure useful.

Human Resources Plan

Success in human resources is the ability to staff your organization with employees who believe in what you are doing, and the skill in motivating them to stay.

Human resources is not only recordkeeping and keeping track of vacation and sick time, but recruiting and filling your organization with the right kind of people. It takes a plan.

This plan should correspond to your financial and marketing goals and organizational structure. Areas it should address include staffing, recruitment, position planning, performance appraisal, career planning, training, compensation/rewards/benefits (see Chapter 5), employee assistance, and records. All of these elements, which in larger firms fall under the jurisdiction of the human resources director, must become the responsibility of one of the principals, who performs these functions on a part-time basis.

Figure 1-19 shows the organizational chart for the Human Resources Division of an actual design firm. The chart applies to firms of all sizes.

As with other plans, your human resources plan should not be an elaborate, 40-page document detailing every process. Instead, focus on the kinds of people you need to attract and the methods to attract them.

STAFFING AND RECRUITMENT

Staffing activities include promoting your firm through methods that reflect your firm's personality. For example, if you are looking for a receptionist, how does your newspaper ad stand out from the crowd so you attract people who are better than the norm? Write an ad that sets you apart from the others. Ask for a "virtuoso on the phone." You will get fewer resumes, but they will be top people.

At the professional level, recruitment may also involve attracting good people from your competitors. While the ethics of this continues to be debated, good employees gravitate to

HUMAN RESOURCES

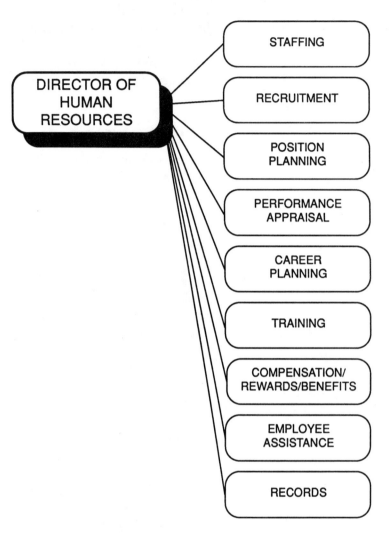

Figure 1-19 Organizational chart of the Human Resources Division. Used with permission.

firms that offer challenging work, a pleasant workplace, and attractive pay, not necessarily in that order. Make them an offer. (See Chapter 4.)

POSITION PLANNING

In position planning, create clear job descriptions with no task associations. Focus on accomplishment, not method. When you list tasks, you allow employees a loophole because they can claim an assignment is not listed in their job description.

Performance-oriented job descriptions are driven by accomplishment. Example: "Your projects will achieve 32 percent profit next year." How the person achieves the goal is up to them. For an illustration of a standard performance-oriented job description, see Figure 1-20. Goal-oriented job descriptions are clear. They also simplify the performance appraisal.

PERFORMANCE APPRAISAL

Measure performance using five criteria:

1. *Actual Performance:* Did you complete contract documents on 80 percent of your projects on schedule?
2. *Work Ethic:* Did you report to work on time? Do you work hard? Do you put in the effort to do your job?
3. *Effectiveness:* Is the work you do effective? Do you get your work done?
4. *Loyalty:* Are you loyal to the organization? Are you loyal to the vision that we have as a company? How is that loyalty measured?
5. *Emotion:* Do you have the right emotional fit with our group? Are your morals the same as ours? That is, Do you really psychically fit with our team?

Avoid performance appraisal systems where employees are numerically rated on forms. Successful smaller firms tend not to have forms, but prefer informal relationships with the staff. Appraisals are direct and regular, sometimes occurring daily as people perform their jobs. Reviews are constant.

An outline of a performance appraisal system by Schmidt Associates Architects appears in Figure 1-21. Forms should be a *record* of the performance appraisal, as opposed to the performance appraisal itself.

CAREER PLANNING AND TRAINING

As a firm you should encourage training and establish training goals. Some firms restrict training budgets to one percent of net billings, according to the *Professional Services Management Journal's* 1989 financial survey.[2] Exceptional firms allocate five times that amount. Stretch employees to become better trained, to complete their university degrees. This motivates

Performance-oriented Job Description

Position: Department Manager
Accountable to:
Responsible for:

General Responsibility

The primary responsibility of the Department Manager (DM) is to make sure that the Department operates in such a way as to meet its responsibilities to:

1. The customers
2. The Company (including other Departments)
3. The employees

In addition, the DM should develop ways of improving the Department's (and the Company's) strategies and operations.

Specific Responsibilities

Marketing

1. Supporting Company marketing objectives and priorities.
2. Developing marketing objectives and plans for Department, in coordination with other Departments.
3. Managing the implementation of Department marketing plans.
4. Assisting own Group Managers in exploiting marketing opportunities.
5. Supporting other Departments in exploiting marketing opportunities.
6. Identifying how the Company can improve its marketing capabilities.
7. Ensuring that Department generates CCRS and other marketing reports.
8. Approving proposals initiated by own Department.
9. Identify how the Company can improve its technical capabilities, and support such efforts.
10. Approve technical reports issued by own Department.

Personnel

1. Supervising and reviewing Group Managers and support staff assigned to department.
2. Assisting and training Group Managers of own Department in obtaining, training, assigning, utilizing, and releasing technical personnel.
3. Determining Department requirements for Group and Project Managers and making promotion and/or hiring recommendations to the President.
4. Review planned salaries of Department members with Administration Department for consistency and for contractual implications.
5. Recommend to the Scientific Career Committee qualified employees within their Departments for promotions into the Technical Specialist or Principal Scientist positions.

Other

1. Identify routine and special facilities needed by the Department.
2. Conduct special projects as assigned.

Specific Authorities

Marketing

1. Negotiate and agree upon job tasks and schedule with technical customer.
2. Provide informal cost estimates to the customer.
3. Agree with other DMs on people utilization for proposal purposes.

Technical

1. Approve all aspects of technical approach.
2. Assign/reassign project management responsibilities within own Department, and between Departments (by agreement with other applicable DMs).
3. Establish appropriate technical liaison with the customer.

Personnel

1. Approve promotions to Senior Analyst and salaries for Department members only.
2. Approve transfers within groups of own Department.

Firm Description

This is a multidisciplinary professional service firm that conducts research and provides technical support to federal government, state government, and commercial customers. Their services consist primarily of operations research, Naval welfare analysis, engineering analysis and feasibility studies, planning computer modeling, environmental analysis, and the development of technical documentation. This firm is located in the Northeast.

Figure 1-20

the staff to stay with you. See Chapter 5, "Compensation," for more information on career planning programs.

To encourage continuing education in your firm, consider these points:

1. Hire people who are motivated to be educated. You cannot force someone to want to become better educated.
2. Put control in the hands of the employee, not the company. Allow employees to take courses that may or may not be directly related to the firm's activities.

SCHMIDT ASSOCIATES ARCHITECTS, INC.
PERFORMANCE REVIEW/CAREER PLANNING

NAME _____
POSITION _____
DATE _____

Everything pertaining to your review and merit increase is personal and confidential.

1. PERSONAL GOALS

    *

    *

    *

    *

    *

2. PROFESSIONAL GOALS

    *

    *

    *

    *

    *

Figure 1-21 Outline of Schmidt Associates Architect performance appraisal system. Used with permission.

38

BEHAVIOR STYLE	ON-THE-JOB OBSERVATIONS AND COMMENTS

1. COMMITMENT OF SELF
 	
  * Demonstrates a positive outlook on life and expects the best.
  * Commits a concept of Lifelong Learning.
  * Maintains a high level of energy.
  * Maintains a high level of purpose.
  * Maintains a high level of determination.
  * Maintains a balance of personal and professional time.
	_____ OUT OF _____

2. COMMITMENT TO PROFESSIONAL EXCELLENCE
 	
  * Pursues "good design" in all efforts.
  * Strives to be the best.
	_____ OUT OF _____

3. SERVICE ORIENTATION
 	
  * Seeks to understand and meet the needs of the clients (client is person/group to whom services are provided; i.e. our clients, owners, users, other staff, Schmidt Associates Architects, consultants, contractors, other associates).
  * Evaluates services to ensure that they are always client oriented.
  * Does not allow personal or job stress to interfere with relations with clients.
  * Shows understanding, sensitivity and empathy in dealing with others.
	_____ OUT OF _____

PAGE 2

Figure 1-21 (*continued*)

BEHAVIOR STYLE	ON-THE-JOB OBSERVATIONS AND COMMENTS
4. COMMUNICATION SKILLS * Gives and receives relevant, accurate information in a timely manner (i.e. delegate effectively). * Presents oral and written information in clear, concise manner. * Keeps manager well informed of activities and needs. * Listens actively and acts on feedback from others.	____ OUT OF ____
5. TEAM RELATIONS * Examines the process of how things are communicated as well as the content of what is communicated. * Demonstrates respect, courtesy and tact for all staff. * Responds appropriately to others' needs. * Others at all levels feel welcome to approach this person for help or advice.	____ OUT OF ____
6. ORGANIZATION SKILLS * Schedules own assignments and tasks so that they can be completed on time. * Prioritizes workload and coordinates own activities with others. * Can size up a work assignment and identify a strategy for accomplishment. * Voluntarily pursues additional responsibility after completion of routine assignments.	____ OUT OF ____

PAGE 3

Figure 1-21 (*continued*)

BEHAVIOR STYLE	ON-THE-JOB OBSERVATIONS AND COMMENTS
7. RESOURCE CONSERVATION * Utilizes time efficiently through proper time management. * Utilizes and maintains equipment and supplies without waste. * Makes suggestions and takes actions to improve productivity and cost-containment. * Shares expertise and experience with others.	_____ OUT OF _____
8. ADDITIONS FROM MANAGER * * * *	_____ OUT OF _____
9. SPECIFIC TASKS TO DO * * * *	

85-100 (Excellent) *Performance clearly exceeds job requirements over a sustained period of time. Makes significant contributions well beyond job demands. Both results, and how they are achieved, are exceptional.*

65-84 (Above Standard) *Fully meets and often exceeds position requirements. Demonstrates full understanding of all required functions.*

50-65 (Standard) *Requirements and responsibilities of the position are handled competently. Usually meets expected level of performance.*

Below 50 (Substandard) *Performance must be improved. Only partially meets job requirements and requires more than minimal help from supervisor and others to perform effectively.*

PERFORMANCE LEVEL _____   TOTAL _____ OUT OF _____

Figure 1-21 (continued)

SCHMIDT ASSOCIATES ARCHITECTS, INC.
PERFORMANCE REVIEW/CAREER PLANNING
PROJECT MANAGER

NAME _____
DATE _____

Everything pertaining to your review and merit increase is personal and confidential.

MAJOR OBJECTIVES	ON-THE-JOB OBSERVATIONS AND COMMENTS
1. OWNER RELATIONSHIPS * Build and maintain Owner rapport. * Know Owner's current objectives and situational factors. * Function as primary communications link between Owner and project team throughout project. * Anticipate Owner reactions and negotiate solutions which mutually satisfy Owner and firm. * Host Owner at routine and special firm events.	_____ OUT OF _____
2. PREPARE PROJECT STRATEGIES * Design the project strategy that meets Owner's goals for results. * Determine the need for project research and fulfill the need. * Develop a clear and concise project plan. * Monitor the success of the project plan and redesign as needed.	_____ OUT OF _____

Figure 1-21 (continued)

MAJOR OBJECTIVES	ON-THE-JOB OBSERVATIONS AND COMMENTS
3. PROJECT TEAM COORDINATION (staff and other consultants who will provide services to Owner) * Summarize Owner objectives and drivers (i.e., budget, schedule, function, spirit, and style of decision makers). * Summarize project strategy. * Lead project team meetings. * Lead design critiques (determine priorities and agendas). * Monitor project process and troubleshoot on behalf of the team. * Review the team's service from project and Owner perspectives. * Build and maintain team rapport. * Establish and influence a positive team attitude.	_____ OUT OF _____
4. PROJECT MAINTENANCE (assure concise, accurate records) * Initiate all project consultant contracts and submittals. * Complete and issue concise and timely meeting notes following all project contacts. * Maintain complete Owner specific files. * Approve changes in contract. * Maintain project compliance within Owner's budget constraints.	_____ OUT OF _____

Figure 1-21 (*continued*)

43

MAJOR OBJECTIVES	ON-THE-JOB OBSERVATIONS AND COMMENTS
5. INSURE QUALITY AND TIMELY SERVICES * Set, monitor and meet all personal deadlines. * Keep project team accountable to Owner deadlines. * Function as the final quality control point of all Owner materials (correspondence, presentations, contract documents, field observation, etc.) * Follow-up with Owner to confirm timely, quality delivery of service.	_____ OUT OF _____
6. MANAGE PROJECT PROFITABILITY * Prepare final Owner's fees with a 20%+ project profit margin in mind. * Process invoices within two working days of approval. * Approve invoices prior to mailing. * Strive to be 80% to 90% billable based upon _____ work week. * Monitor the profitability of work in progress. * Review weekly financial reports.	_____ OUT OF _____

Figure 1-21 *(continued)*

MAJOR OBJECTIVES	ON-THE-JOB OBSERVATIONS AND COMMENTS
7. DEVELOP NEW BUSINESS AMONG CURRENT OWNERS * Awareness of Owner's future needs. * Coordinate with presentation team to produce the polished written proposal. * Prearrange team presentations and coach presenters. * Introduce and summarize the presentation setting the stage for a decision.	_____ OUT OF _____

85-100   (Excellent)   *Performance clearly exceeds job requirements over a sustained period of time. Makes significant contributions well beyond job demands. Both results, and how they are achieved, are exceptional.*

65-84   (Above Standard)   *Fully meets and often exceeds position requirements. Demonstrates full understanding of all required functions.*

50-65   (Standard)   *Requirements and responsibilities of the position are handled competently. Usually meets expected level of performance.*

Below 50   (Substandard)   *Performance must be improved. Only partially meets job requirements and requires more than minimal help from supervisor and others to perform effectively.*

SUBTOTAL _____ OUT OF _____

Figure 1-21 *(continued)*

COMPENSATION/REWARDS/BENEFITS

Insist on fair compensation planning. Do not compensate people arbitrarily: aim for equity in positions, and bonus plans tied to performance, not company profits. Award hard-working employees, not all. Pay 75 percent of the bonus money to the top third, 25 percent to the middle third, and no bonus money to the bottom third. Reward the top people and penalize the nonperformers. (For more details, see Chapter 5.)

EMPLOYEE ASSISTANCE

Societal changes are creating the need for employee assistance programs that adapt to the life-styles of talented employees. Recognize this trend; don't insist on traditional patterns. Childcare and work schedules that revolve around children's school hours might be provided. Evening, flextime, and part-time hours may be offered. Student and team employment (two people sharing one job) are other examples of employee assistance.

Such assistance programs, if they reflect employees' needs, will motivate them to perform and to stay. Figure 1-1, the profile of Meehan Architects, explains how a change in company hours improved productivity.

RECORDKEEPING

Plan your recordkeeping so all your records are succinct. The easiest way for small firms to maintain records is to adapt a standard industry format such as the CSI MASTERFORMAT. This format corresponds to the chapter allocation of all project resources to the CSI numbering system. There are other standards, such as the UNIFORMAT system, still used in Great Britain, that can be useful in setting up your records. Adapting such a system will put you into the mainstream of the industry without sacrificing any efficiency, and your records will be easily translatable from discipline to discipline as you network with other firms in the marketplace. Many client organizations keep their records in the CSI or similar format.

CSI MASTERFORMAT

1. General requirements
2. Site work
3. Concrete

4. Masonry
5. Metals
6. Wood and plastics
7. Moisture–thermal control
8. Doors, windows, and glass
9. Finishes
10. Specialties
11. Equipment
12. Furnishings
13. Special construction
14. Conveying systems
15. Mechanical
16. Electrical

Leadership Transition

The problem with leadership transition in a service business such as architecture and/or engineering is that you cannot just sell your firm and leave. Clients who buy your service count on having you there, especially if you built up the practice.

Leadership selection is one of the most overlooked functions in design firms. You must ask such questions as

Who will carry on your vision into the future?

What kind of a person must you hire as leader to guarantee your firm's future success?

Some firms cannot function without their original leadership, especially if they are star-driven. Address the issue, whether or not you solve it. It is better to have a plan that *rejects* leadership transition than to vacillate on this issue. Be clear about your plan for selecting, training, and cultivating new leaders.

One architect in Tennessee boldly skipped over a generation of 40- to 50-year-olds to pick a new president who was 33. He risked losing 10 or 15 employees because in order to make clear whom he wanted as the future leader of the firm.

LEADERSHIP SELECTION CRITERIA

Define the criteria for leader selection in the firm. Include well-described steps leading to the top position. When clearly stated, the leadership selection plan lets junior employees

---

Rules of Eligibility to be Considered in Becoming an Associate

1. You must have exhibited a willingness to accept responsibility.
2. You must exhibit an attitude of professionalism in the conduct of your responsibilities.
3. You must have exhibited exemplary character, integrity, honesty, fairness, loyalty, dependability, and professional ethics in your working relationships with both those inside as well as outside the company.
4. You must be deemed by the Board of Directors as having gained and maintained the respect of fellow employees.
5. You must have exhibited continued competence in your particular area of expertise. Due to the technical nature of the engineering profession, it is likely that most Associates will be technical employees; however, secretarial, accounting, marketing, business, or other supportive disciplines are not excluded from eligibility.
6. You must be capable of successfully meeting quality, budget, time of completion, and client satisfaction goals on projects in which they are involved.
7. You must have been actively involved in working full time in the engineering/surveying/land planning profession for a minimum of five years.
8. You must have exhibited the ability to be "accepted" by our clients, since those elected to carry the title and exposure which comes with being an Associate are recognized by our clients to be representative of the quality and character of our organization.
9. You must initiate discussion about your intent to become an Associate.
10. Preference will be given to those who have been employees of the company for a minimum of three years.
11. You must be elected by two-thirds of the Board of Directors.

Figure 1-22

know where they stand and what it takes to get to the next rung. Here are 10 criteria for picking leadership in design practices:

1. Clarity of vision.
2. Ability to make things happen.
3. Charisma.
4. Ability to communicate well.
5. Ability to delegate effectively.

6. Courage.
7. Integrity.
8. Desire and drive to succeed.
9. Respect for people.
10. Intelligence.

The above were the results of a recent brainstorming session held at the Beaver Creek Leadership Program with 12 firm principals.

Most firms pick future leaders solely on the basis of subjective opinion. A few, however, have established published criteria for "moving up" in the firm. Figure 1-22 is an example of one firm's criteria in selecting an associate.

ACCOUNTING PLAN

This is a plan detailing the legal/financial transactions for bringing future owners into the firm. Usually referred to as an *ownership transition plan*, it attempts to address the issue of leadership.

LEADERSHIP WANTS AND NEEDS

The company should consider its future and describe the type of leader it needs. Ask: Should we bring in an outside managing partner? Are there people in the second generation we want to target? Should we pick a future chief from the third generation? Or should we decide not to focus on leadership transition and instead on company growth or profits?

Include All the Elements

Your strategic plan must include all six elements. Figure 1-23 is a summary of the six elements of the strategic plan.

CONDUCTING A PLANNING MEETING

The essence of all successful strategic plans is that they are *simple, realistic,* and *easily communicated.* The following simple 11-step process is designed to show you how to conduct a strategic planning meeting, put it in writing, and communicate it to the rest of the firm.

Summary of the Six Elements of the Strategic Plan

1. **Vision**
   Mission Statement
   Culture
2. **Marketing Plan and Direction**
   Measurable Goals
   Focus
   Cost and Organization
3. **Financial Plan**
   Standardization
   Employee Involvement
   Profit
4. **Organizational Plan**
   Market-focused Teams
   Departmental Organizations
   Matrix Organizations

5. **Human Resources Plan**
   Staffing and Recruitment
   Position Planning
   Performance Appraisal
   Career Planning and Training
   Compensation/Rewards/Benefits
   Employee Assistance
   Recordkeeping
6. **Leadership Transition**
   Leadership Selection Criteria
   Accounting Plan
   Leadership Wants and Needs

Figure 1-23

1. Start with Yourself

Make a list of those things you personally want to happen over the next few years. Do you want more income? More challenging projects? A sabbatical? A different role? Write down a description of your personal vision of what the firm and you will look like three, four, or five years from now if all goes as you wish.

2. Establish a Time Span

Long-range planning does not mean 20 years. Think in terms of a 3- to 5-year planning span. This will help make your plan realistic and keep it simple.

3. Involve Others Early

Identify those in your firm with the most impact on its future and ask each to write down their personal ambitions and desires. Then have them describe the firm 3 to 5 years from now.

No need to ask that these written statements be turned in; they are simply to force individuals to think about the issues in anticipation of a group planning session.

4. Pick a Planning Leader

Identify an individual in your firm who is good at conducting brainstorming sessions. The role of this individual is to co-ordinate and conduct a planning session among the senior individuals in your office so as to synthesize the personal goals and desires of the individuals into a concise long-range plan. If no such person is available in-house, bring in a consultant as a catalyst to help you lead the meeting.

5. Set a Date

Schedule a full day's planning session for all those involved in Step 3 above. The session must be outside your facility to avoid interruptions and to underscore your commitment to the planning process. The room should be comfortable and provision made for a flip chart, markers, and masking tape. No more than 10 to 12 individuals should ever be invited to the session.

6. Don't Do Extensive Research

The purpose of the planning session is to clarify goals and direction. Subsequent to the session, assignments can be made to verify specific aspects of your plan through research. Your experience, however, and that of your colleagues should discourage extensive preplanning research.

7. Establish Your Own Yardstick

Using flip chart and markers, begin your planning session by asking all individuals to describe verbally what the firm will look like at 3, 4, or 5 years out. Pick a year (we suggest three) and list very specific items, such as 150 projects, 32 employees, $2 million in gross fees, two new markets, and so on. Be certain to discuss all aspects of the firm—production, marketing, human resources, finance, and management—in terms of goals and targets. Be realistic, yet stretch your expectations a bit.

Also, don't be trapped into cliches such as "growth." If you bought this book, you may actually desire not to grow.

The importance of this step is to actively seek and draw out from those who will get it there the most realistic 3- to 5-year picture of what the firm will be.

8. Set One-year Expectations

After agreeing on 3- to 5-year goals, the leader asks each individual where the firm will be in 1 year, so as to be on track for the 3-year goals. Use the flip chart again, and list in more specific terms exactly where the practice should be in a single year.

9. Give Individual Six-month Assignments

Identify specific individuals within the session who agree and commit to the group to carry out specific assignments in order to begin working toward the goals. Set target *calendar* dates, not elapsed time dates, and establish specifically what is to be done, by whom, and who else will assure that it is done. For example, one possible 3-year goal is to be a recognized expert in a new (for your firm) building type; in one year, you intend to have three projects in that building type, and by January 1, 1991 (30 days), John Smith will have developed a written marketing plan to get the three projects, and Al Jones will have carried out the assignment.

10. Communicate All You've Written

At the end of your session, summarize in outline form on your flip chart your 3-year, 1-year, and 6-month plans. Using the flip chart forces you to be concise and clarify decisions. Take the newsprint sheets back to the firm, and have your long-range plan typed directly from them. Using this method assures that your written plan will be no more than three to six pages long. It will be simple, clear, and easily understood.

Assign each individual in the group session the responsibility to talk with two to four staff people about your planning session and to personally hand out copies of your typewritten plan to them. Do not bind your plan in fancy covers or permanent binders. Instead, mark it "DRAFT: To Be Updated In June 1991" (six months from now). Doing so tells the staff that their input can still have an impact on the firm's direction. When discussing the plan with the staff, the primary objective is to get feedback, not to lay down dogma.

11. Schedule Your Next Planning Session

Before leaving your one-day meeting, pick a specific calendar date six months ahead, a specific location, and specific people for another all-day planning session; repeat the entire process six months later. Following this rule means that you will be devoting two days (16 hours) of your staff time per year to planning, which is a price you *can* afford. It also means that you will respond to the input you receive over the next six months from others on your staff.

REPEAT THE PROCESS PERIODICALLY

By following the planning process, you will see that strategic planning is nothing more than setting goals, establishing 1-year objectives, and assigning 6-month strategies and action plans on how to achieve your goals. A firm that has recently moved to a 6-month planning period is the 25-person firm of the Henderson Group, of St. Louis, Missouri: "We have found that coping with the rapid changes in the development marketplace requires more attention to strategy and operations than ever before. The six-month planning documents include two parts: (1) operations, and (2) work load." Instead of reacting to events, you will be able to take the initiative with a 6-month planning period. You will determine where your firm is going and when it will get there.

More significant than documentation of the goals is the process, which enhances communication of the firm's direction and helps you and your associates measure where you are in relation to your plan. Each person in the firm knows where they want to go and is aware that their actions support it or are a hindrance.

What is true about your plan today may not be true several years from now. Key areas of the plan and the forces that act upon them are in a state of constant change. Periodic reassessment is the only way to ensure that the components of your strategic plan are relevant and respond to your organization's environment. Figure 1-24 is a typical strategic plan.

SUCCESS CHALLENGES

1. Have you really focused on your own personal vision of what you want your company to be? If so, write it down now.

2. Are you communicating your vision to your staff, and do they really believe it?

3. Evaluate your marketing plan—does it directly relate to fulfilling your vision?

4. Look at your financial plan. Are your ratio goals conservative? If so, raise them.

5. Draw a market-focused organizational plan for your company.

6. Does your human resources plan actually draw in high-caliber candidates? If not, why not?

Sample Strategic Plan for the ABC Group

The ABC Group offers planning, design, and management services for the built environment.

Was founded in 1971 by the CEO of the A Group, Inc.; was incorporated in 1979; and is now part of the ABC Group.

The 60 employees include architects, construction project managers, engineers, interior designers, landscape architects and support staff. The ABC Group offers the following services:

Bank planning and design	Hospital renovation and design
Campus planning and design	Library planning and design
Church planning and design	Mental health facility planning and
Construction project management	design
Downtown redevelopment	Office building planning and design
Educational facility planning and design	Parks and recreation planning
Energy management	Retirement facility planning and design
Historic preservation	

Figure 1-24

CLIENT SERVICES

CLIENTS

BRANCH OFFICE

- INTERIORS
- ENGINEERING
- SITE/LANDSCAPE

- GENERAL
- RELIGIOUS

- GENERAL
- HOUSING
- COMMERCIAL
- SPECIAL PROJECTS (REPORTS TO PRESIDENT)
- INSTITUTIONAL
- CPM (REPORTS TO PRESIDENT)

CORPORATE ADMINISTRATION

- SHAREHOLDERS
- BD OF DIRECTORS
- PRESIDENT

- FINANCIAL
- CLIENT DEVELOPMENT
- HUMAN RESOURCES

- OPERATIONS
  - SPECS
  - CADD

Figure 1-24 (*continued*)

55

Memorandum To: The ABC Group Staff
Subject: Strategy Plan
From: CEO
Date: August 29, 1990

This is a follow-up to our February 17, 1990 annual business meeting and the work of the strategic planning session.

We are submitting this first draft for review, comment, discussion, and revision.

OVERVIEW:

- We want to and are committed to providing outstanding professional services
- In keeping with our shared values
- Based upon the continuing work of the "Step Beyond" group

The strategic statements/goals cover the following eight areas:

1. Quality Service
2. Financial
3. Design
4. Growth
5. Business Development
6. Human Resources
7. Facilities
8. Operations

I. QUALITY SERVICES

A. To provide an outstanding quality service to our clients.
B. To provide outstanding technical product.

- Do an annual client survey to measure performance of our service including projects one year after occupancy.
- By October 1, 1992, the results of the survey place us above 80 on a scale of 1 to 100.

2. FINANCE

A. Reduce long term debt by completing payment of our current consolidated loan.
B. Eliminate personal financial guarantees for the ABC Group, Inc., on or before October 1, 1993.
C. Provide financial strength required to grow while meeting "B" above.

Figure 1-24 (continued)

D. Have a 15% operating income (before allocations), which means to be in or above the 75% of design firms operating by the end of FY 1992 and beyond.
E. Provide salaries and benefits within or above 75% of similar firms in our region by October 1, 1993.

3. DESIGN

A. To meet the needs of our clients as a team. (Form, function, time, cost.)
B. To respect the local project environment (contextuality) and our Shared Value #9.
C. To provide alternatives. Every issue should be presented in alternatives. We should state our preference, but the client must have choices to decide.

• Do an annual planned review, starting in 1990, of the various specialties/disciplines with appropriate realistic practical peers to evaluate and measure the above.

4. GROWTH

A. 50% of current discipline efforts to be devoted to prime client service by October 1, 1993.
B. To have an additional specialty team operational by October 1, 1993.
C. To have a second new specialty team operational by 1994.
D. An average growth of 12% per year in the next five (5) years. (17.6%) (85-90 people).

OPTION:

1. Golf course design
2.
3.
4.
5.
6.

• Special organizational emphasis will be devoted to Engineering, Interiors, Civil, and LA to accomplish the above.
• The two (2) new specialty teams are expected to grow out of services/sub-specialties currently provided.

5. BUSINESS DEVELOPMENT

A. To have a minimum backlog of nine (9) months of signed contracts at all times based upon the annual budget.

Figure 1-24 (continued)

B. To have a minimum of nine (9) months of weighted leads based upon the annual budget by June 1, 1990.

C. To have a minimum of a twelve (12) month value of weighted leads at all times based upon the annual budget by October 1, 1992.

D. Be recognized as experts as follows:

Nationally: In two (2) specialty areas

Options: 1. Retirement and mental health

2. Retirement and churches

3.

4.

5.

6.

Options: 7.

8.

9.

10.

Regionally: In two (2) specialty areas and two (2) disciplines

Options: 1. Engineering/Architectural

2. Architectural

3. Mental Health

4. Engineering

5.

6.

7.

8.

9.

10.

Locally: The entire firm

Options: 1.

2.

3.

4.

5.

6.

7.

8.

9.

10.

Figure 1-24 (continued)

E. That each PIC and Discipline Director have a systematic marketing plan implemented by October 1990, including a "family of documents" for public relations.

6. HUMAN RESOURCES

A. To recruit outstanding talent.
B. To train the staff.
C. To enable personal growth by maintaining an effective organization.
D. To have staff satisfaction be equal to or greater than client satisfaction identified in #1A.

- Use a yearly survey administered by an external individual to measure the organization's performance in B and C.
- Use outside recruiting assistance as necessary.
- Special attention paid to "travelers."
- Special attention paid to individuals who find themselves required to provide significant extra effort.

7. FACILITIES

A. With respect to our facilities, it was decided at the Board Meeting on 5/12/90 that we would proceed to expand the 425 building. This will allow us space for the next two to three years.
B. It is our plan that in two to three years the main office would be at a new location in a new facility, either constructed or purchased. This is, of course, contingent upon the firm's financial strength and a positive economy.

- Address image long term.
- Provide statement on long term of branch office.
- Address the concept of Pennsylvania expansion. Make a go/no go decision.

8. OPERATIONS

A. Provide personal computer support to each specialty, discipline and project team by 1993.
B. Adapt spec system to the ABC Group, Inc.
C. Expand and organize the library.
D. Complete building technical standards system.
E. Complete building project management systems.
F. Develop specific standards for design and technical items for each discipline/specialty.

Figure 1-24 (continued)

7. Divide your staff into thirds—top, middle, and bottom—of the top third, which individuals have leadership qualities?

8. Set a date for your annual strategic planning meeting and for the subsequent meeting.

REFERENCES

1. Tom Peters. Nightingale/Conant Sount Management Report, Vol. 1. Chicago, Ill.
2. Practice Management Associates, Ltd, 1989 *PSMJ 1989 Financial Statistics Survey*. Newton, Mass.
3. *Ibid.*, p. 20.

BIBLIOGRAPHY

Building Design and Construction, October 1988. Boston: Cahners Publishing Company.

Frank A. Stasiowski, December 1979. "Do It Yourself Planning." *Professional Services Management Journal*, Vol. 6, p. 12.

Frank Stasiowski, 1987. *Position Descriptions*. Professional Management Association.

Frank A. Stasiowski, November 1989. "Six Strategic Planning Elements." *Professional Services Management Journal*, Vol. 16, p. 11.

2 FOCUSING YOUR PRACTICE

Professionals often "hang out their shingle" without defining their purpose. Usually, their purpose is to "be an architect" or to "be an interior designer." Whether or not there is a need for the service in their community is not even considered. Expressing that need in terms of a specific market for a type of service is far from the minds of most architects and engineers starting a business. As a result, there is a pattern of small firms made up of design professionals who will perform any type of service for any client.

Yet, small firms that are consistently successful focus their practice on a few elemental services unique to its members, and they sell that focused service in the marketplace.

Consider why you are in business. To serve clients? To create monuments? To make money? To provide security for your family? All of these are significant and realistic goals for some design professionals. But they do not necessarily focus the practice.

There are two ways to focus your practice, by project market or type, or by service type. By and large, focusing on providing a service is the more profitable option. Firms marketing an element of their service (facilities planning, selecting art for hotel interiors, providing construction management services) tend to be significantly more profitable than those that sell design services for project types (hospitals, education facilities, etc.). According to the past four years' *PSMJ Financial Statistics* surveys of specialty firms that focus on one client and project type, these firms are significantly more profitable.[1]

The service focus is more profitable because your organization is able to learn much more effectively the language of a single type (or at most two or three types) of client. Every client group has a jargon of its own. For example, in the health care marketplace, one encounters terms such as CON—a Certificate of Need. If you are providing health care services, you must be familiar with this document and CON rate. Small firms that provide a multitude of services to various markets are severely handicapped in communicating with the various types of clients in their own language, compared to the firm that lives, eats, and breathes in one or two markets.

By focusing on a service, you become an expert—for example, as a facilities management consulting firm to hospitals. Chapter 3, "Servicing the Client," further explains the idea of focusing on a service.

ADVANTAGES OF FOCUSING THE PRACTICE

Many small firm principals fear focusing, believing that if they focus on one client type their client base may shrink in a recession. But firms that focus narrowly on a particular service are able to anticipate a recession better than other firms, and as a result are able to move into new specialties faster, thereby avoiding economic downturn.

In other words, the focused firm is able to stay ahead of the market. Earth Technology (Long Beach, California) was, in 1975, the primary geotechnical firm on the West Coast doing underground geotechnical studies for nuclear power plants. In 1979, the nuclear power industry all but stopped building power plants. Today, Earth Technology has moved to site work analysis for hazardous waste. This firm was highly specialized and thus was able to foresee a decline in the industry in enough time to shift quickly to another market focus, ahead of many competitors.

Many small firms avoid making a market shift, fearing their total demise. However, small firms, more than any others, have the ability to move quickly into new markets.

Another focused firm is Thomas Wirth Landscape Architects. Wirth focuses on the kinds of projects he most enjoys—small signatory gardens—and has become renowned at providing this service. A profile of this firm appears in Figure 2-1.

Some firms are able to focus on several areas by dividing into specialized focus teams. Companies of 30 or 40 could divide their resources into two or three teams, each focusing on a particular small market niche.

Profile of a Focused Firm

Firm: Thomas Wirth Landscape Architects
Staff: 6
Specialty: Small, signatory gardens
Address: 20 North Main Street
           Sherborn, Mass. 01770

Thomas Wirth has become a specialist in a small niche of the landscape architecture market, designing small signatory gardens—for example, a garden inside a shopping center. Wirth worked for 10 years on many commercial projects, and developed a preference for designing small parks. "I didn't set out with this in mind," Wirth says of his success. "It just sort of happened." He admits that at a certain point, all his efforts became directed toward designing the smaller garden.

A boon to his success, he says, has been his appearance as the landscape architect for public television's "The Victory Garden," and the writing of his book, *Victory Garden Landscape Guide,* published in 1983. Wirth says the connection with the do-it-yourself home landscaping program has allowed him to further pick and choose his projects.

Wirth contends that he still "does some commercial work." However, he created his own niche, is very content in it, and considers it a fine art.

Figure 2-1

STEPS TO FOCUSING

Focus the practice by choosing a service at which you excel. Look not only at your skill but at your credibility with the client.Compile the past accomplishments of all staff members in your service area; you may have everything you need in-house. Learn everything you possibly can about that service, so that you can become an expert.

By focusing, you learn much more than your competitors about a particular market's needs, wants, and desires, and therefore are perceived to be more valuable to the clients within that marketplace. By being perceived as the expert, you can charge higher fees, employ a much more directed staff, and more easily refuse to take on projects that do not fit the focus of your firm. The steps to focusing are:

1. Targeting clients, not projects.
2. Networking.
3. "Exploding" a niche.
4. Usefulness selling.
5. Learning to say "no."
6. Meaningful marketing.

Each step is addressed in the separate sections that follow.

Targeting Clients, Not Projects

Retaining a consistent work load means retaining repeat clients. Therefore, target clients, not projects. Many small firms move from project to project, never taking the time to really get to know the client. Instead, work hard to build client relationships. Identify clients' personal preferences and get to know each member of their staff. In working closely with a client, you come to understand them so intimately that they end up telling you subconsciously what their needs are, thereby helping you to better market a new project.

Success in a small firm depends on repeat work from satisfied clients. Your ability to create ways to assure happy repeat clients of your choosing is crucial to your future success.

Repeat clients can be retained in several ways, three of which are illustrated below:

One small firm in Hartford, Connecticut, returns to every project six months after construction completion to perform a postconstruction design critique on the project, free of charge to the client.

An engineering firm in the Midwest offers one day of free consulting to its top 10 clients each year.

A West Coast architecture firm runs ads in San Francisco newspapers highlighting clients' projects and companies. Any firm can afford to run ads, especially successful firms. For other suggestions on maintaining clients, see Figure 2-2.

ADD Inc., a Cambridge, Massachusetts, firm, works in interior and office building design, as well as design for health care/biotech, retail mall, and government projects. Although it is not considered a small firm, the small firm principal can learn

---

Suggestions for Retaining Clients

1. Always arrive at meetings 10 minutes early.
2. Always call to confirm meetings.
3. Call current clients at a prescribed time each week (instead of waiting for them to call you).
4. Issue meeting minutes on the day of the meeting.
5. Never switch project managers on a client.
6. Anticipate problems and do the unexpected—such as introducing a client to a new lender when you know your client needs financing, even though you don't really provide such a service.
7. Be prepared with answers for all possible objectives or questions.
8. Admit mistakes quickly and take decisive corrective action.
9. Follow up on all details of the project.
10. Take charge of key routine tasks such as writing the agenda for your weekly client meeting or making the reservation for your client's flight to the job site.
11. Communicate consistently and regularly on project progress as related to client expectations.
12. Make your client representative look good in the eyes of his/her superiors.

Figure 2-2

from it. Most of ADD's business results from maintaining constant client contact. "There's no substitute for face-to-face networking," claims ADD President Wilson Pollock. "They'll never hire you if they don't see you." For example, Pollock travels with one group of developer clients from project to project, fully conversant with the language of the development market.

One way Pollock maintains contact with clients is by sending them direct mail pieces three to four times a year. The mail piece might be a brochure or announcement of an award. This serves to keep the firm's name in front of the client on a constant basis. "You've got to get in and nurse them and talk with their people, "Pollock says. When clients recognize your name because you have sent them repeated information, it dramatically enhances your chances for a meeting.

Persistence is a virtue. Pollock cites a colleague who went to the Corps of Engineers' offices in Washington every three months for three years until he finally was given a design project.

Networking

Small firms often do not command enough dollars of revenue to do marketing on the scale that a big firm can. What they know about is getting work from friends and contacts. Developing your networking skills replaces the need for "big dollars" spent on marketing. Find out what resources are available to you in your locale and make contacts today.

1. *Community Activities.* Small firms should become involved in community activities, specifically those that meet the needs of their clients. In addition to joining the local architects' society, become an associate member of a local association of clients, such as developers, school officials, building managers, clergymen, and garden clubs.

2. *Volunteer.* Don't simply join an association. Volunteer to work on a project unrelated to design services. Join a committee. Volunteer to run a program for the group. Become visible.

3. *Get Published.* Cultivate your image to local newspaper staff and suggest or develop stories on issues useful to your client group. If you are an expert and you appear to speak that client group's language, you will be more readily published. If you lack writing skills, retain a writer to prepare the material. Do not ignore journals that are read by your clients, as opposed to architectural, interior design, or engineering professional magazines, which are more commonly read by your peers than by your clients.

Figure 2-3 is an example of a firm that has successfully networked and promoted its services.

Here are additional suggestions. Always be visible. Make sure that whatever you do in the community gets you that visibility. For instance, if you volunteer to be a Cub Scout Master make sure that newspaper announcements of your activities not only mention that you are the cub master but also that you are the managing partner of ABC Associates, engineers for the city's new wastewater treatment plant.

Network in the circles where your service is bought and get to know as many clients as you can within that circle. This technique will help you build a solid client base upon which to build working relationships. For example, a firm in upstate New York sought to open a branch office in Boston. It built a network by assembling several hospital administrators from

---

Example of Successful Networking

Firm: Summerlin Associates, Inc.
Staff: 28
Specialty: Provides diverse services in civil, structural, and environmental design
Address: 1609 South Broadway
Little Rock, Ark. 72206

Having grown from a one-person operation to a 28-person firm with fees of $1 million a year, firm principal James C. Summerlin attributes much of his success to networking:

"I believe projects have to come to us ... because of my personal relationships and networking in the community. Prior to joining the firm, I had worked in Little Rock as a consulting engineer with another firm for a few years. I have been very active in the professional engineering community, civic work, and have developed a lot of friends and acquaintances who simply helped refer work our way."

Summerlin contends that networking takes a lot of energy. "Some people target a particular group ... others, like me, do everything they can." Specifically, this is what Summerlin did to promote himself in the community:

1. He served on the local planning commission.
2. He was involved in professional societies.
3. Was active socially, in church and the community.
4. He was a member of "Executive Associates," a local networking organization in the town.

Summerlin encourages others to continue to:

1. Be active and visible in the community, whether you're playing tennis or doing business.
2. Serve on local boards and commissions.
3. Join networking associations.

This example shows the importance of becoming involved in client networks much more than peer networks, increasing the likelihood of getting work through a friendship created out of such an activity. Friends give friends work.

Figure 2-3

area hospitals for a roundtable discussion focusing on the needs of the hospital community in the Boston area at that time. The firm's role was to facilitate the discussion within a nonconfrontational, nonsales environment. The objective was to get to know the Boston clients and also to acquaint them with the firm, and the effort was successful. Another firm (Fig. 2-4) set up a network by inviting local potential contacts to become members of its advisory board.

Additional Networking Strategies

Firm: Interior Space, Inc.
Staff: 35
Specialty: Architectural corporate interior planning and design (planning for the corporate work environment only); also provides a facilities management master-planning and design service
Address: 6633 Delmar Blvd.
             St. Louis, Mo. 63130

Interior Space Inc. has successfully networked using a board of advisors. Four times a year, Interior Space Inc. holds a Board of Advisors dinner meeting. It invites only the main facilities person—not those in secondary positions—from Ralston Purina, Anheiser Busch, ITT, and other large corporations. Thus, if the head facilities person is not available, it does not invite the next person below them in rank.

The firm's president, Patricia Whitaker, leads the session, encouraging the advisors to discuss the kinds of problems facilities managers face, and to share ideas. "Corporations are always changing and the only way we can keep up with the change is to meet with facilities managers face-to-face," she says, adding that facilities issues change rapidly because technology, especially that involving computers, is advancing so quickly and the workspace is continually evolving. "We find out what kinds of issues and problems they are facing long before anyone else does so we can provide for these in our design."

The dinner meeting is not to sell the advisors bluntly on Interior Space Inc., but to talk about facilities' needs. Whitaker runs the meeting with only one partner and one other employee. Advisors expect a sales pitch, and are impressed when they do not get one. There is no advertising and no discussion of the design firm's services. The plan is successful, as the firm has gotten work from every session held through mid-1989.

Why has this marketing technique worked? "They all just feel like we're the experts," Whitaker says. The firm adds people from other firms if board members decline to attend. When she has a person in mind to invite whom she doesn't know personally, Whitaker simply calls one of her board who does, and asks to use their name as a reference. No one has ever turned her down.

The advisory board has become the firm's single best marketing tool.

Figure 2-4

Successful entrepreneurs are classic networkers. They enjoy meeting people in every social and economic circle. They have the skill to introduce themselves in a way that is nonthreatening and to be remembered as a valuable person in the client's own marketplace.

Networkers are liked, and they like networking.

"Exploding" a Niche

In the 1990s and beyond, thousands of small businesses will develop by dealing with a specific portion of a larger project or entity. Examples are health care and program planners. Health care planners may be former architects or engineers who provide the upfront services for health care planning that were traditionally part of an architectural or engineering firm's business. This is called "exploding a niche."

Find a narrow service sector in the architecture/engineering marketplace, define it well, and explode that niche. For example, you might narrow your service to selecting art for resort properties. "How many resort properties are there in Sioux City, Iowa, these days?" you may ask. Not very many. Becoming and billing yourself as the expert, however, will attract developers building resorts in all parts of the country and abroad.

The driving force behind entrepreneurship is the ability to control your destiny. One aspect of this is to have one's own business. People want to reduce their overhead, control a much smaller amount of work, and do work that nobody else is doing. The next decade will consequently see a constant focusing on smaller and smaller segments of service, with practitioners alone as experts within that niche.

The trend is toward leanness in organizations—smaller full-time staffs, and access to plentiful, skilled part-time workers and independent contractors. It works out for both parties. The contractor gets a better hourly fee because they are independent and have no overhead, the employer a lower cost because they pay only for the effort directly needed, and the relationship breeds a more intense work effort on the project. See Figure 2-5 for a simple profit/loss statement showing the difference between having more versus fewer people on staff.

Independent Contractors Versus Full-time Staff		
	Annual Full-time Costs, 10 People Full Time	Annual Costs (5 People Full Time and 5 On Call @ 50% Utilization)
Direct salary	$400,000	$200,000
Fringe benefits @ 30%	120,000	60,000
Lost time, 10%[a]	40,000	20,000
Total Cost	$560,000	$480,000
Savings		$80,000

[a]Due to social interaction of lunch, coffee breaks, office parties, and so on.

Figure 2-5

STEPS TO SELECTING A NICHE

To select a niche, look for places where there is either a lack of service, or service that is being provided free. Here is a list of some recent and promising niches:

1. Interior health care architecture.
2. Facilities management for wastewater facilities.
3. Redesign of encapsulated air-handling systems.
4. Energy audits.
5. Hazardous waste audits.
6. Residential kitchen interiors.
7. Luxury yacht design.
8. Graphic signage for specific project types.
9. Financing for low-income housing.
10. Recycling old buildings.
11. Interior design of old movie theaters.

An example of how zoning and other municipal-related activities became a niche for one West Coast firm involved virtual operation of a municipality's entire zoning department. This relieved the community of a tax burden, since there was less staff, and the zoning function was performed more expedi-

tiously, since this arrangement eliminated the political bureaucracy that had surrounded previous zoning department
operations.

AREAS OF SERVICE

In marketing its management services to client prospects, the
modern small firm can focus on any one or two combinations
of the following niches:

Upfront Services

Preproject approval processes: zoning, permits, conceptual-
izing, traffic studies, feasibility studies, marketing studies,
cost studies
Health care planning
Program planning
Environmental impact studies
Market analyses
Construction cost studies
Circulation/traffic studies

Project Services

Facilities management
Financial planning
Securing finances
Construction management
Drafting services

Postproject Services

Construction administration
Materials handling and processing
Scheduling
Budgeting
Quality control on the job site
Value engineering programs

Expand each service within your traditional scope to see if it
can become a specialty. In the 1990s and beyond, there will be
many more small firms focusing on a single aspect of tradi-

tional design services and exploding each niche into full-time businesses.

After you explode a niche, you next plan to export that service.

Usefulness Selling

Meeting in a nonpressure environment, or "usefulness selling," is a valuable way to target and attain repeat clients. One means to do this is to use newsletters and magazines to promote recognition of your firm's name (see example, Fig. 2-6). Another firm that used a newsletter to break into a market is the Jack Johnson Company, featured in Figure 2-7.

Another method is to develop dictionaries for your client. The dictionaries can contain architectural, electrical, mechanical, plumbing, and other terms, with your firm's name and logo on the cover. This is a form of promotion developed by Stanley Engineers, a prominent engineering consulting firm.

Yet another method is to produce a textbook or history book containing examples of how your firm helped in your community. For example, a Bloomington, Minnesota, architectural firm published a town history. The book, which also happens to span the company's 100 years of existence, actually recaptures the history of the whole area, and has become a popular history text in the community.

Ten years ago, Howard, Needles, Tammend, & Bergendoff (HNTB), located in Kansas City, Missouri, introduced itself to the hospital marketplace by starting a newsletter, *Facilities Decisions,* on how to run a hospital more effectively. The newsletter provided useful information—tips, techniques, processes—valuable to hospital administrators. Prompted by former marketing director Frank Zilm, HNTB started mailing the newsletter to hospital administrators, none of whom knew the firm, but many of whom liked the newsletter. It was produced for two years. The firm laid the groundwork for making contacts in the hospital market with a "usefulness selling" technique—the newsletter—making the firm appear to be as informed about the hospital marketplace as any of the competitors.

Zilm created a demand for HNTB through the newsletter. As a result of publishing the newsletter, the company was able to attract clients and create its own niche in the market. The concept is "pull-through marketing"—which means you create

Duffy·Ruble·Momura·Brugger

ARCHITECTS   ENGINEERS   INTERIOR DESIGNERS

THIS PUBLICATION IS A TOOL FOR DRMB TO INFORM CLIENTS AND FRIENDS OF SOME OF THE JOBS WE ARE WORKING ON AND NEWS ABOUT OUR FIRM. WE HOPE IT REMINDS YOU OF OUR COMMITMENT TO ARCHITECTURE, ENGINEERING AND INTERIOR DESIGN PROJECTS MENTIONED HERE AND OTHERS TO FOLLOW IN SUBSEQUENT ISSUES.

SILVER ANNIVERSARY

Our firm was organized on January 1, 1963 by James M. Duffy, President of DRMB.

A review of almost 1500 past projects reflects the design and surveillance of a wide variety of project types: new buildings, additions, renovations and structural repair. Most of the projects have been within the five-state area surrounding Sioux City.

Comments by Duffy regarding a quarter century of architectural practice include: "Architecture is a cultural activity that must be handled as a business. Every client enjoys good design, expects their buildings to be structurally sound, and wants a return on their investment. Listening to the client's needs, obtaining proper academic training, and providing an honest contribution of special talent, are the means of providing proper architectural service."

The team effort by very talented people is the reason for the success-ful twenty-five year practice of the DRMB firm. It also helps to have a group of fine professionals that really "Enjoy going to work".

FIRST FEDERAL SAVINGS

Our firm continues to work on this 45,000 s.f. facility now under construction in downtown Sioux City. W.A. Klinger, Construction Manager on the project, is overseeing the erection of the steel frame and brick and block exterior. At this time, DRMB continues to develop the construction documentation for the building interior.

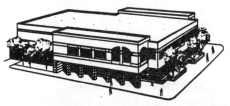

DRMB RETAIL

In the past two years DRMB has been involved in 23 different retail projects. Good clients, seeking creative solutions (Klinger Properties, Inc. to name one) have made this an exciting part of our work. A few of these spaces include Thorpes, Breadbasket, Northwood Gallery, and I Can't Believe It's Yogurt at Marketplace, and Williges, Clothes Tree, Mardell's and Posters Plus at Mayfair.

PLUMS COOKING COMPANY

Plum's Cooking Company at Marketplace features gourmet cooking classes as well as retail sales of food and accessories for gourmet cooking at home. The space features an open market concept. Open wire displays, bright colors, and a canvas awning are a few of the elements which create the dynamic open market atmosphere.

Figure 2-6 Example of promoting recognition of a firm's name. Used with permission. *(Continued on next page)*

DUFFY RUBLE MAMURA BRYGGER
A PROFESSIONAL CORPORATION
ARCHITECTS ENGINEERS INTERIOR DESIGNERS
314 SECURITY BANK
SIOUX CITY IOWA 51101

FOREIGN EXCHANGE

This Mayfair retail space features a pier warehouse theme. The store-front of diagonal tongue and groove hardwood is reminiscent of nautical shipping crates. The red floor is a colorful backdrop contrasting the neutrally colored imports.

JONES EYE CLINIC

Completed earlier this year, Jones Eye Clinic is a dual functioning facility. Approximately 5,600 s.f. of the building serves as an ophthamologist's clinic (eye examinations, etc). 5,200 s.f. of the 14,000 s.f. structure serves as a two O.R. surgical suite.

The building's aesthetics derive from an organic design and use of natural materials. The clinic is nestled in the berms of a well landscaped site and interior spaces featuring laminated wood beams, marble reception counters, and brick fire places offer a welcome change from the clinical atmosphere often found in medical spaces.

The Principal-In-Charge was Owen Mamura and the Contractor was W.A. Klinger, Inc.

GALINSKY RESIDENCE

A dramatic view of the Country Club Golf Course is the highlight of this 3100 s.f. residence. This contemporary design contains vaulted skylit spaces in an open plan. The exterior will be brick and redwood with a large canti-levered deck overlooking the golf course.

James Duffy is the Principal-In-Charge and Bob Young is the General Contractor.

DRMB TRIVIA

Joyce Banka, Architectural Adminis-trator for DRMB, had an unfortunate accident. Joyce fell on a glass; the resulting cut severed tendons, nerves, and muscles in her right hand.

Joyce has since had surgery and anti-cipates 8-12 months of physical therapy and possibly additional surgery. Joyce has shown remarkable ability as a one-handed typist and will continue with the firm on part-time disability until she's fully recovered.

DRMB is happy to announce the addition of a new employee, Jan Lemburg. Jan will be our new full-time secretary/receptionist.

Todd Moss recently received his Iowa Registration by Reciprocity. Todd was previously registered in Wisconsin. Congratulations, Todd!

On Friday, October 23, the entire DRMB architectural and drafting staff attended an in-house training seminar on Contemporary Liturgical Design. Our thanks to Father Brian Hughes for his presentation.

Figure 2-6   *(Continued)*

Using a Newsletter to Break into a Market

Firm Name: Jack Johnson Company
Staff: 35–40
Specialty: Ski resorts, ski areas
Address: 1910 Prospector Avenue
                Park City, Utah 84060

Jack Johnson, president of the Jack Johnson Company, began using a newsletter to break into the ski resort market. "All the articles focused on ski resorts. We featured ski resort projects by other firms. The only editorializing was a one-column article on the back page." Johnson filled the newsletter with short articles ("quick hitters") and numerous pictures.

Circulation of the newsletter helped position the firm into the ski resort niche, but the process took about one-and-a-half years. "People started recognizing the Johnson name and they liked the newsletter. It indirectly put us on the list of firms to be considered for ski resort projects."

The newsletter was sent complementary to various key resort developers. Johnson eventually charged $3 a copy and began receiving money for the newsletter as well. Johnson says newsletters "have got to have a marketing function." His experience shows how a well-planned, well-written, visually appealing newsletter can enhance a firm's image dramatically, especially in new market areas.

Figure 2-7

demand and you pull the market through to you. Usefulness selling and pull-through demand techniques are not expensive. Such techniques allow the small firm to enter a market without spending a great deal of money on elaborate programs and media. Usefulness selling, in particular the newsletter, is a cost-effective way to spread market awareness of your talent.

In other words, provide something useful to your clients that also gives you marketing credibility.

To build a usefulness selling campaign in a small firm, consider what your clients do both during and outside working hours. Hospital administrators do not think so much about hiring architects or engineers as they do about how to manage a facility, pay doctors, manage the parking lot, and compensate the nursing staff. Here, then, is how you can develop a usefulness selling campaign for your company:

1. After two hours of brainstorming, compile a list including all the facts your clients might be interested in learning.

2. Rank that list. Look at the items from top to bottom in terms of what is important to your clients.
3. Collect data from the library and other sources.
4. Communicate that data. Create a newsletter, or simply copy an article and send it with your business card to a group of clients in your marketplace. Limit the group to 50. This is a good number because you can keep track of about that number.
5. Do this about every two months. Then when you decide to call a client prospect, he or she will already be familiar with you and your services.

Learning to Say "No"

Another aspect of focusing your practice is to know when to reject an opportunity. Many design firms accept any work. While often done out of a need to be practical, this tendency will dilute the focus of your company and your ability to achieve your vision. By designing too many different projects for too many varied markets, you spend your most valuable resources, especially time, in areas where you probably should not be. Concentrate instead on areas where you will be most productive. Learn to say no so you can focus on what will get you the biggest return for your input.

Figure 2-8 profiles the Henderson Group, which employs this kind of selectivity in choosing its projects. Likewise, Figure 2-9 presents the philosophy used by the firm of Backen, Arrigoni, & Ross, which never became really successful or distinctive until it began to discriminate between projects it would do and those it rejected.

POSITIVE WAYS TO SAY NO

You must discipline yourself and your firm into saying "no" to clients that either do not appreciate your efforts or fail to match your firm's profile of desired clients. But there is a right way and a wrong way to do this, since a client may have a project in the future that is appropriate for your company. Remember, cater to clients, not projects. Here are a few ways to say no *positively:*

1. *Referrals.* Refer clients to other firms, then follow up to find out if a good job was done. The client will be sur-

---

Being Selective: The Henderson Group

Firm: The Henderson Group
Staff: 25
Specialty: Speculative properties and other diverse services
Address: 100 South Brentwood Boulevard
St. Louis, Mo. 63105

The Henderson Group's focus is on office, industrial, retail, elderly housing, and health care facilities. Services include architecture, planning, interiors, and graphic design.

Says principal Paul J. Henderson: "We focus our efforts and our marketing energies on what we do well. We do not chase, and in cases reject, potential assignments which are significantly beyond the realm of our experience."

The firm's go/no go criteria are based on the following considerations:

1. Number of competitors, and or intensity of effort required to submit bid.
2. Size of project.
3. Profit potential.
4. "High design" potential.
5. Present and future work load.
6. Previous experience with client.
7. Potential to forge new relationships.

Figure 2-8

prised by your care in following up on a referral. You may give away a project, but you will "keep" the client.

2. *Increase the Fee.* Say yes, but raise your price. By raising your price, you either price yourself out of the market for a particular client, or if you do get the job at least you will make a good profit. This also establishes a higher price scale if the client comes back to you at a later date.

3. *Delay the Project.* Quote a higher price and say you won't start it until six months from now, or until you have enough staff free to perform the job.

In the three suggestions above, you are not saying *no*; you are saying *yes, but.* . . . This is much more positive than just saying no. Remember, your primary goal is to target clients, not projects, and this is a way to keep the clients.

Being Selective: Backen, Arrigoni, and Ross

Firm: Backen, Arrigoni, & Ross
Staff: 65
Address: 1660 Bush Street
           San Francisco, Calif. 94109

When a client requests a price quote for services, Backen, Arrigoni, and Ross applies a go/no go policy to determine whether or not to do the project. The four principals of the firm analyze the project carefully, and base decisions to design projects on tangible reasons and criteria: Does the project have financing? Is the project in our niche market? Does the client have a history of paying on time? Does the firm have the people available to do the work?

For reasons of economics, design focus, and lack of potential for repeat work, some projects are not worth accepting, says Marketing Director James Mitchell, and if the firm agrees to do such projects, there are heavy restrictions built into the contract. For example, they have decided to plan for an "orderly retreat" from the condominium market due to its high liability. When the firm takes on a condominium project now, the client must meet the following criteria:

1. They must be substantial enough to pay for the project.
2. They must be familiar with the condominium development process.
3. They must understand the risks involved with developing condominiums.
4. They must pay a fee sufficient to produce a first-quality design as well as quality construction documents.
5. They must grant the firm veto power over the contractor.

Another way of controlling the project is to set added limitations on liability. In some cases, Backen, Arrigoni, and Ross only produces the design for a project, not the working drawings.

Size is another criterion. For example, unless a small project has some interesting characteristics—that is, it is a challenging architectural problem, or the client may provide more, larger projects in the future—you may want to turn it down.

When possible, go for fewer larger projects than very many small ones. Small projects generate too many bills, invoices, and subcontracts for their size. It will cost you almost as much in overhead to do a small project as a medium-sized one.

Backen, Arrigoni, and Ross investigates a client by talking with previously retained architects, asking about past payment practices, working relationships during a project, change order frequency, and possibility for future work. If the four principals of Backen, Arrigoni, & Ross decide to say "no," they give a diplomatic *"we're too busy."*

Selectiveness helps in getting good projects, good clients, and good fees, as the following experience demonstrates. Backen, Arrigoni, & Ross once spent three weeks negotiating with a repeat client, a local university. In negotiating a $600,000 contract, the firm and the university had a $20,000 difference. When the client's negotiator said they were not willing to pay the $20,000 difference, the firm suggested handing the job to another architect. (BAR had already started work on a fee basis.) The university backed down and agreed to the difference. As Mitchell says, "That was the amount we needed to do the good job they wanted, and we weren't willing to do a not-so-good job."

Many firms concede that the least successful jobs are the ones taken at too low a fee. In such cases, the client is often inexperienced at construction and does not realize that the money he pays now will save money later.

Figure 2-9 Source: Backen, Arrigoni, and Ross. Used with permission.

Saying no will

1. Give you confidence that you have the ability to survive without having to accept every project.
2. Show your staff that you have the ability to be strong and that you are committed to your vision.
3. Save you from wasting your time and energies on work you probably shouldn't be doing anyway.
4. Provide a more structured setting in which to plan moves needed to stay successful.

Think of the positive impact that saying no to a few clients will have on your best clients, your staff, and your own well-being. If you feel you must take a project because you have no work, then you are not successful. Revise your planning, marketing, and networking efforts so you will never be in this position. Figure 2-10 contains questions involved in a go/no go decision, as well as a go/no go criteria worksheet.

Meaningful Marketing

Small firms often have neither the time nor the resources to do extensive market research: researching a market, defining its boundaries, assessing the competition, and developing a strategic plan of attack. Most small firms have very primitive marketing plans. They use networking. Yet the arguments for a structured marketing effort are very powerful:

1. Marketing forces your firm to stay aware of developing client expectations. No market is constant or static. You need to anticipate and adapt to changes.
2. Marketing can create a higher demand for services, which allows you to charge higher prices for the same effort. The result is higher profits on the same work.
3. New opportunities appear as you are in touch with the marketplace. (Example: one architectural firm developed a profitable graphics component after identifying the needs of developers during a marketing campaign.)
4. Marketing moves you close to the client community and allows you to become more intimate with the language of the client. It positions you in the client prospect's mind whenever that client needs help.

GO/NO GO CRITERIA

CRITERIA	YES/NO	COMMENT
Requirement — is it real?		
Funds — are they available?		
Is client using a consultant?		
Do we have enough technical know-how?		
Have we had prior contact with client?		
Can we commit maximum effort to the job?		
Do we have the manpower to do the job?		
Do we believe we are the logical winner?		

Figure 2-10a Go/no go criteria worksheet.

Factors Influencing the Go/No Go Decision

1. The client's commitment.
2. Perceived as well as actual needs.
3. Does the client's available budget match their needs?
4. How much personal contact have you had with this client?
5. Who are the real decision makers?
6. Who are your competitors?
7. Do you really have the commitment to win?
8. Are key members of your team available?
9. Will all efforts be enough?
10. Do you have relevant experience?
11. Do you have a sales plan?
12. Could you hire a consultant to do joint ventures?
13. Do you really believe you are the logical winner of this project?

Figure 2-10b

Consider the statistics in Figure 2-11 from the *PSMJ 1989 Financial Statistics Survey*[2] on what percentage of gross and net revenues firms spend on marketing in 1989. The chart shows statistics for firms with and without full-time marketers (designated in the upper left-hand corner of each page).

SEMINARS, PUBLICATIONS, SURVEYS

Once you have identified a niche, you need meaningful marketing tools. As a small firm, you need imaginative ideas rather than traditional expensive tools. Do something different to show that you have knowledge in the niche. For instance, hold a seminar for potential clients, and charge for attendance. Figure 2-12 contains a profile of one firm that successfully uses seminars to spread name recognition. This unique idea may work well for your small firm.

PUBLISH A BOOK ON THE SUBJECT. Gather your notes, supplement with real-life project examples, and type or dictate into a cassette tape recorder. Contact a publisher for guidelines on submitting a viable book proposal. Send it around to various well-known technical book publishers (obtain a list of design and construction publishers from *Books in Print* or the *Literary Marketplace,* available at most local libraries). Then hire a writer to transform this information into a manuscript. Chances are you will not make a lot of money from the book sales, but it is a way to become known as the authority in your niche area.

PERFORM CLIENT SURVEYS. Focus on your client group and perform surveys on information that other professionals in their field want to know about each other. One Texas firm surveyed 130 branch banks to uncover energy-efficient methods that save on air conditioning costs. A St. Louis interior designer annually assesses capital spending plans of the top 100 corporations in Missouri. Client prospects will begin to call you for advice on how to interpret the data, which establishes you as the expert and, when the time comes, the firm of first choice.

PUBLISH A NEWSLETTER. Develop a focused newsletter with informational data. Although you are a design professional and not a publisher, you can hire publishing or marketing con-

MARKETING EXPENSE ANALYSIS

(Firms without full time marketers)	Total Marketing Costs to Gross Revenues		Total Marketing Costs to Net Revenues		Labor as a Percentage of Total Marketing	
Percentage	Median	Mean	Median	Mean	Median	Mean
Overall	2.1	3.2	3.0	4.3	66.7	65.3
Staff Size:						
1–5	2.0	4.0	4.8	6.5	74.0	72.1
6–10	3.6	4.3	4.7	5.2	71.6	74.0
11–15	2.0	2.5	2.6	3.1	62.4	66.8
16–25	2.4	2.2	2.4	2.8	66.0	67.9
26–50	1.9	2.0	2.2	2.4	67.0	66.5
51–100	1.1	1.9	1.2	2.1	65.7	65.0
101–150	NR	NR	NR	NR	NR	NR
151–250	NR	NR	NR	NR	NR	NR
251–500	NR	NR	NR	NR	NR	NR
Over 500	NR	NR	NR	NR	NR	NR
Architectural	2.7	3.7	3.8	5.5	68.2	66.0
Engineering (Prime)	2.3	3.0	3.1	3.9	65.7	67.3
Engineering (Subconsultant)	1.8	2.0	1.9	2.0	70.3	76.7
Engineering (Survey)	1.6	2.1	1.8	2.4	71.0	68.0
A/E	1.5	2.3	1.8	2.3	54.5	60.0
A/E/P	NR	NR	NR	NR	NR	NR
A/I	3.4	4.2	5.7	6.0	56.7	60.2
All U. S.	3.2	4.5	3.9	5.2	66.0	65.4
Northeast	2.3	2.4	2.8	3.1	58.9	61.2
South	2.3	2.6	3.0	3.5	61.2	61.1
Midwest	1.9	3.0	3.1	4.0	68.7	70.3
Southwest	2.0	2.6	2.1	3.0	65.4	65.5
Mountain	3.1	5.1	3.4	4.5	71.3	70.0
West	2.4	3.2	3.3	4.0	69.9	68.7
Private	2.1	3.0	2.8	4.1	68.7	65.0
Government	2.3	3.1	3.0	4.6	65.2	64.7
Mixed	2.4	3.0	3.3	3.9	68.0	65.7
Transportation	2.2	2.8	3.4	4.0	66.4	67.8
Government Buildings	2.1	2.7	3.2	4.0	65.8	66.3
Environmental	4.3	4.4	5.5	5.6	70.2	69.7
Industrial	2.4	3.1	3.4	3.9	68.7	65.2
Commercial Users	2.3	4.7	3.7	5.2	64.2	66.0
Commercial Developers	2.2	3.6	2.8	3.7	65.3	71.2
Housing	2.1	2.9	2.5	3.5	69.1	68.3
Health Care	3.4	4.2	5.7	6.1	67.8	68.3
No Specialty	3.4	3.8	4.4	5.1	65.4	

NR = None Reported

Figure 2-11   Marketing expense analysis from the *PSMJ 1989 Financial Statistics Survey*.[2] (*Continued on next page*)

MARKETING EXPENSE ANALYSIS

(Firms with full time marketers)	Marketing Costs to Gross Revenues		Marketing Costs to Net Revenues	
Percentage	Median	Mean	Median	Mean
Overall	4.4	4.7	5.5	6.1
Staff Size:				
1-5	NR	NR	NR	NR
6-10	NR	NR	NR	NR
11-15	2.3	3.5	4.0	4.4
16-25	3.7	4.2	4.8	5.7
26-50	3.4	4.0	3.7	4.8
51-100	4.6	5.0	4.9	6.1
101-150	4.2	4.8	4.7	5.9
151-250	4.5	4.7	5.8	6.0
251-500	3.5	4.6	4.3	5.8
Over 500	4.1	4.7	5.8	6.0
Architectural	3.7	4.1	5.2	5.4
Engineering (Prime)	4.2	4.4	4.9	5.6
Engineering (Subconsultant)	3.0	3.7	3.6	4.4
Engineering (Survey)	2.9	3.1	3.0	3.9
A/E	4.5	4.8	5.5	5.9
A/E/P	4.7	5.9	5.7	6.9
A/I	4.6	4.8	6.1	6.7
All U. S.	5.0	5.1	6.0	6.3
Northeast	3.9	4.1	5.0	5.3
South	3.4	3.7	4.5	4.6
Midwest	4.3	4.7	5.0	5.9
Southwest	5.5	5.7	4.7	5.1
Mountain	3.6	4.8	6.8	7.9
West	3.8	5.0	4.2	5.8
Private	3.8	4.1	4.6	4.9
Government	4.5	5.0	5.3	6.6
Mixed	4.2	4.5	5.1	5.6
Transportation	2.6	3.4	3.2	4.5
Government Buildings	2.6	3.5	3.4	4.9
Environmental	4.7	4.9	5.9	5.9
Industrial	2.6	3.5	3.8	4.2
Commercial Users	2.7	4.8	4.1	4.1
Commercial Developers	2.6	3.9	3.2	3.9
Housing	2.5	3.5	2.9	3.9
Health Care	3.9	4.5	5.9	6.4
No Specialty	3.7	4.1	4.8	5.5

Figure 2-11 (continued)

(Firms without full time marketers)	Total Marketing Costs to Gross Revenues		Total Marketing Costs to Net Revenues		Labor as a Percentage of Total Marketing	
Percentage	Median	Mean	Median	Mean	Median	Mean
Overall	2.1	3.2	3.0	4.3	66.7	65.3
Staff Size:						
1–5	2.0	4.0	4.8	6.5	74.0	72.1
6–10	3.6	4.3	4.7	5.2	71.6	74.0
11–15	2.0	2.5	2.6	3.1	62.4	66.8
16–25	2.4	2.2	2.4	2.8	66.0	67.9
26–50	1.9	2.0	2.2	2.4	67.0	66.5
51–100	1.1	1.9	1.2	2.1	65.7	65.0
101–150	NR	NR	NR	NR	NR	NR
151–250	NR	NR	NR	NR	NR	NR
251–500	NR	NR	NR	NR	NR	NR
Over 500	NR	NR	NR	NR	NR	NR
Architectural	2.7	3.7	3.8	5.5	68.2	66.0
Engineering (Prime)	2.3	3.0	3.1	3.9	65.7	67.3
Engineering (Subconsultant)	1.8	2.0	1.9	2.0	70.3	76.7
Engineering (Survey)	1.6	2.1	1.8	2.4	71.0	68.0
A/E	1.5	2.3	1.8	2.3	54.5	60.0
A/E/P	NR	NR	NR	NR	NR	NR
A/I	3.4	4.2	5.7	6.0	56.7	60.2
All U. S.	3.2	4.5	3.9	5.2	66.0	65.4
Northeast	2.3	2.4	2.8	3.1	58.9	61.2
South	2.3	2.6	3.0	3.5	61.2	61.1
Midwest	1.9	3.0	3.1	4.0	68.7	70.3
Southwest	2.0	2.6	2.1	3.0	65.4	65.5
Mountain	3.1	5.1	3.4	4.5	71.3	70.0
West	2.4	3.2	3.3	4.0	69.9	68.7
Private	2.1	3.0	2.8	4.1	68.7	65.0
Government	2.3	3.1	3.0	4.6	65.2	64.7
Mixed	2.4	3.0	3.3	3.9	68.0	65.7
Transportation	2.2	2.8	3.4	4.0	66.4	67.8
Government Buildings	2.1	2.7	3.2	4.0	65.8	66.3
Environmental	4.3	4.4	5.5	5.6	70.2	69.7
Industrial	2.4	3.1	3.4	3.9	68.7	65.2
Commercial Users	2.3	4.7	3.7	5.2	64.2	66.0
Commercial Developers	2.2	3.6	2.8	3.7	65.3	71.2
Housing	2.1	2.9	2.5	3.5	69.1	68.3
Health Care	3.4	4.2	5.7	6.1	67.8	68.3
No Specialty	3.4	3.8	4.4	5.1	65.4	

NR = None Reported

Figure 2-11 (continued on next page)

MARKETING EXPENSE ANALYSIS

(Firms with full time marketers)	Labor as a Percentage of Total Marketing Costs		Total Staff to Full Time Marketers	
Percentage	Median	Mean	Median	Mean
Overall	70.7	68.7	33.0	39.1
Staff Size:				
1-5	NR	NR	NR	NR
6-10	NR	NR	NR	NR
11-15	67.8	59.7	12.0	13.5
16-25	69.7	71.2	18.5	18.2
26-50	69.8	70.3	29.0	29.6
51-100	73.0	72.8	40.0	47.8
101-150	69.4	70.3	46.3	46.5
151-250	65.9	68.1	48.0	49.4
251-500	64.3	65.2	37.6	47.8
Over 500	68.0	68.5	30.3	42.7
Architectural	66.2	67.0	23.4	31.6
Engineering (Prime)	73.5	71.0	45.8	45.4
Engineering (Subconsultant)	70.4	70.5	32.0	45.1
Engineering (Survey)	72.3	71.3	32.7	44.3
A/E	69.8	69.9	36.3	41.6
A/E/P	68.7	67.9	28.7	39.1
A/I	66.2	68.3	27.5	30.7
All U. S.	67.3	67.5	30.5	35.9
Northeast	67.9	66.3	36.0	45.2
South	66.2	68.1	32.7	35.9
Midwest	71.3	72.0	34.0	39.7
Southwest	68.3	69.1	26.0	36.8
Mountain	65.2	66.2	35.3	47.0
West	68.0	68.6	28.0	37.5
Private	67.2	66.2	38.0	40.7
Government	73.9	70.3	32.3	40.7
Mixed	69.0	68.6	29.9	35.6
Transportation	68.0	69.2	38.0	45.8
Government Buildings	68.5	69.1	18.0	21.6
Environmental	73.2	71.3	30.3	41.5
Industrial	69.1	70.4	15.7	39.3
Commercial Users	70.2	70.1	30.0	34.8
Commercial Developers	68.3	69.4	22.4	23.4
Housing	69.1	69.5	46.3	57.6
Health Care	68.4	69.2	17.0	26.9
No Specialty	71.0	69.7	33.0	39.5

NR = None Reported

Figure 2-11 (continued)

Using Seminars to Spread Company Name Recognition

Firm: Toby Nadel Architects/Consultants
Staff: 1
Specialty: Roofing and waterproofing problem solving
Address: 4304 E. Genesee Street
           Dewitt, N.Y. 13214

The son of a contractor, Toby Nadel began diagnosing roofing problems quite naturally after leaving a seven-year architectural partnership in which he found himself unsatisfied. "I started advising on building problem solving, and then by 1972 roofing problems took over."

Nadel once attended a midwestern roofing conference, where he was helping an associate sell software. After the convention, he went to a nearby city for an international conference, where he met a French physicist. The Frenchman told Nadel they were looking for an architect who could speak at the convention, "so I borrowed a slide rule, and an architect's catalog, and talked about how and why roofs fail."

After several other speaking engagements, Nadel found that speaking was "fun and got me tons of work." Of his success, he speculates, "I never planned a single thing. My name became nationally known [as a roofing expert] almost overnight." This national recognition was a direct result of his speaking engagements.

Nadel pulls the dichotomous camps of contractor and architect together to solve roofing problems. At first he charged $500 plus expenses, but now says, "Some can only afford to pay the airfare, but I still go. You get a gift in life, and you owe. My absolute rule for success is ignore all the advice and do what you really want to do."

Nadel recognizes that speaking is not for everyone. "Lectures are a wonderful vehicle for securing work, but if you do it for that, you won't have as much success." Humor and interest are the main reasons why Nadel enjoys speaking to countless contractors, architects, owners, and engineers on roofing diagnosis.

Figure 2-12

sultants to produce a professional-looking product. The newsletter is a good way to establish credibility, and expert information is usually readily available at your local library or from other sources such as client periodicals, consultants, actual project histories, past clients, and so forth. See also the section called "Usefulness Selling" (earlier in this chapter) for advice and examples on how publishing a newsletter can enhance your image.

Figure 2-13 contains a listing of the features of an effective newsletter.

WHEN TO HIRE A MARKETER

Small firms generally hire their first full-time marketer when they have grown to between 20 and 30 staff members, and that person is usually a marketing coordinator. Beyond that, design firms hire one marketing staff person per 20 employees, for firms of up to 150 people.

Note that "marketing staff person" means only those engaged full time in direct or support marketing functions. It does not include technical professionals or principals (unless full time in marketing), or the marketing director. It does include outside prospectors, the marketing coordinator, in-house public relations/graphics, and clerical support.

Characteristics of Effective Newsletters

Forty newsletters were culled from a larger number of publications obtained by Practice Management Associates, Ltd., and yielded the following typical features:

- Nearly two-thirds use 2 to 3 colors.
- About 20% are willing to pay for four-color printing.
- White is the preferred paper stock color.
- Blue and red/burgundy are popular second colors, and almost all use black ink for the body type.
- The 8- × 11 in. size is overwhelmingly the favorite.
- Most paper is 80-lb weight, with 100 lb the second choice.
- A four-page length seems to work for most firms, with six-page "gatefolds" and eight pages next in popularity.
- One-third are self-mailed.
- Half are mailed quarterly. The majority of the balance produce fewer issues, but two publish monthly.
- Most of the newsletters are written in-house, though in many cases not by professional writers; but more than half appear to be designed and produced outside.

A recent study of company newsletters revealed that quite a few firms both write and typeset their copy on in-house word processors/computers/composers. The results are mixed, but at least the technology is being used.

Figure 2-13

Use your own judgment in applying the figures above to your situation. For example, there is more marketing staff per employee in firms that are just venturing into marketing, that have an aggressive program, or that compete in the municipal market. On the other hand, there are less marketing people in firms where the technical staff does the selling, or where the firm receives large projects or significant repeat work from the same clients. Figure 2-14 summarizes some marketing hints.

CREATING A MARKETING PLAN

Before your small firm even thinks of developing a formal marketing plan, here are five steps to take:

1. *Create Professional-looking Materials.* Although brochures alone should not represent the bulk of your marketing effort, a brochure can project the image of having your act together, even if you're not totally organized. If you already have a brochure, refer to Figure 2-15 for tips on how to improve it.

Marketing Hints

- Place a one-line advertisement in the local *Yellow Pages* for client's convenience in finding your telephone number.
- Research to develop a unique market niche.
- Develop a one-page direct mail piece that emphasizes the value of your service.
- Target markets for existing facilities surveys.
- Follow up finished projects with a final meeting; send a questionnaire to client to leave job on "up" note.
- Plan appearances in the media that focus on the client rather than your profession. Consider books, articles, television appearances, and lectures to public groups.
- State your mission up front in your brochure or marketing package.
- Consider changing the name of your service to avoid being pigeonholed. For example, take out the words "architects" or "engineers" from your firms name and substitute "facilities planners," "hospital planners," etc.
- Talk with large out-of-state firms to make contact for small job referrals.
- Use present clients to expand your future client base.
- Utilize the uniqueness of your firm (e.g., minority- or woman-owned) to target clients—especially those who are required to aim for such participation.
- Identify unique services needed by "new" clients (i.e., clients with new project types).

Figure 2-14

Brochure Usefulness

Ninety percent of all design firm brochures are made for other design professionals instead of for clients. Do clients really want to see tabloid pictures of hundreds of your projects? This is misusing your valuable time and money. Ask yourself if your brochure really works for your clients by considering the following questions:

1. What use will your client have for your brochure?
2. When your brochure reaches your client's desk, specifically what will he or she do with it?
3. What specific items are contained in your brochure that provide continual benefit to your client in *his* or *her* business?
4. Do you think that your client's brochure files are similar to those kept by your specification department for building products?
5. Is your brochure more than 10 pages? If so, does your client ever read it?
6. Do the pictures in your brochure have captions?
7. Are there dated "headshots" of principals who may have since left your firm?
8. Is there any "useful" information in your brochure that would prompt your client to keep it as a reference tool?

Figure 2-15

2. *Improve Your Mailing List.* Use your miscellaneous holiday cards, gift cards, and reception invitations to compile a comprehensive computerized mailing list of clients, prospects, and friends of the firm.

3. *Start with Some Inexpensive Public Relations.* Send brief, one-page, double-spaced press releases on new personnel, new contracts, or design awards to local media and associations. Send announcements on senior personnel and major awards to your entire mailing list. See Appendix A for a listing of media prospects for architects, engineers, and interior designers, and/or places to obtain such lists.

4. *Set Out a One-year Action Plan.* Once you have some of these basic elements in place, you can objectively review where you came from, where you want to go, and how to get there. (See Fig. 2-16.)

5. *Establish Measurable Goals.* Don't plan to contact 20 developers if you haven't contacted one in the past year. Review and correct your plan every three months. Consider addressing major image problems (name change,

---

One-year Action Plan

Goal: To secure 3 projects in the health care industry within 12 months.

Tactics	Measurement
1. Call 100 clients in each of 3 building project types to determine anticipated health care projects now planned.	1a. Develop lists by 2/1. 1b. Assign 50 calls each to 6 people by 2/15. 1c. Calls made by 3/1.
2. Assemble list of real projects in each area.	2. Measure potential fee dollars of each project.
3. Assign each PM a contact list of 15–20 real contacts.	3. Do on 4/1.
4. Contact 5 clients per week.	4. Measure on 6/15.
5. Make a total of 10–20 presentations on real projects.	5. Between 6/1 and 9/1 meet weekly on Mondays to assess.
6. Have a first project.	6. Not later than 7/1.
7. Assess overall plan.	7. Do on 9/1.

Figure 2-16

substantial growth where you are still seen as small, etc.) with a direct mail piece.

Only now should you consider creating a formal one- and three-year marketing plan.

Writing the Marketing Plan. Although planning the marketing effort was discussed in Chapter 1 ("Marketing Plan and Direction"), the specifics of the plan are now discussed in more detail. The marketing plan is the final step toward putting your vision into action. This is where you write down exactly how you are going to reach that vision, and this strategy should be broken into tangible, yearly goals.

The purposes of the marketing function are to

1. Decide what services to offer to which clients.
2. Prepare the market plan.
3. Perform public relations, possibly including advertising.
4. Review and create sales tools such as brochures, newsletters, and so forth.
5. Outline cold prospecting.

6. Find project leads.
7. Sell particular projects.
8. Perform client follow-up.

The marketing plan is a written plan outlining target markets and projected yield for a specified period of time, usually one year. It should address the marketing effort and define responsibilities for its implementation.

The elements of a marketing plan should include

1. A goals statement.
2. An overall marketing program.
3. Identification of specific markets.
4. Overall administration or marketing control.
5. Budget.

GOALS STATEMENT. Before setting your goal, perform some preliminary analysis to ensure that the goals are both realistic and specific. Without some framework, blue-sky goals creep in, such as "attain excellence in the hospital market," or "grow 50 percent this year."

To perform such an analysis, look at your internal strengths and weaknesses. Be brutally honest. Also perform some research (e.g., via telephone calls to a few past clients) as to your image among present and potential clients. If you are a new firm with a short track record, this may be all you have to do.

If the firm has a marketing history, analyze the results of past efforts. Some suggested areas to consider are

- Practice mix by type of project, client, and geographic area.
- Profitability for each of these markets.
- Proportion of repeat work and clients.
- Number of proposals submitted and interviews attended, and the resulting success ratio.
- Marketing costs compared to annual revenues and bookings.
- Effectiveness of supporting functions such as public relations, marketing tools such as brochures, and written presentation materials as well as verbal presentations.

Next look at your external environment:

- What external factors will affect your market? Look at, for instance, the economy in general, the bankruptcy of a client, new government regulations, or the opening of new branch office by a major national firm.
- What government actions will affect client activities or regulate their operations?
- What economic or social factors will create or eliminate markets?
- What actions are the clients themselves taking to expand business and become more competitive?
- What factors are affecting clients in their selection of planning and design firms?

Some firms hire an outside consultant to perform this marketing research, but for the small firm the most effective market research is by your technical experts in the particular field. For example, your chief mechanical engineer is in the best position to research the solar energy market.

Having performed some marketing analysis, you are ready to set goals. Be realistic, clear, and specific: "Increase revenues to $550,000"; "Achieve a pretax return on sales of 15 percent"; "Enter the Southwest market," and the like.

OVERALL MARKETING PROGRAM. Most important for the small firm developing a marketing plan is *time management;* in other words, determine what effort will best achieve the results you want. To translate overall marketing goals into specific marketing tasks, list objectives that will get you to your goals. Note that a market is defined as: project type + client + geographic location

Sample objectives include

"Elderly housing work for nonprofit clients in Iowa and Minnesota: increase fees in this area to $400,000, achieve a 20 percent return on sales (ROS), and limit marketing costs to $30,000."

"Spend $20,000 in direct labor responding to Corps of Engineers and Navfac RFP's announced in *Commerce Business Daily's (CBD)* weekly release. (CBD is a weekly digest of government contract procurements and contract award notices. It is customized to your area, and includes

Federal Supply Classification Codes. The telephone number for *CBD* is (301) 961-8777.)

"Have three projects published in national design magazines."

"Set a quota for making cold calls: Make four prospecting calls a week."

As a small practitioner, also remember to delegate everything you can to your employees, even if you only employ part-timers or a limited number of people.

IDENTIFICATION OF SPECIFIC MARKETS. Included in this section are a statement of each market (who, what, why), geographic particulars, the markets' size and potential for growth, expected share and "edge" in those markets, and how each market will be pursued. The latter section should include employee responsibility, intensity, methods, schedule, and fees.

OVERALL ADMINISTRATION OR MARKETING CONTROL. Plan how often you will hold meetings and who will attend. Appoint a leader of marketing, either yourself or another key individual in the firm. Update the plan regularly, perhaps every six months and at least once a year. Make economic projections based on the marketing program.

BUDGET. As a small firm your bottom line on marketing spending may be "What do I have available from the overhead?" Consider principal's prorated time, marketing support salaries, materials, postage, telephone, travel, and entertainment. One way to discover how much money you have for marketing is to allocate eight percent of your gross billings for the past year to marketing. (See Fig. 2-11 for percentages of money spent on marketing.)

As a small firm, allocate funds prudently. To ensure that you are not overspending, provide for an accounting program for time and expenses to track your spending. See Appendix B for a sample marketing plan.

FOCUS THE EMPLOYEES ON SELLING

Members of the firm need to develop the skills to procure and maintain clients to put the marketing plan into action and sustain the success of the company. Although not everyone is good at face-to-face sales efforts, each plays a part in the success of your small firm. Your whole company should develop sales skills in case your current client base shrinks.

Before explaining selling techniques for the small firm, it is important to clarify the terms "marketing" and "selling." There is considerable confusion about the difference between marketing and sales; smaller firms often use the term "marketing" when in fact they mean "sales." This can be very confusing. Marketing is client-need-oriented and sales is project-commitment-oriented.

Marketing, as defined in the *Professional Services Management Journal* and the *A/E Marketing Journal,* is the activity of planning, organizing, directing, and controlling the marketing effort to secure clients. Marketing is focused on the needs of the client. It involves market research strategy and direction. Sales involves the face-to-face activity of securing a project. This is done by the project manager, the principal, or whoever will actually convince the client to choose the firm for a given project.

Marketing, in the truest sense, is the analysis of client needs to determine a strategy to go after and meet those needs with services and professional talent.

THE PRINCIPAL. The principal is often among the best salespeople in the firm. Here's how to use your principal(s) as a resource:

- Contrary to popular wisdom, encourage the principal to say "I" often. Only he/she can say to the prospect, "I have people who can commit to your project."
- Position the principal as an expert who comments in the media on design issues that matter to your firm. Principals have that extra credibility by virtue of their position.
- Value tough questions by the principal to you about your marketing effectiveness. Such confrontational behavior reminds staff of the obligation to justify their actions.

TECHNICAL PEOPLE. Technical professionals on occasion talk with the client and are in a good position to sell your firm's services. It makes sense to expose them also to experienced salespeoples' advice. As an introduction to sales techniques, begin with one or two selections from a variety of books on the subject. Consider

- *Back to Basic Selling: Unique Sales Tips,* Robert Taylor, Prentice-Hall, (201) 767-5937 ($8.95), 1985.
- *The Best Seller: The New Psychology of Selling,* Ron Willingham, Prentice-Hall (hardcover $19.95, paperback $6.95), 1983.
- *The Four Minute Sell,* Janet G. Elsea, Simon & Schuster. (Out of print, but you may be able to find it at your local library.)
- *How to Master the Art of Selling,* Tom Hopkins, Tom Hopkins International, 1980, (800) 528-0446.

These books provide tools to help you train technical people to sell. Read them and remember that as a small firm entrepreneur you must always be selling. Even while you are drafting, formulate plans for your next client meeting, brainstorm your next presentation, or mentally envision yourself winning your next presentation.

PROJECT MANAGER AS SALESMAN. The project manager has distinct responsibilities to help ensure a continuing supply of work. The following is a list of sales activities for the project manager:

Extras: Be aware of actual and potential extras and charges on a project. There is a definite opportunity to sell these to a client.

Additional Services: Offer services outside of those for which the client has contracted. The project manager should make sure the client is aware of all services the firm offers.

Other Projects: Actively seek other projects from clients. Ask about other activities of the client firm to find out about possible projects.

Client Maintenance: Establish a program for regular client contact after a project is complete. Call them once a month, make sure they receive your holiday cards, send regular announcements, put them on your monthly newsletter list. Make sure that the project manager personally calls them at least once a year and takes out a member of the client firm for lunch at least once a year. Invite the client to occasions such as your firm's annual party or company softball games, or obtain hard-to-get sporting event tickets for them. Encourage the project manager to keep the client aware that you exist.

Other Likely Clients: Ask clients if they know of other potential clients and projects. Direct referrals are excellent sources of work.

Network Building: Develop a reputation and awareness about the firm among project managers' acquaintances. When they have a project, they should think of your firm. Encourage project managers to make liberal use of their business cards.

NEVERTHELESS, DON'T LET EVERYONE SELL. Not everyone should have a chance to be involved in *face-to-face* sales efforts. Identify those who are especially good at it and use them often. But since even star performers will "bomb" with some clients, this group should be diverse, so your prospects will have a better chance of being matched with an appropriate person in your firm.

Your best bets are those individuals who

- Like to meet people and have many contacts and acquaintances.
- Are prepared to champion new ideas within your firm.
- Recruit well.
- Are enthusiastic about their work.
- Run good meetings.
- Are politically smart.

Save these special sellers for situations requiring persuasion: presentations, interviews, and selected meetings. Assign marketing functions to less sales-oriented individuals, who can prepare photographs and slides of past projects, write project histories, or fill out government forms.

MANAGING YOUR CLIENT

To best manage current and prospective clients using your work force, consider breaking up your staff into in-house marketing and marketing-sales client managers:

1. *In-house Marketing.* In-house staff perform marketing support such as proposal response writing, brochure generation, development of marketing materials, research and development, and creation/maintenance of information systems.For

very small firms, such support may be one of the duties of your administrative assistant.

2. *Client Managers.*   Field marketing staff make direct contact with potential clients; that is, they sell. Unlike typical salespeople, however, their participation does not stop once the job is secured. As an added bonus to the client, the client manager should continue to be involved in the job by visiting the site regularly and attending major job meetings with the project manager.

Here are some additional sales hints:

- Make face-to-face contacts.
- Hire project managers (engineering and architecture) who will be responsible for acquiring a given level of revenue.
- Put these sales expectations in writing.
- Review performance expectations at predetermined stages.
- Use direct contact with project managers and principals.

Client managers actually *manage* the client by leading client meetings, establishing contractual relations with consultants, anticipating changes in work for the client, and meeting unexpected client demands. The client manager should develop and nurture the client's trust from the signing of the agreement all the way through to occupancy of the completed project. Developing secure, long-term relationships will result in contracts. This is a new concept in the design professions: using client managers will distinguish your firm from the competion.

HONING TELEPHONE SKILLS

Sales efforts for the small firm must be lean and efficient. The small practitioner can achieve real sustained success by the judicious honing of telephone skills.

Compare the management and growth of a practice with portfolio investments. You do not react to every hot tip or attempt to manage a portfolio so large as to be out of control. To be small and stay small, one must be selective and focus on connecting with a limited number of potential clients at any given time.

Call directly the person you want to reach. If you are a structural engineering or interior design firm, for example, locate a listing of architectural firms and seek to be considered when they accept multidiscipline assignments. Determine if there are particular architects whose design approach or style is congenial and put them on your prospect list.

A reasonable effort should be restricted to four calls a day, no more than 20 a week. This allows you adequate time for long telephone conversations in which you and the prospect can take each other's measure and begin to relate to one another. If the chemistry is wrong, you can tell early on and both you and the prospect will have saved a lot of time and expense.

Plan the calls with a checklist and write out answers to possible queries or objections. Why are you "the better mousetrap"? If you cannot answer most questions positively, don't make the call. Figure 2.17 contains typical client objections

---

Client Objections/Answers

1. **"Your price is too high."** This is a common objection. Do not become defensive and start to justify your price. Instead, focus on the scope of work that's being provided for the price. Tell the client they are getting better quality and better service than the competition provides for the same price. Give the client the choice of reducing the price by reducing the scope of services. Tell them the price quoted reflects the highest standard. This is a positive defense when the client objects to price.

2. **"The schedule is too long."** A client will often say this when the firm has built into the schedule expected delays or client changes. To defend this, ask the client what their preferences are for the schedule. Given their restrictions, advise them that it is possible with less reviews or an increased intensity in the reviews, which may cost more money. Another alternative is to suggest that you will work overtime to shorten the schedule and that you will have to charge more money to cover the associated costs.

3. **"You're putting too much emphasis on quality."** Again, do not become defensive. Suggest to the client that they help define the quality level so that you can understand the client's quality expectations.

4. **"You're putting the wrong people on the project."** This can be difficult to overcome, especially if you have committed people to the project in the proposal and presentation stages. A firm can win or lose a project based on the people they put on the job. You can overcome this objection by guaranteeing to the client that a certain principal or the company president will oversee the day-to-day project progress. Most clients, especially when dealing with small firms, want the principal to be involved in the project. One of the key advantages that a small firm has over a large one is that it can allocate the principal's time to a particular project much more readily than a larger firm.

Figure 2-17

and some possible answers. Figure 2-18 is a sample marketing call report form, and Figure 2-19 a client contact memorandum.

Here are some ways you can prepare for the call:

1. Know your purpose.
2. Research telephone techniques.
3. Attitude of enthusiasm.
4. Communicate that you'd like to help solve problems, not just find projects.
5. Make observations, and *listen.*
6. Ask open-ended questions, not ones that can be answered with only a yes or no.
7. Use positives, not negatives.

SUMMARY

Focusing the practice is a very important element in staying small successfully. Firms that exercise prudent judgment and control end up stronger over the long haul.

Target clients, not projects; network in client circles, not peer circles. Say no to projects and clients that do not match your focus. Find a narrow niche and be the biggest in that niche. To accomplish this, utilize usefulness selling, that is, providing useful information to clients. Use distinctive marketing tools, such as surveys, articles, newsletters, books, and seminars to encourage focusing.

SUCCESS CHALLENGES

1. Are you really working on securing clients or are you working on securing projects? The key indicator is whether, after you complete a project, you keep in touch with a client.
2. Are you developing networking activities that allow you to meet more and more people on a routine basis?
3. Are you developing "usefulness" marketing tools such as a client newsletter to provide a backbone to your marketing effort, or are you simply providing selling tools such as project photographs and advertising brochures to your staff?

BUSINESS CARD

MARKETING CALL REPORT

ORGANIZATION _____

NAME _____

TITLE _____

ADDRESS _____

_____

PHONE _____

DATE _____

POTENTIAL PROJECT _____

INFORMATION	ACTION TO BE TAKEN

BROCHURE _____

REFERRED BY _____

RELATED _____

MAILING LIST   YES _____ NO_____

BY _____

Figure 2-18   Marketing call report form.

CLIENT CONTACT MEMORANDUM

Date : _____ Division : _____ Contact By : _____

Type of Visit : ☐ Office ; ☐ Telephone : ☐ Other _____

1. Company : _____

2. Address : _____

   _____

3. Division or Department Contacted : _____

4.

	Person(s) Contacted	Position / Title	Telephone Number	Add to Mailing List?
a.				
b.				
c.				

5. Objective of Visit : _____

6. Project or Prospect Identified : _____

7. Who is Decision Maker? _____

8. Summary of Discussion : _____

   _____

   _____

   _____

   _____

   _____

   _____

9. Is Proposal to be Prepared? _____ ; Date : _____; Est. Dollar Value : _____

10. Commitments to Client : _____

11. Literature Left : _____

12. Action to Follow (What? By Whom? When?) : _____

   _____

   _____

Distribution (Attention) : ☐ Corporate Marketing _____

☐ Houston _____ ;   ☐ Const. mat. _____ ;   ☐ New Orleans _____

☐ Little Rock _____ ;   ☐ St. Louis _____ ;   ☐ Ventura _____

☐ San Francisco _____ ;   ☐ TERA _____ ;   ☐ London _____

☐ Saudi Arabia _____ ;   ☐ Singapore _____ ;   ☐ Other _____

Signature : _____

Figure 2-19 Client contact memorandum.

4. Are you learning to say no to clients in a way that helps focus your marketing response by eliminating clients you should not be courting?

5. How does the focus of your practice reinforce your vision of where your firm should be?

6. Examine the *services* you now provide. List three that could be expanded into focused niches in which you can be perceived to be a real expert.

REFERENCES

1. Practice Management Associates, Ltd, 1986–1990. *PSMJ Financial Statistics Survey*. Newton, Mass.

2. Practice Management Associates, Ltd. 1989. *PSMJ 1989 Financial Statistics Survey*. Newton, Mass. pp. 75–78.

BIBLIOGRAPHY

Jim Morgan, 1984. *Marketing for the Small Design Firm*. New York: Whitney Library of Design.

Paul E. Pritzker, October 1978. "The Small Firm." *Professional Services Management Journal*

Ruth Stockman, August 1989. "For Small Firms . . . Starting from Scratch." *A/E Marketing Journal*

3 SERVICING THE CLIENT

Students go to architecture or engineering school hoping to become renowned for great design. From day one in a job, graduates want their names associated with the world's greatest designs, whether a bridge design to span the widest river, a wastewater treatment design for the newest technology or the design of the most brilliant high-rise facility. The ego-driven design-orientation is part of any design professional's background.

Design, however, from the client's perspective, becomes a feature, not a benefit. All clients expect the firm they select to produce high-quality design. Unfortunately, to the client, good design is like a spark plug in a Corvette. Spark plugs do not sell Corvettes. Sex, glamour, and life-style sell Corvettes, as do speediness, color, and image.

In design, it is the *service* element of the business that will keep the small firm in successful practice over the long run. The most successful design firms in the marketplace become known for the service they provide, while also providing a high level of quality in design.

It is easy to distinguish good service from bad. When you drive up to a gas station, the attendant either washes your windshield and checks your oil, or he doesn't. It's a black-and-white issue. But, there is more: perception becomes reality. You must not only provide good service; you must be perceived as doing so.

In design, the quality of service can be measured by

Schedule
Does the firm set up a realistic initial schedule?
Does the firm perform according to the schedule?

When it cannot adhere to it, is the firm honest, up-front, and swift in notifying the client of this?

Budget

Is the firm meeting its design budget and its projected construction cost budget? Budget and schedule go hand in hand. If the firm is meeting its schedule but exceeding its budget, it is spending too much just to meet the schedule. Set a realistic budget, and suggest to the client contingencies within the budget. Consider a three to five percent construction contingency to make up for changes in the budget later in the project.

Performance

Is the firm technically qualified?

Is it selling its qualifications realistically?

Does it go beyond its technical capabilities?

Does it fulfill the budget and schedule promises?

Managing Meetings

Does the firm set up meetings, or is it simply reacting by attending already-scheduled meetings?

Does the firm arrive to meetings on time?

Does it cancel meetings?

What is its active role in serving the client? Clients want leaders who will take charge of a project, and set up job meetings with contractors.

Does the firm take control of meetings by arranging them, setting the agenda, and leading them?

Does the firm follow up with action after the meetings?

Doing Satisfactory Working Drawings

Are the drawings realistic?

Are they clear to the contractor?

Is the contractor pricing the jobs appropriately based on the quality of the drawings?

Bidding

Provide more than enough drawings to the contractors.

Telephone contractors to inquire about questions/problems

with the plans. (Be careful—legally you must communicate equally with all bidders.)

Involve the owner/client in the bidding process, within an interview scheme. Allow each bidder to interview the owner to better ascertain mutual understanding of project scope.

In general, all of the above point to reinforcing communication during bidding.

Construction

Document daily project activities.

Appoint a project site representative to be on site and to document performance on the job. This includes monitoring the schedule, material delivery, and daily activities.

Keep the client aware of the project's progress.

Photograph the site from the same angles, producing a photographic history of the entire project. Pick five, six or seven key points on the site and photograph at these points every day. This record can be invaluable during any liability disputes later on.

Photographs are invaluable to understanding "covered up" materials such as concrete, reinforcing bars, and so on.

Hold regular on-site job meetings with owner's representatives to review aspects of construction.

Successful design firms have an ability to perform on schedule and stay within the budget to a degree that may exceed their own targeted projections. They are realistic when they

- Target project performance.
- Establish project schedules and budgets with enough leeway to achieve their goals.
- Are able to convince their staff that schedules and budgets can be met.

This chapter explains how your small firm can be profitable if it focuses on providing a good service rather than on design; ways to be responsive to your client to provide better service; how to establish a quality-control program to ensure quality as part of providing that service (and to avoid liability); and suggested ways to innovate your activities so the client perceives your firm as providing exemplary service.

SERVICE VERSUS DESIGN

Small firms often try to be a little of everything. They want to have some outstanding element of each arena—that is, of design *and* service. According to studies by the Coxe Group, it is far better to *make a choice* as to what type of firm you want to be: an ideas firm (design-focused), a strong-service firm (gray-hair firm), or a strong-delivery firm (referred to as a service firm in this text). The Coxe Group of Philadelphia has researched and identified these three types of firm technologies and also two types of value systems. The choice of technology and values will affect every aspect of organization and project delivery, and ultimately, your firm's profitability. Figure 3-1 contains a description of these classifications and explains the Coxe Group's test results showing that successful firms make a choice on one focus or another. Firms that don't make choices cannot possibly succeed in *all* areas and therefore are not among the most profitable. Develop a clear notion of what your firm does best, and plan your organization accordingly. Make a choice. For the very small firm, establishing a design reputation may be difficult; you first need to develop a good reputation. The easiest and fastest way to do this is to deliver. Provide good service and you will become well known. Whether or not you can grow from there to provide good service and win design awards depends on many variables, some of them out of your control. For the small firm, it is far better to begin by focusing on providing good service. A firm that can promise to finish a job on schedule and within budget will stand out in an industry where these criteria have often not been met.

LITTLE THINGS THAT COUNT BIG

Providing good service begins with the little details, which actually convey the spirit of the firm's focus to the client. The following list may contain some items you *think* you are doing—but do you stand out from the competition in each of these areas? If you do *not* differ from your competitors in each element, review and change your procedures. There may be some lessons, for example, in the profile of the Scott Companies in Figure 3-2, a firm that dares to guarantee schedule and budget or it won't take its fee. Here are some little things that you can do to upgrade bad or mediocre service to good service:

CATEGORIES OF DESIGN FIRMS

The Coxe Group Management Consultants (Philadelphia) delineates three types of technologies and two types of value systems within design firms. By technologies, they refer to the focus in which projects are delivered. The three types are

- *Strong-idea (brains) firms,* organized to deliver singular expertise or innovation to unique projects. Project technology for this type of firm flexibly accommodates the nature of any assignment, and often depends on a few outstanding experts or "stars" to give final approval.
- *Strong-service (gray hair) firms,* organized to deliver experience and reliability, especially on complex projects. Their focus is to provide comprehensive service to a client that is closely involved in the process.
- *Strong-delivery (procedure) firms,* which provide efficient service on similar or more routine assignments to clients which seek more of a product than a service. This firm repeats previous solutions over and over again with highly reliable technical, cost, and schedule compliance. [Referred to as service firms in this text.]

A company's technical emphasis may shift during the following process:

1. New ideas come from strong-idea firms.
2. As they become understood and accepted in the marketplace, the ideas are then applied widely by strong-service firms.
3. When the idea becomes routinized and is in demand by many clients, strong-delivery firms will start to provide the service, where repetitive projects and efficiency are stressed.

Thus firms should periodically review their status on this continuum to ensure that they are keeping the focus where they want it to be.

The technology of a firm affects
- Project progress.
- Project decisions.
- Staffing (middle and lower).
- Marketing (choice of market).
- Products being sold.
- Prices.
- Management style.

The choice of technology shapes the design process, and it is becoming recognized that all really successful firms have a clear, consistent project-delivery process that fits into one of the above three categories.

The other area that shapes a firm's service delivery system is its values. Do you run your business as a "practice" or as a "business"? This can make a difference in

1. Organizational structure.
2. Decision-making process.
3. Staffing (top level).
4. Marketing strategies of firms.
5. Identifying clients.

Figure 3-1 Source: The Coxe Group Management Consultants, Weld Coxe, Nina Hartung, Hugh Hockberg, Brian Lewis, David Master, Robert Mattox, and Peter Piven. Used with permission. *(Continued on next page)*

6. Organization of marketing.
7. Rewards.
8. Management style.

To determine what your firm is, look at your bottom line:

- *Practice-centered business:* Your major goal is the opportunity to serve others and produce examples of the discipline you represent. Your bottom line is qualitative: How do we like what we're doing? How does the job serve the client's needs? Our needs?

- *Business-centered practice:* Your major goal is a quantitative bottom line, focusing on the tangible rewards of your efforts. How did we do? How much money did we make?

Many firms succeed in any combination of these technologies and values, but the objective is that you should have one. You should choose your particular focus based on your individual preferences and goals. The Coxe Group surveyed 100 firms of different sizes, markets, and organizational formats. The results of that survey showed that firms that have a clear notion of what they do best (technology) and a common set of goals (values) succeed—for themselves and their clients.

Figure 3-1 (continued)

1. Provide good telephone service, that is, are calls to the company answered in a pleasant/unique manner? For instance, employees of one firm answer the telephone with "Good morning, it's a great day. This is ABC Associates." You may think this is trite or cute, but the concept is to instill a positive feeling in listeners before they even speak. In so doing, you can short-circuit angry people and perhaps change their present frame of mind and intentions.

2. Respond quickly to letters and other materials. Things to consider: What is the time frame implied by "a quick response"? When you instruct an employee to send a letter "immediately," does he/she think three days is a quick response, or does the letter go out in that day's mail?

3. Follow up on details. You will be remembered for the small details, recalling the name of a client's spouse or the birthday of a client's child (see the next section, "Responsiveness"). But details also include remembering that the bathroom is to be done in chrome, not brass.

Service: The Approach of the Scott Companies

Firm: The Scott Companies Architects Interiors Engineers, Inc.
Staff: 35
Specialty: Retail, health care, multi-unit housing, educational facilities, and
            government work
Address: 601 S. Lake Destiny Road
            Suite 400
            Maitland, Fla. 32751

"Very few schools educate design professionals on the business end of running a practice. But not everyone is going to be a design-oriented architect." Instead, success in a small firm is a process of client satisfaction, maintains Ray Scott, president of the Scott Companies.

Scott was formerly a partner of Catalyst, a design-focused firm. "We sold design—our focus was 'Let's do award-winning architecture.' The problem with this focus is that after 7 or 8 years, you realize that concentrating on design eats up the fees. We won a lot of awards, but we didn't make a lot of money. All projects were over budget and over schedule. We ignored other aspects of business, such as service and client satisfaction. When the project went out for construction, the situation tended to be adversary. Clients were one-time, maybe two-time clients. I'd say 60% were satisfied, 40% were not. Externally we won a lot of awards, but internally we weren't breaking even."

Scott left Catalyst in 1984 to start his own company. The new firm now has what he calls "100% client satisfaction . . . Our focus is 'Let's serve the client.' We are now able to meet the budget and the schedule. We thought we'd surprise clients by delivering on time (not usually expected in design). We promise a lot, but our whole key is to deliver, too. Many design firms promise, but don't deliver."

Initial design presentations are more flexible at the Ray Scott Company. "In the design focused firm, we developed a single solution and presented it to the client with the comment that 'this is the best design.' In our service firm, we develop rapidly 5, 6, or 7 sketches, put them on the conference room wall, and ask the client, 'Which one do you like?'" This technique works very well, Scott says. "For our first shopping center, we put 12 sketches on the wall. We were hoping for one, but the developer liked two others, and chose those for his next two shopping centers."

The key, Scott says, is ego: "A service firm has to hang ego on the door and satisfy the client." Ninety percent of all clients do not care about an award-winning building if they don't receive good service: "They just want a nicely designed building." Organizations wanting an award-winning building comprise probably only 5% of all clients, and there is great competition nationally for such projects. For small firms, a service focus is more profitable.

The difference can be seen in the bottom line—profit. After 7 years in business, Scott says, Catalyst was worth about $150,000, had 35 people, 4 partners, and never broke $1 million in gross fees. The Scott Companies Architects Interior Engineers, Inc., in contrast, has a $2 million business value after only 4 years and has increased its gross fees by $1 million each of those 4 years.

The firm's success also hinges on its commitment to hiring the best available staff. "Everyone in our office is licensed. It affects your direct cost, but alleviates the money spent problem-solving later in a project." Hiring quality employees affects the firm's ability to service its clients. The company's low level of change orders on jobs also reduces the negative aspects of the construction project. "We've even had projects with no change orders," claims Scott.

Figure 3-2

4. Be open and warm to all clients. Make them feel they come first even though you may have 14 other clients.

5. Thoroughly document things such as meeting minutes, telephone calls, meetings with product suppliers, mistakes and/or changes on the job, and contractor questions.

6. Never hide from a problem. Be up-front. There is no use in pretending a problem doesn't exist merely to avoid client conflict.

7. Make sure your telephone number is on *all* pieces of correspondence, to encourage contacts and queries from the client.

8. Make sure every piece of paper that crosses your desk is dated, to be certain that you can provide an accurate time/dated record of all activities if called on by your client to do so.

9. If you have an important telephone conversation, record it, with permission, so you can later recall its key elements.

10. Be certain to record telephone and Fax numbers of all key people on a project so that they can be reached.

11. Install a car phone in your project managers' cars so they are accessible in a crisis. You may even consider bringing a portable phone when you travel by plane.

12. Learn how to send Faxes so you don't depend on others in your office in an emergency or crisis.

13. Develop a key contact list of pertinent building departments so you can call the right person in a crisis.

RESPONSIVENESS

Responsiveness is critical to being perceived as providing outstanding service. The small design firm must known its clients intimately in order to court long-term relationships, which are important to success (as explained in Chapter 2, under "Targeting Clients, Not Projects"). There is nothing more embarrassing and detrimental to client perception of responsiveness than getting into a conversation with a client, who has mentioned his/her spouse previously (in detail), only to forget that spouse's first name when it comes time to ask, "How is (blank) anyway?" To show your clients how much they are valued, set up a filing system to record personal facts. One way to do this is suggested in Harvey Mackay' *Swim With the Sharks Without Being Eaten Alive.*[1] Mackay, who owns an envelope corporation, has a 66-question customer profile for each customer that his employees come into contact with. Because it is impossible to answer every question in one telephone call or visit, the questionnaire is kept in the file and filled in as the firm gets to know the client. The list includes such things as the spouse's name; birthdays of the client, spouse, and children; nickname; and college fraternity. (See Fig. 3-3 for a CEO customer profile form based on Mackay's questionnaire.) Developing such a list for your organization will make you appear more concerned, more responsive, and more service-oriented. Responsiveness helps retain repeat clients.

QUALITY CONTROL

Naturally, providing good quality is a large part of providing good service. Along with establishing education standards for your staff and encouraging continuing education, you should set up an organized quality-control program. A comprehensive quality-control system will help to limit liability. The following pages are based on David Kent Ballast's *Guide to Quality Control for Design Professionals.*[2] They are a good introduction to quality control for the small design firm.

Overview

The current liability crisis affects nearly all design professionals, more and more of whom are involved in litigation. Insurance costs skyrocket, and everyone is sensitive to how they practice and what liability exposure they have. The causes of this situation are varied. Some blame the litigious nature of society, others point to the cyclical nature of the insurance business, and still others blame the design professionals themselves for poor performance.

Whatever the cause, many design professionals are exploring ways to avoid litigation, but litigation is primarily a way to sort out who can be legally blamed. Reduce your errors and you have gone a long way toward solving the liability crisis. Setting up a rigorous quality-control program is the best way to reduce errors and thereby reduce litigation.

Practice Management Associates, Ltd.

CEO CUSTOMER PROFILE

CUSTOMER

1. Name_____

   Nickname_____

   Title_____

2. Company Name_____

   Address_____

   City, State, Zip_____

3. Home Address_____

4. Telephone: (Work)_____(Home)_____

5. Birth date and place_____

   Hometown_____

6. Professional Licenses in_____ :_____ :

7. Secretary's Name_____Tel Ext_____

EDUCATION

8. College_____

   Graduation Date/Degree_____

9. College Honors_____

   Advanced degrees/School_____

10. College fraternity/sorority_____

    Sports_____

11. Extracurricular college activities_____

    Noteworthy sports awards_____

12. If customer didn't attend college, is he/she sensitive about it?_____

    What did they do instead?_____

13. Military service_____

    Discharge Rank_____

    Attitude towards being in the service_____

    Vietnam Veteran: Yes_____No _____

FAMILY

14. Marital status_____ Spouse's name_____

    Previously Married: Yes_____ No_____ # of Times_____

15. Spouse's education_____

Figure 3-3 Practice Mangement Associates' CEO Customer Profile form based on McKay questionnaire. Used with permission. *(Continued on following pages)*

Spouse's Job/Career_____

16. Spouse's interests/activities/affiliations_____

_____

17. Wedding anniversary_____Year Married_____

18. Children, if any, names and ages_____

_____

19. Children's education_____

_____

20. Children's interests (hobbies, problems, etc.)_____

_____

Special Notes About Family_____

_____

BUSINESS BACKGROUND

21. Previous employment: (most recent first)_____

Company _____

Location_____

Dates_____Title_____

Company_____

Location_____

Dates_____Title_____

22. Previous position at present company: Title_____

Dates_____

23. Any "status" symbols in office?

24. Professional or trade associations

Office or honors in them

25. Any mentors?

Name of Assistant/Secretary

26. What business relationship does he/she have with others in our company?

_____

27. Is it a good relationship?_____Why?_____

_____

28. What other people in our company know the customer?_____

_____

29. Type of connection_____

Nature of relationship_____

Figure 3-3   (continued)

30. What is client's attitude toward his/her firm_____
_____

31. What is his/her long-range business objective_____
_____

32. What is his/her immediate business objective? _____
_____

33. What is of greatest concern to customer at this time: the welfare of the company or his/her own personal welfare?_____

34. Does the customer think of the present or the future?_____
Why?_____

SPECIAL INTERESTS:

35. Clubs or service clubs_____

36. Politically active?_____Party Importance to customer_____

37. Active in community?_____How?_____

.   Religion_____Active_____

38. Highly confidential items not to be discussed with customer (e.g. divorce, member of AA)
_____

39. On what subjects (outside of business) does customer have strong feelings?_____
_____

LIFESTYLE:

40. Medical history (current condition of health)_____

41. Does customer drink?_____If yes, what and how much? _____
_____

42. If no, offended by others drinking?_____

43. Does customer smoke?_____If no, object to others_____

44. Favorite place for lunch_____
Favorite place for dinner_____

45. Favorite type of cuisine_____

46. Does customer object to having anyone buy his/her meal?_____

47. Hobbies and recreational interests_____
What does customer like to read?_____
What type(s) of books?_____

48. Vacation habits_____
Airline Preference: First Class_____Coach_____
Hotel Preference_____Room Type_____

Figure 3-3   (continued from previous page)

Rental Car Preference_____

Does family travel with customer?_____

49. Spectator-sports interest: sports and teams_____

_____

50. Kind of car(s)_____Color_____

51. Conversational interests _____

52. Whom does customer seem anxious to impress?_____

_____

53. How does he/she want to be seen by those people?_____

_____

54. What adjectives would you use to describe customer?_____

_____

55. What is he/she most proud of having achieved? _____

_____

56. What do you feel is customer's long-range personal objective?_____

_____

57. What do you feel is customer's immediate personal objective?_____

_____

SUPPORT OF PMA

58. Does customer subscribe to:

   PSMJ_____AEMJ_____Details/Plus_____Job Mart_____

59. Has customer purchased/participated in surveys?_____

   Which_____

60. Has customer purchased publications? _____

   Which_____

61. Has customer attended a trade show?_____

   Which_____

62. Has customer attended education programs?_____

   Which_____

63. Does customer's firm actively support our products/services? _____

64. Has customer of firm had any bad experiences with our service?_____

_____

65. Location/Dates of CEO Programs attended_____

_____

Figure 3-3 *(continued)*

THE CUSTOMER AND YOU:

66. What moral or ethical considerations are involved when you work with the customer?

_____

67. Does customer feel any obligation to you, your company or to your company's competition?
    If so, what?_____

68. Is he/she primarily concerned about the opinion of others?_____

69. Or very self-centered_____Highly ethical _____

70. What are the key problems as customer sees them?_____

_____

71. What are the priorities of the customer's management?_____

_____

    Any conflicts between customer and management?_____

_____

72. Can you help with these problems?_____How?_____

_____

73. Does our competitor have better answers to the above questions than we have?_____

_____

ADDITIONAL NOTES:

Figure 3-3   *(continued from previous page)*

Quality control revolves around good project management, which involves four key areas. These key issues can be applied to every area of the project, from predesign through post-occupancy evaluation:

Budget Control: Well-run firms clarify the difference between client expectations and reality for each expenditure to be made during both design and construction. Misconceptions often lead clients to seek legal counsel when costs exceed anticipated expenditures.

Scheduling: Honesty about elements of a project that are within a firm's control and those that are not is critical. Many delays caused by outside agencies have been blamed on design firms, and many mistakes have been made by design professionals trying to make up time in fear of a client's wrath.

Coordination: Regular communication with all project team members is probably the single most important element of a good quality-control program. Good communication assures that little problems don't grow large, and that big problems are handled quickly.

Records Management: Maintaining a well-documented trail of written communication about all aspects of a project assures that each liability claim can be properly defended. Creating such documentation also helps each person to understand a project better.

Providing good-quality standards must be a part of providing good service. A quality-control program can help to

- Prevent errors and resulting claims and litigation.
- Satisfy owner requirements (insurance and quality control).
- Help you practice better and offer the most competitive service possible.

What is Quality Control?

The level of performance implied with good quality is established by tradition, standard practices, and legal precedent. Quality control attempts to assure that the normal correct project-delivery tasks and the management of those tasks and supporting office activities proceed according to plan, as free of error as possible. Quality control can be thought of as "management of management."

Checking and approval systems differ for each type of design business. Whatever type of business you run, however, there are some guidelines to setting up a quality-control program:

1. Top management must support and encourage a quality-control program. You cannot "assign" the task to someone and then forget about it.
2. One person or a small committee should be given the responsibility to guide the daily efforts of the program.
3. Everyone in the office must be involved. This is especially true when the firm is first being formed; solicit suggestions from all employees concerning problem areas and how procedures can be modified to improve things. A

quality-control program thrust upon employees will not work. "Quality circles" are especially useful in motivating and involving employees.

4. Review past problem areas. Start with a list of those things that cause your firm the greatest difficulties or that have the potential to do it the most damage.

5. Once you understand your office's unique problem areas, set up priorities and a schedule for action. Only you can do this, since every office is slightly different and since you won't be able to solve everything at once. Use the past-problem list as a starting point. You may find that improving your standard agreements is the most needed action or that documentation needs to be improved.

6. Finally, stick with your program. Monitor it continuously, eliminating what doesn't seem to be working and keeping what helps the most.

An effective quality-control program takes time and money to set up and maintain. Even for the smallest of firms, it may mean the inclusion of checklists for each phase. As the small firm grows, the quality-control system grows tool and the payoff will be fewer errors, reduced liability exposure, efficiency, and improved service to your clients.

How to Set Up a Quality-control (QC) Program for the Small Design Office

PREDESIGN STAGE

The first step in a quality-control program is to look at a client and the feasibility of the project and make a "go/no go" decision. Does the client want too much? Has the client come to you with unreasonable expectations or demands? Answering such questions is the first step in your quality-control program because even if you need the work, a project could end up costing you more money than you might earn.

In reviewing the client's expectations and budget, consider also whether your firm can complete the proposed project. Look at

- Number of personnel.
- Experience in the proposed project type.
- Current work load.

Be sure you are not presenting your firm as a "specialist" in an area if it is not true. You will be held accountable for a higher standard of practice than a "general" design firm.

Review the client's proposal carefully. Does he or she want you to use existing plans? If so, review possible pitfalls with the client, and protect yourself in the agreement or contract. In submitting your proposal, include a detailed list of services included in the cost. Do not attach previous cost estimates or preliminary estimates to the contract. These may bind you to design a facility within a certain cost limit.

Consider also scheduling. In addition to normal scheduling activities, identify any special requirements or possible delays. List these in writing and submit them to the client, explaining that this is not all-inclusive. Items causing delay might include

- Elevators.
- Hardware.
- Special finishes.
- Mechanical equipment.
- Construction strikes.
- Seasonal weather factors.

Finally, choose a team. Estimate their average experience level by taking the total number of years of experience of all team members and dividing by the number of team members. If the resulting number is less than five years, you may want to add more experienced people to the team or closely supervise the work.

PROPOSALS

The proposal generally includes a firm's proposed approach to a project. As such, it often serves as the basis for the formal written contract. It follows that your proposal should be subject to the same kind of quality-control check as any other part of the practice. Figure 3-4 is a checklist of items to consider when writing the proposal. Use this checklist as a guideline to draw up your own, to be reproduced and followed each time you write a proposal.

CONTRACTS

Your first line of defense against exposure to liability is your contract. Spell out exactly what your client can expect of you

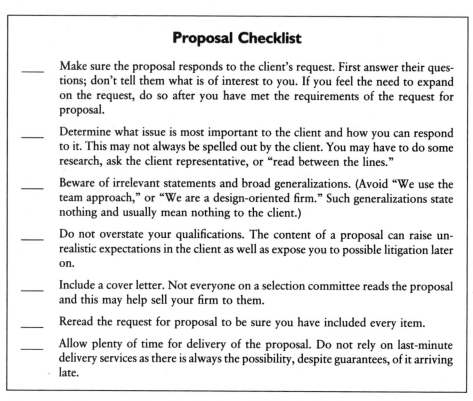

Proposal Checklist

____ Make sure the proposal responds to the client's request. First answer their questions; don't tell them what is of interest to you. If you feel the need to expand on the request, do so after you have met the requirements of the request for proposal.

____ Determine what issue is most important to the client and how you can respond to it. This may not always be spelled out by the client. You may have to do some research, ask the client representative, or "read between the lines."

____ Beware of irrelevant statements and broad generalizations. (Avoid "We use the team approach," or "We are a design-oriented firm." Such generalizations state nothing and usually mean nothing to the client.)

____ Do not overstate your qualifications. The content of a proposal can raise unrealistic expectations in the client as well as expose you to possible litigation later on.

____ Include a cover letter. Not everyone on a selection committee reads the proposal and this may help sell your firm to them.

____ Reread the request for proposal to be sure you have included every item.

____ Allow plenty of time for delivery of the proposal. Do not rely on last-minute delivery services as there is always the possibility, despite guarantees, of it arriving late.

Figure 3-4   Source: *Guide to Quality Control for Design Professionals,* by David Kent Ballast, Newton, Mass.: Practice Management Associates, Ltd., 1986. Used with permission.

and what you can expect of your client. State responsibilities and the level of professional services you will provide. In addition, be sure your contract protects your rights to collect fees due.

Since laws and regulations vary from state to state, you should consult an attorney on all legal matters. Figure 3-5 is a checklist of general considerations applicable to most contract situations.

QUALITY CONTROL FOR THE ACTUAL WORK

Because every design practice differs in the details of the work process, it would be difficult, if not impossible, to include here every phase of work and a checklist for each one. There are publications available with checklists and other advice, such as the aforementioned *Guide to Quality Control for Design.*[2]

Contract Checklist

____ Base your contract on standardized contract forms developed by the American Institute of Architects, the Engineers' Joint Contract Documents Committee, or other professional organizations. While you should develop your own contract to best clarify your needs, these contracts represent the most current standards of practice and needs of the practicing professional and are important reference points.

____ Never start work without a signed contract, even if it is being negotiated and near completion. Unforeseen circumstances can cause the project to be cancelled, leaving you with no basis for collecting fees on work already done.

____ When modifying any standard form, consult an attorney. This is the least expensive kind of "insurance" you can buy.

____ If your client insists on using another contract form consult an attorney. Compare it to your contract, paying particular attention to its provisions. Don't hesitate to insist on changes necessary to protect your interests.

____ Make sure your contract is coordinated with the General Conditions of the contract and other applicable contract documents.

____ Clearly spell out the scope of services. Do not hesitate to attach a detailed list of services you will perform.

____ Include a detailed description of the owner's responsibilities for delivery of whatever the owner is to provide for the project. Clearly identify the due dates and exactly what data is to be provided.

____ Do not perform services based on a "purchase order," "service order," or other preprinted form.

____ Verify that the contract does not contain any language that connotes perfection. Be on the lookout for the following words and clauses that refer to your performance and obligations:

- Guarantee and warranty
- Supervise
- Inspect
- Insure and assure
- Comply with applicable regulations and ordinances
- Complete drawings and specifications
- Will provide "as-built" drawings. (Instead provide "record" drawings.)
- Control
- Direct
- Oversee
- Guide
- Approve
- Right to stop work

____ Check for words that imply an indirect promise of performance, such as "adequate," "safe," "satisfactory," and "suitable."

____ Check for words that connote extremes, such as "all,", "best," "complete," "every," "highest," "none."

____ Check for ambiguous words and phrases.

Figure 3-5 *Source: Guide to Quality Control for Design Professionals,* by David Kent Ballast, Newton, Mass.: Practice Management Associates, Ltd., 1986. Used with permission. *(Continued on next page)*

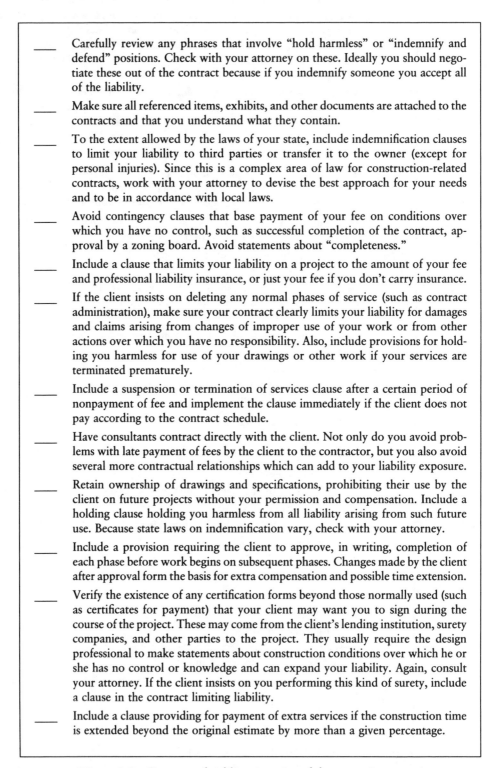

_____ Carefully review any phrases that involve "hold harmless" or "indemnify and defend" positions. Check with your attorney on these. Ideally you should negotiate these out of the contract because if you indemnify someone you accept all of the liability.

_____ Make sure all referenced items, exhibits, and other documents are attached to the contracts and that you understand what they contain.

_____ To the extent allowed by the laws of your state, include indemnification clauses to limit your liability to third parties or transfer it to the owner (except for personal injuries). Since this is a complex area of law for construction-related contracts, work with your attorney to devise the best approach for your needs and to be in accordance with local laws.

_____ Avoid contingency clauses that base payment of your fee on conditions over which you have no control, such as successful completion of the contract, approval by a zoning board. Avoid statements about "completeness."

_____ Include a clause that limits your liability on a project to the amount of your fee and professional liability insurance, or just your fee if you don't carry insurance.

_____ If the client insists on deleting any normal phases of service (such as contract administration), make sure your contract clearly limits your liability for damages and claims arising from changes of improper use of your work or from other actions over which you have no responsibility. Also, include provisions for holding you harmless for use of your drawings or other work if your services are terminated prematurely.

_____ Include a suspension or termination of services clause after a certain period of nonpayment of fee and implement the clause immediately if the client does not pay according to the contract schedule.

_____ Have consultants contract directly with the client. Not only do you avoid problems with late payment of fees by the client to the contractor, but you also avoid several more contractual relationships which can add to your liability exposure.

_____ Retain ownership of drawings and specifications, prohibiting their use by the client on future projects without your permission and compensation. Include a holding clause holding you harmless from all liability arising from such future use. Because state laws on indemnification vary, check with your attorney.

_____ Include a provision requiring the client to approve, in writing, completion of each phase before work begins on subsequent phases. Changes made by the client after approval form the basis for extra compensation and possible time extension.

_____ Verify the existence of any certification forms beyond those normally used (such as certificates for payment) that your client may want you to sign during the course of the project. These may come from the client's lending institution, surety companies, and other parties to the project. They usually require the design professional to make statements about construction conditions over which he or she has no control or knowledge and can expand your liability. Again, consult your attorney. If the client insists on you performing this kind of surety, include a clause in the contract limiting liability.

_____ Include a clause providing for payment of extra services if the construction time is extended beyond the original estimate by more than a given percentage.

Figure 3-5 Contract checklist. _(continued from previous page)_

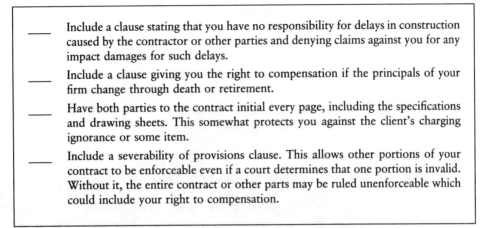

_____ Include a clause stating that you have no responsibility for delays in construction caused by the contractor or other parties and denying claims against you for any impact damages for such delays.

_____ Include a clause giving you the right to compensation if the principals of your firm change through death or retirement.

_____ Have both parties to the contract initial every page, including the specifications and drawing sheets. This somewhat protects you against the client's charging ignorance or some item.

_____ Include a severability of provisions clause. This allows other portions of your contract to be enforceable even if a court determines that one portion is invalid. Without it, the entire contract or other parts may be ruled unenforceable which could include your right to compensation.

Figure 3-5 Contract checklist. *(continued)*

While such sources contain ready-made checklists for quality control, you can also develop your own. Be sure to include every step in the design process:

Programming
    Zoning
    Building codes
    Handicapped accessibility
Design
    Actual design
    Selection of materials and products
    Technical "design" of individual components and details
Construction documents
    Working drawings
    Project manual
    Specifications
    Coordination checking
Bidding
Substitutions
Contract administration
    Site observation
    Shop drawings and change orders
Start-up, operations, and maintenance
    Project close-out
    Client follow-up

Postoccupancy evaluation
   Office performance
   Professional services evaluation
   Consultants/contractors evaluation

Also consider including records and information management in the above list.

Current Methods of Quality Control

There are some methods of quality assurance being used today that are worth mentioning. Since these techniques are relatively new, they should be given careful consideration before including them in your quality-control process.

QUALITY-CONTROL CIRCLES

The idea of the quality-control circle, begun in Japan in the 1960s, has been successfully applied in many industries. A quality-control circle is a group of employees that regularly meet to identify, analyze, and solve problems related to their work. The premise is that employees are valuable resources and may know, better than management, their immediate quality-control problems and how to solve them. Benefits from this process include increased motivation, improved communication, teamwork, more involvement by employees, and higher productivity. The circles should meet once a week for an hour, be flexible enough to accommodate everyone's schedules, and membership should be voluntary.

There are some additional guidelines to quality-control circles, shown in Figure 3-6. Also see the reference sections at the end of this chapter for some publications about quality circles.

PEER REVIEW

A rapidly developing aspect of quality control is peer review. This technique improves the quality of practice by having its policies and procedures examined by a group of professional colleagues. Peer review does not assess the design quality in the office, but rather the firm's ways of delivering services.

One exemplary source of peer review is the American Consulting Engineers Council (ACEC). ACEC has developed a peer review program manual, trained reviewers, and set in motion the actual review processes for many members.

Guidelines for Quality-control Circles

1. The concept and process must have top management support, including a commitment to seriously consider suggestions made by the quality circles. Any middle management that exists in larger firms must also support the idea.
2. The quality circles must be ongoing activities.
3. Quality circles are not just gripe sessions, they are problem-solving units.
4. Everyone on the committee should get training in problem-solving techniques.
5. Size should be kept small. For larger firms or ones with several service areas, you should consider more than one circle.
6. Although quality circles can work with any size firm, they are more appropriate to medium- and larger-sized firms. A twenty to thirty person firm could probably benefit from one small quality-control circle. Larger firms may institute more.
7. Quality-control circles should be considered a means to help employees develop and generally improve the quality of working as well as the quality of the work output.

Figure 3-6 Source: *Guide to Quality Control for Design Professionals,* by David Kent Ballast, Newton, Mass.: Practice Management Associates, 1986. Used with permission.

As it now exists, ACEC's program involves a team of highly qualified professionals who review a firm's written policies of management, development and maintenance of technical competence, human resources, project management, financial management, and business development. The team then visits the office to determine whether employees understand all policies and procedures. Finally, they deliver a verbal report to the firm's principals. This is an interesting concept, even if you feel your firm is too small for such an audit. For more information, consult *The Peer Review Program Manual,*[3] published by the ACEC, or call them at (202) 347-7474.

Excess Perfection

Watch out for overkill, however. In a survey of clients, consultant Martin McElroy found that "many corporate officers took note of a tendency for design professionals to perform (and design) to self-imposed standards that are more costly than necessary to meet the client's requirements."[4] This is the infamous "excess perfection syndrome." (See Fig. 3-7). While it is important to provide excellent service, you must tailor the services to the expectations of the client, because that is all he or she will pay for. Prevent your staff from providing the same level of service for every job or client. That means some jobs get the Chevy treatment and others the Cadillac.

Even the Chevy jobs must meet a standard company quality. For this reason, be sure to use seasoned personnel as quality-control resources. Project managers often do not make good use of the firm's technical resources (in other words, quality-control staff), citing cost. When project managers must absorb this cost within their budgets, they minimize the time technical staff spend on the project. This is false economy.

At a 1989 roundtable, one firm suggested an approach to this problem:

> Take a set percentage of the fee from all projects and pool these funds for quality control. The quality-control staff then charges time to this pool, rather than to individual projects.

This solution resulted in project managers using senior staff earlier in the project, when they can contribute more. By removing the cost factor, they found the quality-control function more readily accepted as a resource. On the other hand, overhead increased.

Successful firms are distinctively different in the quality control they provide. Emphasize quality control as a process, not as an act after the fact. Figure 3-8 contains 10 quality-control tips. Figure 3-9 is a building code checklist, to be used for quality control.

INNOVATE EVEN NORMAL ACTIVITIES

Again you must realize the importance of standing out. Avoid being seen as part of the herd in the way you practice. In today's marketplace, you encounter the same contracts, pricing strategies, and services. None is distinctively different. Position yourself as different in each area of service you perform. Distinction will give you the biggest and fastest return. It will augment the client's perception of your firm providing good service; therefore, it serves as the reason why the client should give you a project. Such distinction allows you to be alone in a niche (see Chapter 2), and to develop widespread reputation for being in this niche. And, of course, when you are alone in

Excess Perfection Syndrome

Most technical professionals suffer from the "excess perfection syndrome." Design professionals often do more than is really necessary on a particular task.

For example, a project manager is assigned to study the feasibility of installing snow-making equipment at a ski area. To size the pumps, he must know the difference in elevation between the lake and the top of the mountain. The project manager sends out a survey crew to level up and down the mountain. They close within a tenth of a foot and charge the project $2000. However, they could have looked at a U.S. Geological Survey map and charged the project $10.

Note that this discussion is not about perfect versus imperfect work. This is about *degrees of excellence.* Also, less than 100% perfection does not mean poor quality control with resulting liability claims. It might very well mean cutting the designer off at 90% and giving the remaining fee to the checkers to catch the mistakes.

The excess perfection syndrome is graphically illustrated below. In the early stages of a task, increased effort causes pronounced increases in excellence. But as the task approaches 90% perfection, the point of diminishing returns is rapidly reached. In other words, you do lose money in the form of man-hours with very little real improvement of the project.

The question the project manager should constantly ask is, what level of excellence is really needed at this particular time? In the conceptual stages, maybe only 80% is necessary, while for a complex structural system, maybe 98% or higher is needed. However, it is not ever possible to achieve 100% perfection.

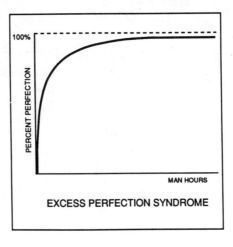

EXCESS PERFECTION SYNDROME

Figure 3-7 Source: "Excess Perfection Syndrome," *The Best of PSMJ, 1979.*

Ten Quality-Control Tips

1. **Encourage those actually doing the work,** not just the principals, to stamp or seal documents. Responsibility and initial quality rise with the signing of plans.

2. **Adopt a formal checking system,** instead of relying on the experience of individuals. Develop or use a more formalized procedure such as a building code checklist. (See Fig. 3-9.)

3. **Build into a project's schedule and budget the time and costs** of review by individual(s) not involved with the initial design.

4. **Have a final design review** after all documents are prepared. Late changes can have a major impact on quality.

5. **Get staff to job sites** as a continual training process. This is especially important for designers and drafters working on details.

6. **Make sure cost estimates are accurate.** Develop in-house expertise, use an outside expert cost estimator when necessary, and continually update and check the cost of items with suppliers and contractors.

7. **Schedule postconstruction design reviews** between the client's site representative and designer.

8. **Do not switch project managers** in mid-project.

9. **Don't allow field decisions to be made under pressure.**

10. **Have your firm undergo a peer review** by your professional association to come up with more ways to improve quality.

Figure 3-8

---

a market niche, you can price your services as high as the market will bear.

Here are eight ways to be different:

1. Give portable telephones to all technical staff.
2. Guarantee to meet client schedules and budgets or you won't take your fee.
3. Install portable Fax machines in project managers' cars.
4. Guarantee to respond to client calls within a half hour.
5. Produce renderings on all projects.
6. Build models of all projects.
7. Put a CADD terminal in your client's office.
8. Buy an airplane to guarantee your availability at remote job sites.

Some firms put distinctive characteristics into every aspect of doing business. For example, everyone might participate in

Building Code Checklist

(Based on BOCA Code)

Project: _____ Date: ____

Occupancy Requirements

☐ Use . . . . (table 6, 203-213)
☐ Fire District Restrictions . . . . (302, 303, 856.42)
☐ Height and Area Limitations . . . . (table 6, 305-308)
☐ Special Occupancy Requirements . . . . (see attachment #1)

Fire Resistance Requirements

☐ General Fire Resistance Requirements . . . . (table 5, 9, 214-218)
☐ Special Fire Resistance Requirements . . . . (907)
☐ Fire Stopping . . . . (924.0, 912.0, 914.0, 888.5)
☐ Stairway Construction & Enclosure . . . . (618.8)
☐ Shaft Enclosures & Venting . . . . (516.0, 1020.0, 913.0)
☐ Refuse Chutes . . . . (1125.0)
☐ Refuse Vaults . . . . (1129.0)
☐ Boiler Room Enclosure & Venting . . . . (111.1)
☐ Fire Walls . . . . (909.0)
☐ Spray Booths . . . . (412.0)
☐ Volatile Flammable Storage . . . . (403.0)
☐ Roof Structures . . . . (932.0)

Fire Protection Requirements

☐ Sprinklers . . . . (1213.1)
☐ Standpipes . . . . (1207, 1209, 1210)
☐ Horizontal Fire Lines . . . . (1211)
☐ Fire Access Panels . . . . (863.0)
☐ Fire Alarm Systems . . . . (1217, 1219)
☐ Fire Ventilation System . . . . (521.0)
☐ Fire Extinguishers . . . . (1218.0)

Figure 3-9 Building code checklist for purposes of quality control. *(Continued on next page)*

Exit Requirements

☐ Number of Exits . . . . (610.0, 614.1-614.4)
☐ Exit Capacity . . . . (610.0)
☐ Length of Travel . . . . (609)
☐ Location of Exits . . . . (609.0, 614.5)
☐ Swing of Doors . . . . (614)
☐ Hardware . . . . (614.9)
☐ Width of Doors . . . . (614.3)
☐ Width of Corridors . . . . (612.3)
☐ Width of Stairs . . . . (618.2)
☐ Stair Landings & Platforms . . . . (618.3)
☐ Stair Treads & Risers . . . . (618.4)
☐ Handrails . . . . (618.5)
☐ Stairway Doors . . . . (618.6)
☐ Monumental Stairways . . . . (618.7)
☐ Stair Construction . . . . (618.8)
☐ Roof Access . . . . (619.0)
☐ Smokeproof Towers . . . . (620.0)
☐ Stairway Light & Ventilation . . . . (514, 516)
☐ Exit Lighting . . . . (624.0)
☐ Emergency Lighting . . . . (625.3, table 15)

Light & Ventilation Requirements

☐ Light & Ventilation of Rooms & Areas . . . . (507-513)
☐ Unpriced Industrial Buildings . . . . (517.0)

Structural Requirements

☐ Structural Design . . . . (chapter 7)
☐ Materials & Tests . . . . (chapter 8A)
☐ Steel, Masonry, Concrete, Gypsum & Lumber . . . . (chapter 8B)
☐ Building Enclosures, Walls & Wall Thickness . . . . (chapter 8C)
☐ Lateral Wall Bracing . . . . (841.0)
☐ Wall Thickness . . . . (873.0, 878-881)
☐ Foundation Walls . . . . (882.0)
☐ Retaining Walls . . . . (883.0)
☐ Isolated Piers . . . . (884.0)

Figure 3-9   *(continued)*

Building Code Checklist

Attachment 1

Special Occupancy Requirements

☐ Explosion Hazards . . . . (402)
☐ Volatile Flammables . . . . (403)
☐ Liquefied Petroleum Gases . . . . (407)
☐ Pyroxylin Plastics . . . . (408)
☐ Flammable Film . . . . (409)
☐ Combustible Fibers . . . . (410)
☐ Combustible Dusts, Grain Processing & Storage . . . . (411)
☐ Paint Spraying & Paint Booths . . . . (412)
☐ Dry Cleaning & Dry Dyeing . . . . (413)
☐ Private Garages & Airplane Hangars . . . . (415)
☐ Public Garages & Airplane Hangars . . . . (415)
☐ Motor Vehicle Service Stations (gas stations) . . . . (416)
☐ Motor Vehicle Repair Shops . . . . (417)
☐ Places of Public Assembly . . . . (418, 419)
☐ Amusement Parks . . . . (420)
☐ Stadiums & Grandstands . . . . (421)
☐ Drive In Movies . . . . (422)
☐ Tents & Temporary Structures . . . . (423)
☐ Parking Lots . . . . (424)
☐ Radio Towers . . . . (425)

Figure 3-9 *(continued on next page)*

signing contracts. Traditionally, architect/engineer firms use boilerplate contracts that tend to be signed in a very routine and traditional manner at a private meeting with a client. To be different, you could make the contract-signing a celebration.

Another idea is to handwrite meeting minutes and pass them out the day the meeting takes place. This distinguishes you from other firms, whose minutes are typed and resemble every other standard piece of paper. If you then must have them

Zoning Ordinance Checklist

Project:_____Date:_____

☐ Zone_____
☐ Use_____
☐ Prohibited Uses . . . . (24F)
☐ Minimum Lot Size_____
☐ Reduction of Lot area . . . . (26A1)
☐ Lots Less Than Minimum Area . . . . (26A2)
☐ Area Per Dwelling Unit_____
☐ One Main Building on Lot . . . . (26A4)
☐ Requirements for Mixed Occupancy . . . . (73G)
☐ Height _____
☐ Height Exceptions . . . . (72)
☐ Front Yard_____
☐ Side Yard_____
☐ Rear Yard _____
☐ C Zone Abutting an R Zone . . . . (51C)
☐ M Zone Abutting an R Zone . . . . (61C)
☐ Lot Coverage_____
☐ Corner Setback . . . . (26A5)
☐ Yard and Area Exceptions . . . . (73)
☐ Required Parking Space . . . . (24C)
☐ Off Street Loading . . . . (24D)
☐ Public Parking Areas . . . . (24E)

Figure 3-9 *(continued)*

typed, you have at least eliminated the time pressure put upon your typing pool for such an activity.

Still another idea is to give all project managers beepers so they can be reached at any time.

For back-room activities, rather than doing drawings on vellum right away, postpone starting final drawings until key decisions are made and do all drawings on yellow tracing paper prior to going to full working drawings. This allows your clients the luxury of making more changes without costing you incredible amounts to meticulously change working drawings.

Very few design firms agree to guarantee their work. Most firms do not supervise, they observe; they don't inspect, they review. A dramatic departure from traditional liability wisdom comes from a Boston structural engineering firm, the LEA Group, which guarantees that its roof structures will not leak for 5 years. According to Eugene Eisenberg, CEO of the firm, "We will guarantee the roof if we have full-time inspectors (engineers) present and control over installation." Have they ever fired a contractor for installing the roof incorrectly? Yes, they have. This service guarantee also costs considerably more money, Eisenberg says, but for some it's worth the price. "In one case, the executive offices were right below the roof, where they had rooftop parking, so there was a need for waterproofing. They didn't want to have to worry about leaks and cracks in the executive area." In most cases, he says, the guarantee lasts for five years.

The LEA Group has taken the increased liability risk to be distinctively different. LEA has certain terms and conditions under which the guarantee applies. Clearly, if you choose to offer such departures from normal contractual procedures, have terms to protect you.

Personal touches make lasting impressions. Have you ever sent a rose to the client's accounts payable clerk when the client pays a bill quickly? You can bet that next time your bill will get paid first.

Some examples of firms that dare to be different, and thus provide excellent service, appear in Figure 3-10.

Being distinctively different makes you easily recognizable and remembered by potential clients, whether you are a firm that does art selection for hotels only, interior hospital architecture, facilities management for chemical plants, or restoration of old movie theaters. Narrowly focus your capability, and prospects will remember you. So will the media. When you are different, it is easier to get published.

As a key part of your service, look at how you hire your staff. Employees who focus on design alone and treat clients as a necessary evil do not belong in your service-oriented firm. Hire extraordinary people who understand the importance of the client and make it a point to concentrate on service as well as design. The next chapter addresses hiring and firing.

Providing Excellent Service

Western Technologies in Arizona gives out papers to its project managers, allowing clients to page them directly at any time, thereby providing constant communication.

An environmental consulting firm in Michigan gives each project manager a portable telephone and requires them to carry it 24 hours a day.

A Boston firm photocopies meeting minutes for every job meeting on the on-site contractor's copier. They give everyone present copies of the handwritten minutes as the meeting ends. This expedites any actions to be taken by meeting attendees.

One firm faxes all correspondence to clients as it occurs within their firm. Using a fax can expedite the speed with which any internal office or project-related correspondence can be acted upon.

Figure 3-10

SUCCESS CHALLENGES

1. When did you last examine how your service is different from that of your competitors?

2. Do you really know what *service* your competitors provide?

3. If you are providing a largely generic service, similar to every competitor in your marketplace, how can you change that today to make it be, *and* to have it appear, better?

4. How can you respond more effectively to clients (through correspondence, on the telephone, personal attention, and in other ways)? Set yourself apart. Say "service" above all.

REFERENCES

1. Harvey Mackay, 1988. *Swim With the Sharks Without Being Eaten Alive.* New York: William Morow & Company, Pp. 43–53.

2. David Kent Ballast, 1986. *Guide to Quality Control for Design Professionals.* Newton, Mass.: Practice Management Associates, Ltd.

3. American Consulting Engineers Council. *The Peer Review Program Manual.* Washington, D.C.

4. Martin McElroy, October 1987. "Management: The Architect as FM—Fiction and Fact." *Architectural Record.* Also Martin McElroy, June 1984. "Marketing: How Big Corporations Choose Design Firms." *Architectural Record.*

BIBLIOGRAPHY

Alexander Hamilton Institute, 1983. *Quality Circles: A New Approach to Productivity.* New York.

Bureau of Business Practice, 1981. *Quality Circles: A Dynamic Approach to Productivity.* Waterford, Conn.

Weld Coxe et al., May/June 1986. "Charting Your Course." *Architectural Technology.*

International Association of Quality Circles, 801B. W. Eighth Street, Cincinnati, Ohio 45203.

Noto Saski and David Hutchins, eds., 1984. *The Japanese Approach to Product Quality: Its Applicability to the West.* Oxford, N.Y.: Pergamon Press.

4 PERSONNEL

HIRING

Hiring staff is always a basic ingredient of a good professional practice, but nowhere is this more true than when assembling the staff of a small design firm. The strategic planning aspects of human resources are addressed in Chapter 1. The current chapter describes how to recruit exceptional people, how to keep them motivated to perform, how to recognize when a person has reached a peak with you, and why you shouldn't tolerate nonperformance. Successful firms are also not afraid to bring in new people above loyal longtime employees.

One trap that entrepreneurs fall into is to hire those less smart than themselves, those who are not as aggressive, and those who merely follow instructions. They then fail to extend them to their full ability, or neglect to expose them to clients or to inside business information, for fear they may leave and start their own business. Instead, you need to hire those smarter than you, those whose talents in their area far surpass yours: for example, hire a great specification writer, or hire the best civil engineer or project manager in your city. You can only benefit from hiring someone who has skills you do not possess. R. G. Vanderweil Engineers, of Boston, is a firm that believes firm principal hiring top performers has contributed significantly to its success.

As W. L. Vanderweil states: Ours is a 'peoples' business, and a firm's success or failure is largely measured by the quality of its staff. With this in mind, we strive to treat our staff equally and fairly at all levels, and pay at the top end of the scale for people in our field. Every few years we take salary and benefits surveys of our competitors to make sure we are competitive. We skew our benefits to reward those employees with the most seniority, as they are the ones who have gotten us where we are and will keep us there. Even in slowdowns, we will hire an outstanding prospect, as they are extremely difficult to find and you need them to build business. Probably most importantly, we give people at all levels as much responsibility as they can handle and push them to learn and grow as rapidly as possible. We create goals for them designed to challenge and motivate them, and reward them according to their performance.

Figure 4-1 is another example of a firm that believes in hiring the best.

Hiring the Best

Firm: Schmidt Associates Architects, Inc.
Staff: 25–30
Specialty: Architecture, landscape architecture, interior design, planning
Address: Wil-Fra-Mar Building
           320 East Vermont Street
           Indianapolis, Ind. 46204

Wayne Schmidt, president of Schmidt Associates Architects, contends that talented people flock to a talented firm and vice versa: "Success both for individuals and the firm is achievable when the firm is managed profitably to provide for staff development, up-to-date tools and facilities, and strategic planning."

The firm grew from a one-person operation in 1979 to 25–30 people in 1990. A strategic plan is in effect that targets 10% growth each year to the year 2000. Schmidt maintains a positive work atmosphere by focusing on the importance of each employee as an integral part of the total team, developing an environment where ideas thrive. To help employees achieve individual excellence, Schmidt has done away with traditional performance review forms. Instead, each employee receives a career planning guide to evaluate how well he or she is meeting the professional and personal goals they set for themselves every six months. (See Fig. 1-21 for Schmidt's performance evaluation form, and Figs. 5-6 and 5-7 for an overview of its career tracking program.)

Figure 4-1

CONTROLLING YOUR EGO

One of the biggest challenges when hiring smart people is controlling your ego. Understand that as entrepreneur/main partner/key person in the small design firm, your main role is as leader. Orchestrate the firm as a coach does a football team made up of a group of stars. The coach cannot try to run every play of the game; the team would soon be losing every game of the year. His job is to create a team to take on the other teams and win the game.

In professional architecture and engineering, your job as head of a small firm is to hire stars. Make sure that you are in control of the shots, but that your stars are carrying out the plays—day in, day out—to manage the clients and their projects.

Another way in which you must control your ego is in giving others in the firm recognition. The principal of a firm in Cambridge, Massachusetts, was considered a "guru" by many of his peers, except for one bad habit. He would employ staff who would work as much as 80 hours a week on project work and produce a great product after tremendous amounts of effort. As the project was completed, the firm's publicity campaign would highlight the principal, who in fact had very little input into the project whatsoever, with no recognition going to the actual designers and other staff. The firm soon found itself to be a seedbed for other new firms. Employees would leave and start their own firm or join other competitive firms. It ended up as a fine training ground, but a poor example of a successful small design firm.

HOW TO ATTRACT TOP PEOPLE

Always look for the best people. As one infamous developer advises, if you find a good person in a competitor's organization, find a place for them in your organization and "steal" them, rather than waiting for the opportunity for openings in your organization and hoping they'll apply.[1] Look for good people in other firms, including branch offices of these firms, and "steal" them.

How do you "steal?" One way is to place an advertisement in the newspaper and hope that person from the competitor's office will call you. You may take that a step further by putting the advertisement in the newspaper and then directly contacting the employee.

If you feel direct recruitment is unethical, remember you cannot force anyone to go against their wishes. Staff members won't leave their present companies to join yours unless it is clearly in their best interest, or you have misrepresented the opportunity offered.

On the other hand, other firms may be attempting to directly recruit your employees. To guard against losing top performers, concentrate on making your organization into the best possible place to work by emphasizing open communication and clarity of direction and by constantly letting everyone know where they stand. That way, if an employee meets a competitor at a local AIA meeting and is approached about a position, or gets a call from a former classmate working at another design firm looking for talent, your employee will remain in your fold.

Identify the stars in other companies and attract them to your team. If you are small, you cannot afford to wait.

One method used by some small firms is a signing bonus. This is more common in marketing and CADD areas than design, drafting, or specification writing. The advantage of the bonus to the firm is that the salary level can stay at about the existing level, and the bonus is in essence a one-time expense.

Develop a process for meeting competitors' top performers. Here are some suggestions.

- Do joint ventures to work directly with your competitor's top people.
- Within peer associations, always be on the lookout for stars from other firms who may be dissatisfied.
- Look into other firms' compensation plans to see how they compare with yours.
- Discover ways to identify people in the competitor's firm that would fit into your organization.

DEVELOP TOP PERFORMERS FROM WITHIN

"There isn't anyone in the office who can bring a project in on schedule and on budget, keep clients happy, and hustle new work when things are slow. I want you to find a person who can do those things. Oh, yes, he should be registered, willing to work for a modest salary until he proves himself, and shouldn't be much more than 35 years old so he'll fit in with the rest of the staff. What I want is a real go-getter, somebody who'll be able to take over my job some day and if you can find him, I'm prepared to offer him an associate partnership!"

Search firms hear this description of Mr. Perfect so often they have dubbed him The Man on the White Horse (TMOTWH). TMOTWH has no faults. He manages well. He's technically competent. He is handsome, a born leader, and people like to work for him. He can charm an angry client in 30 seconds flat. He can identify a prospect, write a proposal, lead a presentation, and get a job that all your competitors have been lusting after. There's only one problem: TMOTWH doesn't exist.

Where do search firms find candidates for such positions? Usually, the person who is hired away from a firm has been passed over by his or her present boss for promotion to associate or other higher position in the present firm. The only way to climb up the career ladder is to change jobs, with a title and an instant higher level of responsibility at a new office. So he/she changes jobs. The old firm now must find a replacement and calls a search firm.

"Twofers," and How to Avoid Them

What occurs next is known as a "twofer" situation. This happens when two employees working in different firms are each talked into quitting their present job and going to work at the other place. Twofers only count when each person receives an increase in salary, position, and authority. This occurs more frequently than search firms like to admit, and clearly each firm is better off if such a job swap does not take place. In this situation, the time required for a newcomer to become accepted by present clients and the effort involved in acclimating him/herself to the firm's practices are a waste. In addition, to the higher salary add the search firm's fee (which may go as high as one-third of annual salary), the expense of relocation, the time it takes to interview, and the extra perks. All of this may total 60 to 70 percent of the person's annual salary.

To avoid twofers and/or searching outside for TMOTWH, assess which current employees have top-performer potential and groom them for a senior position *within* your firm.

Look for three common traits in top performers:

1. Enough technical competence to assure professional registration in your state.
2. An extroverted personality.
3. Common sense.

To turn a staff member with these three attributes into a top performer, consider this:

1. *Assessment.* Analyze the good and bad things about a person. Make a list of technical skills the person needs to learn or improve, plus a list of social or personality traits that may need changing. Now write down ways such changes can be implemented.
2. *Appraisal.* Advise the employee of areas in performance and personality that could be improved. Outline these areas in detail, but in a nonthreatening and noncritical way. Together with the employee, agree on steps to be taken to erase technical deficiencies and improve social and personality traits.
3. *Motivation.* Clearly explain why the employee should improve in these areas—that he/she is being considered for advancement or promotion by salary or title, such as becoming an associate, which carries with it higher salary or profit participation or other perks such as use of a company car. Even if there are few tangible perks, most staff will be motivated to improve with the promise of management participation. (See Fig. 1-22, which presents one firm's criteria for becoming an associate.)
4. *Coaching.* Work with the employee on a daily basis to make the improvements. Help improve job-related areas by assigning work that will give the employee familiarity in new areas. Nothing sharpens project management skills better than assigning more projects to manage. Also, *give constant feedback.*
5. *Reward.* When the first promotion or increase takes place, the coaching process doesn't stop, but continues until you feel completely comfortable in every respect with the employee, to the point of turning over more responsibility.

Never underestimate the importance of people skills. A survey of firms that promote from within and successfully retain valuable staff stresses the importance of personality traits.

These must be at least equal to technical competence as a prerequisite to admitting people to upper management. In a small firm especially, you have to offer more to a client than just the promise of doing a good job. A client must feel secure about your firm and like dealing with your contact person if the relationship is to continue.

ANNOUNCE POSITIONS WITHIN

When you feel you must look outside, how you search for an outsider can have a direct impact on your employees' morale. Announce plans to look for an outsider to your staff *before* you begin to search. This accomplishes two important goals. First, it gives an opportunity to any current employee who feels qualified for the position to talk to you about the job before it is offered to an outsider. Nothing is more damaging to staff morale than to have the principal announce that a new person has already been hired to fill a position an employee would have liked but did not know was available.

If a current employee does inquire about a position, be honest with them if you don't think he or she is ready for the assignment. Be prepared to suggest steps you can take together to help the employee work toward the level of competence required to attain such a position within your firm. If your candid feeling is that the person is unlikely ever to meet that level, you have an obligation to share that feeling, even if you turn out to be wrong.

The second goal of announcing openings is that of possible referrals from your staff. Someone may know of an outside candidate, leading to an introduction and subsequent hire. Employee referral is one of the most satisfactory methods of recruiting and among the least expensive.

If you fail to find an employee in-house or by referral, then and only then should you consider advertising the position, contacting a search firm, recruiting directly, and so forth. See Figure 4-2 for tips on advertising positions, Figure 4-3 for questions to ask in an interview, and Figure 4-4 for making an employment offer.

When you give your staff the first opportunity to apply for a position, and later to try to help you fill it, they will accept the newcomer more warmly and will be more willing to accept him/her as a team member.

Job Advertising Do's and Don'ts

Do write ads that will attract the readers' attention quickly.

Do include you company name, address, and telephone number, as well as your company contact person.

Do request details on the candidate's current compensation package.

Do provide information on any unusual benefits your company has to offer.

Do make sure your receptionist/switchboard operator/secretary knows how to respond to calls or visits.

Do run regular advertising for the positions you historically have had the hardest time filling.

Do send a letter to all who respond to your ad within one week.

Do track responses to your various advertising efforts to determine what medium attracts the greatest numbers and quality.

Don't include salaries or salary ranges.

Don't oversell your company or your opportunity.

Don't give the position a title that misrepresents the real duties and responsibilities, e.g., Marketing Management Administration Specialist instead of Secretary.

Don't include discriminatory language such as "attractive," "young," or "he."

Don't ask for salary expectations in the new position.

Figure 4-2

DELEGATE!

Entrepreneurs tend to believe that no one can perform as well as they. The solution is to make the *goal* clear to the subordinate before you delegate the task, then let this person find the right *method* for reaching that goal.

Here are five types of tasks to delegate:

1. *Something That You Cannot Do.* For example, if you have to design a wastewater treatment facility as part of a project and you have no experience at this, you must obviously hire an engineer who is a specialist.

2. *Technical Tasks Someone Else Can Do as Well as You.* Let that person do the task so you can get on to more important issues. Even though you can calculate structural beam depths, it may be more important for you to handle client communications and to delegate the actual calculations to another engineer.

Interview Questions

The goal of any employment interview is to find out what a candidate is really like. Asking questions that can be answered with "yes" or "no" will not accomplish this goal. As an interviewer, you should do about 20% of the talking and 80% of the listening. These questions will help you uncover what you need to know about a prospect:

1. Tell me about yourself.
2. What are your greatest accomplishments?
3. What do you want to be doing 3/5/10 years from now?
4. Why did you go into this field?
5. What tasks do you like to do?
6. If we talked with your co-workers, what would they tell us about you?
7. Why should we hire you over someone else?
8. What is motivating you to make a change (if the candidate is currently employed)?
9. What do you like/dislike about your present position?
10. What is your least favorite activity?
11. If you worked for us and we told you that we wanted you to move to Fargo, N.D., what would your reaction be?
12. What is a typical workday for you? How long is it?
13. What motivates you to do an outstanding job?
14. What in the work you currently do encourages a lack of motivation?
15. What do you like to do in your spare time?
16. What do you think is more important—technical abilities or communication and management skills? Why?
17. Do you aspire to be an owner in this or any other organization? Why?
18. Please rank the following in their order of importance to you:
    a. the quality of your work
    b. the timeliness of your delivery
    c. giving clients what they want
19. Name some of your accomplishments.
20. Name some of your worst failures. What are you doing to make sure they don't happen again?
21. Do you plan on continuing your education? If so, what do you plan on pursuing?
22. What is more important to you—getting along with people or getting things done?
23. What do you feel is the most pressing issue facing the design profession today?
24. What kinds of projects do you like best? Why?
25. How do you feel about CADD?
26. Have you ever used CADD on a job?
27. How do you feel about working evenings and weekends if the job requires it?

Figure 4-3   *(continued on next page)*

28. How do you feel about travel?
29. What are you doing to improve your knowledge of your field?
30. Is there anything else we need to know about you?
31. Could you give us the names of your supervisors at your previous job? Are they still there? Do you have their phone numbers?
32. How do you feel about working with people who are younger/older than you?
33. If we made you an offer, when could you start?

Figure 4-3   Interview questions. (continued)

3. *Technical Tasks Someone Else Can Do Almost as Well as You.* Be certain that you guide and coach. For instance, if you have been responsible for specifying all details for structural columns, and you now have a new engineer, let him/her do the preliminary drawings, then review the final drawings together.

4. *Technical Tasks Someone Else Can Do Adequately.* Make sure you delegate items that won't harm the project. Consider assigning someone to assemble drawings from predrawn standard details that are locked into your CADD system so they cannot be destroyed.

5. *Project Management Tasks.* This is one of the easiest areas to delegate. Such tasks include assembling meeting minutes, preparing a preliminary budget, developing or implementing the schedule. Put yourself into a reviewer role.

Make a point of having a good staff of part-time workers on call. As a small business person, you cannot afford to hire all on a full-time basis. Work up the flexibility to delegate to a staff of part-time or independent contract employees. This way other firms or individuals can work on part of a project whenever you are short-staffed. (Fig. 4-5 gives some insight into the differences, which are not always obvious, between an "independent contractor" and an "employee.")

Delegating means flexibility. You can accomplish more and spend less by working with a group of such outside contractors than with a full-time staff.

Instructions When Delegating

Instruct your employees to ask you the following when you are delegating:

1. What happens if you are away and I have a question about this task? Whom should I consult?
2. What is your absolute deadline for completing this task?
3. Will there be review meetings between now and the final deadline?
4. Is there anyone else who can help me work on this task or should I do it all alone?

Making an Employment Offer

Cover these 15 points when extending an offer of employment:

1. Position title.
2. Duties and responsibilities.
3. Name and title of person to whom employee will report.
4. Office location: the location of the particular office/branch to which the employee will be assigned.
5. Base pay—salary expressed in weekly, biweekly, or monthly terms, or the hourly rate.
6. Whether overtime will be paid, and, if so, whether it is straight overtime or time-and-a-half overtime, or a combination.
7. Benefits.
8. Date by which to accept or reject offer.
9. Start date.
10. Work hours.
11. Dates of first performance/salary reviews.
12. Perks, such as use of a company vehicle, which expenses are covered, and any personal use limitations.
13. Specifics of the relocation package, if any.
14. Potential for the person to advance beyond the position they are being offered.
15. Confirm offer in writing immediately upon extending it verbally.

Figure 4-4

Defining "Independent Contractors" and "Employees"

The IRS has a tight definition of those who rate as "outside contractors" rather than "common law employees." You may be held responsible for payroll taxes for more individuals than you think. Here are some of the tests applied by the IRS to determine employment:

1. A worker who is required to comply with another person's instruction is an employee.
2. Provision of training is normally seen as an advantage that comes with employment.
3. A continuing relationship may indicate employee–employer status.
4. Establishment of set hours of work is a control factor for employment purposes. If you control a person's hours, then a person is not an independent contractor.
5. Full or substantially full time work is not necessarily the mark of an independent contractor.
6. Work performed on the employer's premises is an indicator of employment, especially if the work could be performed off the premises.
7. The requirement of regular verbal or written reports may indicate control that comes with employment.
8. Payment by the hour, week, or month rather than by a lump sum is associated with employment, especially if it is not just for the convenience of a lump sum payment.
9. Working for only one firm is the mark of an employee.
10. The right to fire an individual or terminate his/her services can be interpreted as employment. An independent contractor normally cannot be terminated without violation of a contract.
11. Unless the individual offers services to more than one firm and to the general public, a business relationship may be considered as employment.

Your firm should review its relationship with outside contractors to see if an employment status has been reached. The IRS is examining such issues closely in order to increase revenues, especially FICA taxes. A firm failing to file taxes and reports may be held liable for both interest and penalties. If in doubt, review IRS Rev. Rule 87-41.

Figure 4-5

5. What do I do if I am pulled off this task by another supervisor?

This will ensure that you retain control over the project and its priority. It also is the difference between delegating and merely abdicating.

PROBATION PERIOD

As you hire new staff, be sure to set up a restrictive initial three-month period in which you immediately test new hires' abilities. On the first day, everyone is eager to perform. But do not wait two months before you give out tough assignments; do it right away. Also, make sure the new person is learning how to accomplish tasks as quickly as possible and, after the learning period, is achieving meaningful results on jobs that need to be done.

Always give employees a salary target. For example, start the new employee at a somewhat smaller base salary for the first three months. Then implement tough performance standards, to be met rigidly. At the end of the next three months, offer an immediate raise (say, $3000), followed by another three-month probationary period. At the end of that period, give another raise if the employee met your expectations. This way the new employee knows what he/she can expect to be making at the end of nine months.

It should also be made clear during probation that if the employee fails to perform, he/she can be dismissed.

There is some merit in setting up such a moderately threatening framework for the new employee. Put the person to the test right away; don't tolerate nonperformance. Nonperformance is very expensive to you as a small firm.

FIRE INCOMPETENTS

It is difficult to find good staff, and when you have had someone with you for a long time it's hard to let them go. It is much easier to keep a mediocre person than it is to fire someone and have to look for a replacement. But as a small firm you cannot afford to pay someone to perform a mediocre job.

Successful small firms must have rigid standards of performance that are adhered to on a routine basis. For example:

- All projects will be done on budget and on schedule.
- Whatever the client wants comes before what the firm wants.
- Team performance supersedes individual performance.

- Good design cannot be achieved exclusive of project profitability.
- Communication effectiveness is the cornerstone of client service.
- Client expectations will be explored and understood fully before starting any project.
- The firm's contractual relationships will achieve all profit and cash-flow goals.

Those who do not adhere to your expected performance criteria (after warnings) should be dismissed. One way to monitor performance is to conduct an annual review with each staff member, focusing on the interview itself, not on standardized forms. Forms should merely be records of the review process, not the process itself. To monitor day-to-day performance, set up monthly informal meetings with each employee to review the performance of a particular set of goals established mutually by both parties.

The willingness to fire is important to staying small successfully. One firm even dares to enforce an annual 10 percent turnover. If, at the end of the year, the partners find only a 6 percent turnover, they fire 4 percent of their staff to meet the quota. It may seem unkind at the end of the year to terminate 1 out of every 10 people, but the impact on motivation, performance, and service is considerable. Although you may not feel the mandatory turnover rate policy is fair, it is an ingenious way to maintain top staffers and fire bad ones.

EMPLOYMENT CONTRACTS

With the increasing importance of a clear understanding of the employer–employee relationship, many more small firms are now choosing to enter into employment contract with key employees. The primary beneficiary of such an agreement is the employee, who receives a documented and explicitly clear written agreement on his or her role in the firm. Figure 4-6 is a typical employment contract from a small firm. Expect more firms to adopt such agreements in the future as one means of attempting to keep key people in light of the increasingly predicted dearth in design professional personnel.

THE CAVENDISH PARTNERSHIP, INC.
145 Main Street
Ludlow, Vermont 05149

EMPLOYMENT AGREEMENT

EMPLOYMENT AGREEMENT by and between THE CAVENDISH PARTNERSHIP INC., (Company) and ****, (Employee).

For good consideration, Company shall employ and the Employee agrees to be employed on the following terms:

1. **Effective Date:** Employment shall commence on ***, 19**, time being of the essence.

2. **Duties:** Employee agrees to perform the following duties:

*****

Employee shall also perform such further duties as are incidental or implied from the foregoing, consistent with the background, training and qualifications of Employee or may be reasonably delegated as being in the best interests of the Company. The Employee shall devote full time to his employment and expend best efforts on behalf of the Company. Employee further agrees to abide by all reasonable Company policies and decisions now or hereinafter existing.

3. **Term:** The Employee's employment shall continue for a period of *** years, beginning on the effective date of this agreement and ending on ****, 19**.

4. **Compensation:** The Employee shall be paid the following compensation:

a) Annual salary: $_____, paid on the payroll schedule existing for other employees.

b) Such bonuses, vacations, sick leave, and expense accounts as stated in the Company manual for other management personnel or as may be decided by the Company if said items are discretionary with the Company.

5. **Termination:** This agreement may be earlier terminated upon:

a) Death of Employee or illness or incapacity that prevents Employee from substantially performing for *** continuous months or in excess of *** aggregate working days in any calendar year.

Figure 4-6 Typical employment contract from a small firm. Used with permission.

SUMMARY

The successful small businessperson needs to understand the necessity to grow *through* and *with* others, not alone. This involves suppressing your ego, and "growing" individuals within your organization, helping them develop often greater talents than you have. "Successful managers use all their strength by recognizing, developing, and utilizing the physical,

b) Breach of agreement by Employee.

6. **Renewal:** Should employee remain in the employ of the Company after the termination date of this Agreement, the terms of this Agreement shall remain in full force effect, except that the continued term of employment shall be at the will of the parties, and can be ended at any time, for any reason, by either party.

7. **Miscellaneous:**

a) Employee agrees to execute a non-compete agreement as annexed hereto.

*** b) Employee agrees to execute a confidential information and invention assignment agreement as annexed hereto.

*** c) Employee agrees that during the term of this agreement and for a period of ** years thereafter, Employee will not:

i) Induce or attempt to induce any employee to leave the Company's employ;

ii) Interfere with or disrupt the Company's relationship with any of its employees;

iii) Solicit or employ any person employed by the Company.

d) The agreement shall not be assignable by either party, provided that upon any sale of this business by Company, the Company may assign this agreement to its successor or employee may terminate same.

e) In the event of any dispute under this agreement, it shall be resolved through binding arbitration in accordance with the rules of the American Arbitration Association.

f) This constitutes the entire agreement between the parties. Any modifications must be writing.

8. **Equal Opportunity:** During the performance of this Agreement, the Company will not discriminate against any employment because of race, color, creed, religion, sex, national origin or handicap.

The Company will comply with the applicable provisions of Title VI of the Civil Rights Act of 1964 as amended, Executive Order 11246 as amended by Executive Order 11375 and as supplemented by the department of Labor Regulations (41 CFR Part 60). The Company shall also comply with the rules, regulations, and relevant orders of the Secretary of Labor, DOT Regulation 49 CFR 21 through Appendix C, and DOT Regulation 23 CFR 710.405 (b).

The Company shall comply with all of the requirements of Title 21, V.S.A., Chapter 5, Subchapter 6 and 7, relating to fair employment practices to the extent applicable.

Signed under seal this *** day of *****, 19**.

THE CAVENDISH PARTNERSHIP, INC.

_____   _____
Witness   Principal

_____   _____
Witness   Employee

Figure 4-6 Typical employment contract. *(continued from previous page)*

EMPLOYEE NON-COMPETE AGREEMENT

FOR GOOD CONSIDERATION, and in consideration of my being employed by THE CAVENDISH PARTNERSHIP, INC., I, the undersigned, hereby agree that upon my termination of employment and notwithstanding the cause of termination, I shall not compete with the business of the Company, or its successors or assigns.

The term "not compete" as used in this agreement means that I shall not directly or indirectly own, be employed by or work on behalf of any firm engaged in a business substantially similar and competitive with the Company.

I further agree that this Agreement shall:

1. Extend only for the following geographic territory:

    ●●● For a radius of fifty (50) miles from the present location of the Company.

2. Shall be in full force and effect for ●● years(s), commencing with the date my employment with the Company will have terminated and notwithstanding the reason for termination or the party terminating.

Signed under seal this ●●● day of ●●●●, 19●●.

_____   _____
Witness   Employee

Figure 4-6   *(continued)*

mental, and spiritual talents of their subordinates." This quote comes from *Top Performance,* by Zig Ziglar.[2] In this book about "developing excellence in yourself and others," Ziglar states that your success as a manager will be measured by the number of your employees that eventually pass you by on their way up the ladder to success.

SUCCESS CHALLENGES

1. Rank your employees according to top, middle, and bottom thirds by performance, not by position. Reflect why you are keeping those in the bottom third. Are all those in the top third adequately compensated for their efforts?

2. How is your training program organized? Is it clearly different from those of your competitors?

3. Are you managing your benefits package differently?

4. Are you able to attract employees because of your distinctive personnel policies?

CONFIDENTIAL INFORMATION AGREEMENT

IN CONSIDERATION of being employed by THE CAVENDISH PARTNERSHIP, INC. (Company), the undersigned hereby agrees and acknowledges:

1.   That during the course of my employ there may be disclosed to me certain trade secrets of the Company; said trade secrets consisting of:

    a)   Technical information: Methods, processes, formulae, compositions, inventions, machines, computer programs and research projects.

    b)   Business information: Customer lists; pricing data; sources of supply; and marketing, production, or merchandising systems or plans.

2.   I shall not during, or at any time after the termination of my employment with the Company, use for myself or others, or disclose or divulge to others any trade secrets, confidential information, financial or other data of the Company in violation of this Agreement.

3.   That upon the termination of my employ from the Company:

    a)   I shall return to the Company all documents relating to the Company, including but not necessarily limited to: drawings, blueprints, reports, manuals, correspondence, customer lists, computer programs, and all other materials and all copies thereof relating in any way to the Company's business, or in any way obtained by me during the course of my employ. I further agree that I shall not retain any copies of the foregoing.

    b)   The Company may notify any future or prospective employer of the existence of this Agreement.

    c)   This Agreement shall be binding upon me and my personal representatives and successors in interest, and shall inure to the benefit of the Company, its successors and assigns.

    d)   The unenforceability of any provision to this Agreement shall not impair or affect any other provision.

    e)   In the event of any breach of this Agreement, the Company shall have full rights to injunctive relief, in addition to any other existing rights, without requirement of posting bond.

Dated:_____

_____   _____

Witness   Employee

Figure 4-6   Typical employment contract. *(continued from previous page)*

EMPLOYEE INVENTION AGREEMENT

FOR GOOD CONSIDERATION, and in consideration of the undersigned being employed by THE CAVENDISH PARTNERSHIP, INC., (Company) the undersigned hereby agrees, acknowledges and represents:

1.   The undersigned, during the course of employment, shall promptly disclose in writing to the Company all inventions, discoveries, improvements, developments and innovations whether patentable or not, conceived in whole or in part by the undersigned or through assistance of the undersigned, and whether conceived or developed during working hours or not, which:

a)   Result from any work performed on behalf of the Company, or pursuant to a suggested research project by the Company, or

b)   Relate in any manner to the existing or contemplated business of the Company, or

c)   Result from the use of the Company's time, material, employees or facilities.

2.   The undersigned hereby assigns to the Company, its successors and assigns, all rights, title and interest to said inventions.

3.   The undersigned shall, at the Company's request, execute specific assignments to any such invention and execute, acknowledge, and deliver any additional documents required to obtain letters patent in any jurisdiction and shall, at the Company's request and expense, assist in the defense and prosecution of said letters patent as may be required by Company. This provision shall survive termination of employ with the Company.

Signed under seal this ** day of ****, 19**.

_____   _____

Witness   Employee

Figure 4-6   *(continued)*

5. Do you know of a top employee in another firm you would like to hire? Make the contract.

REFERENCES

1. Donald J. Trump, 1987. *Trump: The Art of the Deal.* New York: Random House.
2. Zig Ziglar, 1986. *Top Performance: How to Develop Excellence in Yourself and Others.* N.J.: Fleming H. Revell Company.

BIBLIOGRAPHY

Charles McReynolds, March 1982. "Finding Top Performers." *Professional Services Management Journal,* Vol. 9, p. 3.
Mark C. Zweig, 1988. "How to Be Your Own Search Firm." *Professional Services Management Journal.*

5 COMPENSATION

Successful firms compensate their staff with more than money. An analysis of payroll burden based on annual total revenues, annual net revenues, and direct labor is shown in Figure 5-1. Figure 5-2, analysis of general overhead expenses, also includes data on payroll burden. This chapter presents some ideas for motivating and rewarding employees for performance, and highlights some innovative small firm business policies.

MOTIVATING DESIGN PROFESSIONALS

There is a conception that to motivate design professionals bonuses or other forms of incentive compensation are necessary. Indeed, Hal Ahlberg of Dallas-based Professional Service Industries, which acquired a series of 5- to 10-person firms in the geotechnical field, has challenged the validity of this concept by instituting an instant policy upon acquisition—that of eliminating all incentive bonuses. He began paying his staff at market or slightly above, based on the salaries in the communities where the firms were located. Believing that design professionals are more motivated by recognition and control of more interesting project work, he found he lost no staff and, in fact, started to acquire more because he compensated the loss of bonuses by giving his staff more autonomy on their projects, bigger and better jobs, and more final say in project outcome.

Ahlberg's philosophy is that a bonus is the employer's way of borrowing money from the employee interest-free, until year-end, when such bonuses are due anyway. Instead he feels you should pay people a fair salary and motivate them with quality projects.

This analyzes payroll burden expense, again using the three baseline computations. (Since the items were individually analyzed, this schedule is not additive.) Note the largest individual expenditures were labor, fringe benefits, payroll taxes and time off (vacation, sick leave and holiday).

ANALYSIS OF PAYROLL BURDEN

Percentage	Based on Annual Total Revenues		Based on Annual Net Revenues		Based on Direct Labor	
	Median	Mean	Median	Mean	Median	Mean
Mandatory Payroll Taxes	3.5	3.5	4.4	4.4	12.2	12.2
Vacation, Sick Leave, Holiday	3.7	3.7	4.6	4.6	12.9	12.3
Group Insurance	2.1	2.2	2.8	3.0	7.3	7.3
Annual Pension Expense	1.4	1.8	1.7	2.3	3.9	5.2
All Other Fringe Benefits	.6	.8	.8	1.0	2.3	2.6
Total Payroll Burden (without bonus)	10.2	10.6	13.2	13.0	37.2	36.9
Bonus, Incentive Payments, Profit Sharing	4.5	6.0	5.4	7.2	8.5	9.5
Total Payroll Burden	14.1	15.0	17.1	18.1	47.0	49.0

Individual items are not additive

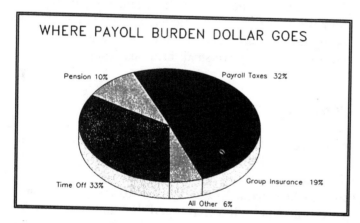

Time off and payroll taxes are the largest portion of payroll burden.

Figure 5-1 Analysis of payroll burden, from the *PSMJ 1989 Financial Statistics Survey.*[1]

Ahlberg's success with the firms is demonstrated by the fact that he acquired them for a total of $12 million over a two-year period starting in 1984, and sold the entire firm in December 1986 for $42 million, for a net gain of $30 million.

A small firm principal can learn from this example of a larger firm. Ralph Pierce, a principal of Harley, Ellington, Pierce, & Yee (HEPY), of Southfield, Michigan, invites employees from the firm to breakfast with him once a week. They talk about what they want, and he listens. Then he writes a personal letter to each employee explaining why certain concerns can, or cannot, be dealt with. Such meetings are a form of reward in themselves, and can be morale builders for design firms. More ideas on motivating design professionals appear in Figure 5-3.

ANALYSIS OF GENERAL OVERHEAD EXPENSES

Percentage	Based on Annual Total Revenues		Based on Annual Net Revenues		Based on Direct Labor	
	Median	Mean	Median	Mean	Median	Mean
Indirect (non project) Labor	9.8	10.5	12.3	12.8	35.1	35.9
Computer Cost	.6	.9	.8	1.2	2.2	3.6
Payroll Burden (without bonus)	10.2	10.6	13.2	13.0	37.2	36.9
Cost of Space	4.0	3.9	5.0	5.1	14.4	14.8
Telephone	.8	.8	1.0	1.1	2.6	2.9
Professional Liability Insurance	3.6	4.0	5.2	5.7	13.8	16.4
Interest Expense	.6	.8	.8	1.0	2.2	2.8
Bad Debt Expense	.5	.7	.6	.9	1.8	2.4
Training and Education	.3	.4	.4	.5	1.0	1.4
Legal and Accounting	.6	.7	.8	.9	2.2	3.0
Production Supplies	.8	.8	1.0	1.1	3.0	3.5
Office Supplies	.9	.9	1.2	1.2	3.2	3.6
Marketing Costs	3.4	4.0	4.2	5.2	11.8	14.8
All Other General and Administrative	4.9	5.4	6.2	6.6	16.7	18.2
Total Indirect (overhead) Expenses	43.5	42.8	53.8	53.4	149.7	146.3

Individual items are not additive

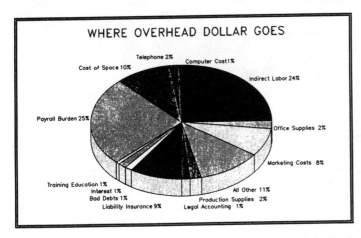

Payroll burden and indirect labor are the largest portion of overhead expenses.

Figure 5-2   Analysis of general overhead expenses, including payroll burden, from the *PSMJ 1989 Financial Statistics Survey.*[2]

Motivating Design Professionals

One way to motivate is not to demotivate. The following checklist helps you avoid demotivating ambitious, achievement-conscious professionals:

1. Encourage them to complete what they start—don't assign more project/tasks than can be completed with above-average effort.
2. Don't assume your staff cannot handle an unfamiliar project.
3. Keep your people informed. Tell them about the firm, their department, new or lost projects. Pass on both good and bad news.
4. Be frank about individual performances. Give thorough performance appraisals when they are due, but also have regular informal conversations to let employees know how they are doing and what their future is.
5. Give commitments regarding advancement. Tell employees what it will take for them to advance to the next level. Then back up your commitments; do not rationalize lack of action.
6. Give plenty of stroking. Frequent verbal praise, memos to personnel files, letters, bulletin board postings, etc., all help keep motivation levels high.
7. Explain why people are promoted. Most companies fail to take advantage of this great opportunity to reinforce patterns of behavior they want to perpetuate.
8. Offer your best people a piece of the action. Most design firm principals will share information about ownership with their best people, but few get around to offering it.
9. Build management expertise from within, if possible. Promote from within when you can for management positions.
10. Reward performance, with tangible rewards. Tie compensation as much as possible to performance. Do not allow your top people to be dragged down by your nonperformers.

Figure 5-3

BENEFITS

A comprehensive benefits package is often a good motivator. Some companies opt to pay no benefits at all. Instead they pay salaries high enough for employees to purchase their own benefits. Sometimes known as a flex plan, this accomplishes two things: the employee gets a higher rate of pay and the employer saves money otherwise spent on group benefits. Hoskins Engineers, a firm that offers no benefits, is profiled in Figure 5-4.

If you choose to include benefits, be sure they are equitable. As of January 1989, firms are legally obligated to demonstrate that their fringe benefits are not discriminatory. This means that individuals must be grouped into two classifications: those earning under $50,000 per year and those earning $50,000 or more per year.

Benefits and costs for each of these groups must be proportional. For instance, you can no longer give top management significantly different benefits such as country club dues, expensive cars, multiple vacations, or high life-insurance coverage without running the risk of having the IRS tax a portion of those benefits as compensation. If you do not pay such taxes on these benefits, members of the highly paid group will have to

---

Profile of Firm That Offers No Benefits

Firm: Hoskins Engineers, Inc.
Staff: 10
Specialty: Engineering for diverse client base, including contractors, developers, private individuals, architects, other civil engineers, insurance companies, and attorneys
Address: 501 S. Bascom Avenue
           San Jose, Calif. 95128

Hoskins Engineers, Inc., founded in 1973, currently makes extensive use of subconsultants. This practice provides expertise in many disciplines while managing a volatile work load.

The principal's underlying philosophy is that an individual is paid for working. This translates into a management style that does not pay for sick leave, health benefits, vacation, etc. Depending on the overall performance and cash position of the firm, certain holidays are paid. The one benefit that is offered is a generous profit-sharing and pension plan. Three years of service are required for eligibility. Thereafter, between 20 and 25% of an individual's salary is contributed to the plan. Vesting is immediate at 100%. Hourly compensation is augmented by frequent performance bonuses.

Hoskin's philosophy is worth considering if you are a small firm and you are looking to save money on overhead, payroll burden in particular. There are many ways to compensate your staff creatively.

Figure 5-4 *Source:* Hoskins Engineers, Inc.. Used with permission.

recognize a portion of their benefits (free health insurance, etc.) as income. Suggestions for coping with this new law follow:

- Minimize the number of optional benefits (e.g., dental coverage), since each option creates a separate plan group that must be tested.
- The new law makes part-time employees who work an average of 17.5 hours per week count toward compliance. If you have staff who meet this test, offer them group insurance coverage.
- Eliminate any extra coverage for managers and principals that could be considered discriminatory.
- Expect to spend $2000 to $2500 in data-gathering and paperwork for each plan you offer.

Because of the high cost of compliance, this new law is expected to curtail the cafeteria-style plans with many options.

Figure 5-5 summarizes some benefits that several typical small design firms are offering.

FACTORS AFFECTING EMPLOYEE TURNOVER

The following are results of a 1989 survey by *A/E Job Mart:*[3]

Salary was the number one reason stated for seeking a new position. Of 288 respondents, 27 percent believe they are not paid enough.

Even though for 73 percent, money wasn't the motivating factor for leaving a job, almost 100 percent expected a salary increase for a new position. While the majority expected a 10 percent increase, 26 percent expected 20 percent or more. Only 11 percent didn't see money as a motivating factor for changing jobs, and didn't expect to increase their salary. Although money was important to many, there were these other reasons for leaving a position:

- Lack of advancement opportunity   24%
- Lack of professional/technical growth   17%
- No appreciation for what they do   12%
- Inability to get ownership   6%

Other reasons for discontent in their current position included

Benefits Offered by Some Typical Design Firms

The Cavendish Partnership, Inc.
145 Main Street
Ludlow, Vt. 05149
Staff: 22
% gross payroll for direct labor: 30%
Notable benefits: Pays 50% of health, life, and disability; offers ski-lift tickets to employees

Eley Associates Architects
418 East Capital Street
Jackson, Miss. 39201
Staff: 13
% gross payroll for direct labor: 22%
Notable benefits: 21 days of: vacation, sick leave, and holidays; bonuses based on profit

Arizona Engineering Company
419 North San Francisco Street
Flagstaff, Ariz.
Staff: 8
% gross payroll for direct labor: 26.6% plus 5% for profit sharing
Notable benefits: Offers paid medical insurance

Duffy, Rubble, Manura, & Brygger
314 Security Bank Building
Sioux City, Iowa 51101
Staff: 14
% gross payroll for direct labor: 18%
Notable benefits: Pays 80% insurance premiums, including disability and life

R. C. Byce & Associates, Inc.
487 Portage Street
Kalamazoo, Mich. 49007
Staff: 29
Notable benefits: Floating holiday: when a holiday falls on a Tuesday or Thursday, a floating holiday will be taken Monday or Friday.

Figure 5-5 Note: Based on information submitted at the seminar "Staying Small Successfully," given by Frank Stasiowski at Beaver Creek, Colo., February 21-26, 1988.

- Not being kept informed about happenings in the firm   19%
- Feeling unappreciated   17%
- Having too much responsibility and not enough authority   13%

Many respondents work for firms where top executives control the information and perks and leave other ranks uninformed and unrewarded.

Look over the above points and see how many of these undesirable qualities you can eliminate from your firm's policies. Chances are that policies you think of as traditional and normal are in fact bringing employees motivation down, hence productivity and profitability. Successful firms go beyond traditional practices, and the difference fuels employees to stay and work harder and better.

Mobility

The 1989 *A/E Job Mart* survey[3] also emphasized the fact that we now live in a mobile society and relocation is no longer a big deal. Only 17 percent said they would not relocate. Thirty-eight percent said they would be willing to relocate outside their region; 45 percent were willing to relocate within the region.

Those prepared to relocate for a job expected some form of relocation compensation. Most preferred compensation for certain expenses, while a small percentage (5 percent) would settle for a cash relocation allowance.

Salary

In successful small firms, the spread between the salary of the owner(s) and those of the employees is relatively narrow as compared with that in unsuccessful firms. In successful firms, the second person in command is earning about 80 percent of the salary of the top person in command. This is a well-balanced compensation scheme. If a compensation scheme favors the top owners in spite of good performance by junior employees and there is a wide spread (30 to 50 percent between owners' and the next-ranking employees' salaries), there is often a high turnover rate, low morale, and other related problems.

TIMING PAY RAISES

Part of the compensation package includes motivating design professionals with pay raises. Some urge separating discussion about the granting of salary increases from performance evaluations. Others feel this approach could be worse than not having performance evaluations at all.

The problem with separating performance and salary discussions is that to most employees in design firms the only recognition for good performance *is* increased salary. Not talking about it is like talking about the scope of a new project for a client without discussing the fee.

You should discuss both performance and money during the same meeting but structure the meeting differently from the standard performance evaluation:

1. Begin performance reviews by concentrating on the future. Ask each employee to bring to the meeting a written list of goals for the next six months. The employee should note what will be done and when.
2. Listen. Make the employee explain even the most absurd idea.
3. Ask probing questions, but don't tell the employee what you think until all of the employee's goals are *fully* explained to you.
4. Come to a mutual agreement with each person on goals and objectives, and then ask each employee to tell you what they think they are *worth* if all goals are met satisfactorily. Whether it is below or above your figure, you should discuss it and agree upon an amount.
5. After agreeing upon the amount, discuss how the difference between current income and future income will be paid. Should part be salary and part bonus, or should all be bonus?

If you have been open about setting up a mutually agreed-upon scope of work with each individual, and if the amount and terms of payment are clearly understood, the employee will be able to self-evaluate prior to the next session and tell you whether or not any increased compensation was earned. This process is like writing a contract with a client.

This approach is feasible, but has two drawbacks:

1. It takes time, and requires that each person be allowed to set up individual goals.
2. It takes courage and honesty to discuss salary as part of a performance review if you have never done it, espe-

cially in light of the commonly held opinion that you should separate such discussions.

INCENTIVE COMPENSATION

Incentive plans should be set up with one thing in mind: to recognize superior performance. W. L. Vanderweil of R. G. Vanderweil Engineers explains how this is done within his firm:

> A key to our success is the emphasis we put on marketing to existing clients to generate repeat business. Of our six principals, only the principal who is in charge of operations gets a bonus that is heavily weighted towards profitability. The others receive the major part of their bonus from marketing existing clients and the amounts of repeat business they bring in. We do find that money is a very good motivator, particularly when you pay bonuses that are very significant in proportion to an employee's salary, as we do. This emphasis on repeat business makes the key people in our firm focus on keeping the client happy. By doing this we get most of our business from existing clients (83 percent in 1988) and also find that their referrals result in a fair amount of new business. To date, this philosophy has served us well.

Avoid the following compensation practices, since they are known to result in poor profitability:

1. *All employees get the same raise.* When profits drop, some firms limit all raises to a given percentage. But this way you reward your worst and your best performers equally. Eventually, the good performers will either leave for a firm that rewards performance, or their performance will drop to average, since it makes no difference to their salary. Equal raises look fair and appealing, and not having to apportion limited salary dollars will save time, but it will only prolong poor financial performance.

2. *Bonus plans that pay the same percent of salary to all eligible participants.* The same factors apply as in #1 above.

3. *Pay bonuses where the average is five percent (or less) of salary.* If you make $40,000 a year, will a $2000 (or less)

bonus really motivate you? Compensation studies have shown 15 percent of salary to be the minimum necessary to trigger a significant positive staff reaction. This is especially true if bonuses are tied to performance. If you are going to hold out bonuses as a reward, make sure they are big enough to get an employee's attention.

During hard times, when there are not enough salary and bonus dollars to satisfy every employee, you must be even more careful to make sure good performers are rewarded more favorably. This means your poor and average performers may get no raise or bonus at all.

Incentive Bonuses

Incentive bonuses, used to reward key people, should be at least 10 to 15 percent of a person's salary.

When budgeting, set aside 10 to 15 percent of your total expected salary expense for incentive bonuses. Although this figure may seem high, you will receive the benefit of superior performance before spending your first bonus dollar. The very fact of establishing the budget underscores your commitment to your key staff.

Begin cautiously. A poorly established and managed plan is worse than no plan at all. Start by carefully defining each job in your firm and make sure that your people understand clearly what is normally expected of them. Establish regular performance appraisals to confirm your understanding and theirs of what is meant by normal expected performance. After standards are set, define your bonus incentive reward process clearly.

One Midwest firm rewards its project managers on a per-project basis using a formula that includes variables for profitability, quality of design, service to client, and the performance of their staff.

Another firm gives team bonuses to an entire project team when it achieves better performance than expected. This helps build team spirit. Your plan must reflect your goals for reward based on your process for delivering service. If you perform services as a team, reward the team, not an individual. If you act as individuals, reward individually.

Do not vary from standards. Do not reward one project manager $500 and another $1000 for superior performance on similar projects, despite the second manager's greater experience. *Never* consider longevity as a factor in making incentive rewards. Doing so will demotivate a hardworking younger employee.

Consider using bonus rewards other than monetary reimbursement:

- Added vacation time.
- A paid trip for the top achiever and family.
- Books or subscriptions.
- Extra education such as seminars and night courses.
- Special use of company recreation facilities, such as country club privileges for a month.
- A company car.

Two other ideas that are not incentive-related but positive include:

- Profit sharing. This rewards all, including poor performers.
- Christmas bonuses. Personnel often count on this as a salary requirement.

Finally, be sure to communicate your incentive plan to the entire staff.

Stock Bonuses

With growing cash-flow problems, there is another method available to incorporated design firms. It consists of issuing to employees bonuses in the form of stock instead of cash. Doing so allows a firm to take an immediate deduction on its books for the expense of the stock bonus without actually paying out any cash. Thus, cash flow is preserved and taxes deferred.

One Northwest engineering firm provides its employees with both cash and stock as an annual bonus. For each dollar of bonus, the employee receives 40 percent in cash and 60 percent in stock. This move allows the employee to pay personal income taxes with the cash and at the same time lets the company take an immediate deduction for 100 percent of the bonus value while paying out only 40 percent in cash.

The additional benefit derived from such a plan is that it encourages all employees to increase the value of your stock by working harder to make the firm profitable. Paying a stock bonus requires a well-developed ownership and leadership transition plan that allows for stock distribution among key employees on this basis. Closely held businesses with one or two partners may find it difficult to incorporate such a bonus arrangement.

Quarterly Bonuses

A variant on this theme is a quarterly incentive compensation plan that pays each project team a bonus based on accrual team profitability for the past three months, even if cash is not yet collected.

A Northwest engineering firm using this plan pays 50 percent of the actual bonus earned each quarter and puts 50 percent into a revolving five-quarter pool, which is paid out over five quarters based on collections and subsequent quarterly performance. This avoids the dilemma created should a team encounter a losing quarter.

Such a frequent payment plan is best for using money as a reward. The closer the timing of the reward to the activity for which it is given, the greater the motivation.

Deferred Bonuses

The end of the fiscal year is often the time to distribute bonuses. One type of bonus is deferred compensation. Under this program, regular weekly pay is lower than market rates, or at least less than the value the firm applies to the individual's efforts. This discrepancy is made up at the end of the fiscal year with a cash bonus payment that is widely distributed throughout the firm.

There are a number of advantages to using a deferred bonus program as part of your total compensation progam:

1. Deferred compensation reduces cash flow out during the year until the end of the fiscal year, when the firm may have more cash available. This can help borrowing requirements during the year or alternatively make more cash available for short-term investment.

2. Firmwide compensation can be linked to profitability, by tying individual compensation to the overall financial achievements of the firm. This is an excellent way to motivate employees to act in accordance with the profit objectives of the firm.

3. In price-competitive marketing situations, you can quote lower hourly rates for your employees. This may need to be offset by a higher multiplier to cover eventual bonus payments, budgeted as part of your overhead, but you have an initial advantage over competitors.

4. By delaying compensation for a year, you are able to tie compensation more effectively to actual performance. Deferred compensation payments can be adjusted up or down depending on the individual employee's actual achievements.

5. Because payments are made at the end of the fiscal year, employees are encouraged to stay with the firm until that time rather than lose the bonus.

6. Deferred compensation is an allowable cost under federal procurement policies. You need to document *your intent* to pay the bonus or show that you historically have paid deferred compensation without reference to stock ownership.

7. By deferring compensation and combining it with more discretionary bonus payments, you are able to make bonuses significant enough to truly motivate employees the following year. Small bonus payments are poor motivators.

8. Deferred compensation can serve as an enforced savings program for employees. By allowing a company to take an immediate expense reduction, this puts aside a future amount of compensation for an individual.

Bonus payments may also be used for such items as IRA contributions or stock purchases for those seeking equity positions in the organization.

CAREER TRACKING

Successful design firms create career tracks for employees. This recognizes that your firm is made up both of professional management positions and technical positions and that both must be rewarded. Successful firms reward their professionals according to their respective career tracks.

In firms that use career tracking, salary levels are assigned by ranges, and all are paid within those levels. No one knows exactly how much each individual makes, but the salary level structure is a published document that shows the ranges corresponding to job positions within the firm. This is feasible even in the smallest firm. The career tracking plan of Schmidt Associates Architects, a 25-person firm, is shown in Figure 5-6. The company's career planning form for its architects is presented in Figure 5-7.

CREATE AN ATMOSPHERE OF ACHIEVEMENT

As a design firm principal, you should try to create an environment of achievement in your firm. The purpose is to get your staff motivated. Do not, however, start a massive motivational campaign. Instead, start with yourself. Look at the little things you can do daily:

1. *Listen more than you talk.* Practice by learning to ask more questions.
2. *Tell employees or project teams often that they are doing a good job, if they are.* Appreciation and recognition are the most valued but least available commodity in most design firms.
3. *Thank staff and their spouses for overtime work.* A nice touch is a handwritten thank-you note home to a spouse. Such a practice will set you apart from the average.
4. *Be seen.* Take your coffee break and walk around the back room. It is not a waste of time, but a sound motivator.
5. *Start each project with a team meeting* to discuss goals for the project, goals of the client, and specific goals of each team member. If the team assumes "ownership" of the project requirements, the time you spend in such a meeting will be amply returned by the participants.
6. *Stay flexible.* When one of your staff works until 2 A.M. on a project, accept it when he/she comes in late the next

SCHMIDT ASSOCIATES ARCHITECTS, INC.
ARCHITECTURAL/INTERIORS/LANDSCAPE ARCHITECTURE CAREER PATHING MODEL

7 C.E.O.
- DRIVE STRATEGIC DECISIONS
- PRIME FISCAL RESPONSIBILITY
- PROVIDE LEADERSHIP TO COMMUNITY
- INSPIRE FIRM GOALS AND ATTITUDES

6A PARTNER
- MENTOR FOR STAFF DEVELOPMENT
- MANAGE LIFELONG LEARNING (INTERN STAFF)
- MANAGE INTERN STAFF CAREER PLANNING
- DESIGN/MONITOR SYSTEMS FOR QUALITY CONTROL
- PARTICIPATE IN CORPORATE POLICY DISCUSSION

6B MANAGING PARTNER
- DEFINE MARKETING DIRECTION
- DEVELOP AND MANAGE ANNUAL SBU BUSINESS PLAN
- DEFINE DELIVERY PROCESSES
- FORMULATE AND MANAGE ANNUAL BUDGETS
- SET CORPORATE POLICY
- MENTOR/MANAGE PROJECT MANAGER AND PROJECT ARCHITECT DEVELOPMENT

5 SENIOR PROJECT MANAGER
- NURTURING RELATIONSHIPS WITH ASSIGNED CLIENTS
- PARTICIPATE IN PRESENTATIONS FOR PERSPECTIVE CLIENTS
- MANAGE SIMULTANEOUS PROJECTS

4 PROJECT MANAGER
- ESTABLISH PROJECT GOALS
- MANAGE FOR PROFITABILITY
- DELIVER PROJECT WITHIN OWNER'S BUDGET
- COACH/MENTOR PROJECT TEAM
- FACILITATE A POSITIVE DESIGN PROCESS

3 PROJECT ARCHITECT/SENIOR STAFF
- PLAN THE WORKFLOW TO REACH PROJECT GOALS AND TIMELINE
- COORDINATE THE IMPLEMENTATION TEAM (INTERNAL & EXTERNAL)
- COACH THE TEAM IN TECHNICAL EXECUTION
- PROVIDE QUALITY DESIGN ALTERNATIVES

2 INTERN STAFF
- ENHANCE TECHNICAL SKILLS
- DELIVER SERVICE WITHIN TIME OBJECTIVE
- CONTRIBUTE TO TEAM IN CONTENT AND PROCESS

1 ORIENTATION
- ESTABLISH A WORKING STYLE COMPATIBLE WITH FIRM VALUES
- DEMONSTRATE COMPATIBILITY IN BASIC TECHNICAL SKILLS
- INTERACT WITH TEAM EFFECTIVELY

Figure 5-6 The career tracking plan of Schmidt Associates Architects. Used with permission.

CAREER PLANNING: SCHMIDT ASSOCIATES ARCHITECTS - ARCHITECT

NAME:_____ DATE:_____

PERSONAL GOALS:
1
2
3
4
5

PROFESSIONAL GOALS:
1
2
3
4
5

COMMITMENT:

	1	2	3	4	5	6	7	8	9	10
1. Attitude towards Self										
2. Commitment towards Self-improvement										
3. Attitude towards Work Ethic										
4. Attitude towards Client Relationship										
5. Attitude towards Architecture										
6. Attitude towards Peers										
7. Level of Energy										
8. Level of Purpose										
9. Level of Determination										
10. Attitude towards Community										

COMPETENCE:

	DIRECTIVE 1 2 3 4 5 6 7 8 9 10	COACHING 1 2 3 4 5 6 7 8 9 10	SUPPORTIVE 1 2 3 4 5 6 7 8 9 10	DELEGATION 1 2 3 4 5 6 7 8 9 10
1. Communication Skills in Listening				
2. Communication Skills in Speaking				
3. Communication Skills in Writing				
4. Competence in Specific Thinking				
5. Competence in Comprehensive Thinking				
6. Proficient in use of Micro-Computers				
7. Competence in Alternative Development				
8. Leadership Ability with Peers				
9. Competence in Architecture Business				
10. Competence in Synthesis				
11. Strategic Planning/Thinking				
12. Ability to Delegate				
13. Skill at Organization				
14. Competence in the Design Process				
15. Competence in Building Construction				
16. Leadership Ability with Clients				
17. Leadership Ability with Allied Profes				

OTHER:

	1	2	3	4	5	6	7	8	9	10
1. Awareness of Patience										
2. Sense of Good Humor										
3. Ability to Influence										

Figure 5-7 The career planning form for architects at Schmidt Associates Architects.

morning. Learn who are your morning versus your night people, and realize that a night person may work all night but has trouble coming to the office on time in the morning.

7. *Never tolerate poor performance,* or you will encourage your best performers to do less, and end up with a group of nonperformers. When people do not perform, tell them immediately. The second time let them know it is the second time, and the third time consider termination.

8. *Ask yourself: Do all staff members really know what is expected of them?* If the answer is yes, you probably don't have anything to worry about. If it's no, begin planning performance criteria and revise job descriptions to reflect expected performance.

SUMMARY

Successful small firm entrepreneurs recognize performance as a key issue. There are five elements to measure in performance:

1. Hard work.
2. Work effectiveness.
3. Loyalty to the company.
4. Work ethic.
5. Emotion.

One of the most difficult entrepreneurial challenges is to replace a loyal hardworking staff member who has reached their maximum capability in a growing firm. Successful firms are able to hire people and position them over employees of long standing as the company grows. Many firms build around loyalty in the absence of any other performance standards only to find their profit growth severely limited by a group of people who have maximum capability. The Peter principle—Dr. Laurence J. Peter's theory that "in a hierarchy individuals tend to rise to their levels of incompetence"—hurts these firms dramatically.[4] How a firm motivates its employees is a measure of its success in the marketplace.

The simplest form of motivation is *recognition.* Praise your staff for the smallest examples of good performance. Do it in writing so they can show it off at home. On the other hand, reprimand privately and verbally promptly after poor performance.

SUCCESS CHALLENGES

1. Does your second in command receive 80 percent of your salary, or is there too wide a spread to encourage close team relationships?

2. Does your bonus system really motivate people to perform, or are you wasting your money on Christmas and other expected bonuses? How could you restructure the same bonus money in a way that would really motivate staff to perform?

3. Are you giving bonuses to 100 percent of the people in your firm, or are you only giving bonuses to the top performers as you should?

4. If you could do as much work in the marketplace with less people, how can you compensate people less to help you do so? Do you use independent contractors to accomplish some of the tasks full-time salaried people are doing now?

5. Can you employ two part-time people rather than one full-timer, thereby saving on the overhead of fringe benefits and the lack of productivity that occurs during a full eight-hour day put in by one person?

6. As you look to the future, do you have in place compensation plans that allow for career tracking—for both the technical and management professionals to advance in their respective directions—with defined, appropriate salary levels?

7. Do you have a training program that will allow you to retain key people who are now highly compensated but unchallenged?

REFERENCES

1. Practice Management Associates, Ltd., 1989. *PSMJ 1989 Financial Statistics Survey*. Newton, Mass. p. 34.
2. *Ibid.*, p. 35.
3. Practice Management Associates, 1989. *A/E Job Mart*. Newton, Mass.

4. Dr. Laurence J. Peter, 1985. *Why Things Go Wrong or The Peter Principle Revisited.* New York: William Morrow & Company.

BIBLIOGRAPHY

"Deferred Bonus." *Professional Services Management Journal,* October 1984.

"Don't Forget Motivation." *Professional Services Management Journal,* May 1983.

"Incentive Bonuses." *Professional Services Management Journal,* June 1979.

"Money Can Motivate." *Professional Services Management Journal,* August 1988.

Dr. Laurence J. Peter, 1986. *The Peter Pyramid.* New York: William Morrow & Company.

"Quarterly Bonuses." *Professional Services Management Journal,* August 1988.

"Stock Bonuses." *Professional Services Management Journal,* April 1983.

"Timing Pay Raises." *Professional Services Management Journal,* November 1981.

6 MANAGING THE BOTTOM LINE

As Wayne Schmidt, president of Schmidt Associates Architects, Indianapolis, says, "Running a sound business which is efficient, results-oriented, cost-effective, and accountable to timeliness is as important . . . as providing top quality professional skills."

William Carpenter, former CEO of a very successful firm, Sirrine Engineers in South Carolina, once said that "profit is the only measure of successful design." Carpenter's philosophy was that no matter how you define success, the "bottom line" is the ultimate yardstick for measuring it. Thus, a focus on bottom-line financial performance, which includes setting and managing budgets, prices, contract terms, and financial results, is an integral part of becoming and staying successful. A significant profit goal is a must in every firm's planning process. As stated in Chapter 1, average small firm profits are in the 9 percent range. However, outstanding firms have goals of 25 percent, and, because they are aiming for higher than average goals, they naturally produce higher-than-average results. This chapter tells you how to achieve the profit goal you set in your strategic plan (Chapter 1) through simplified financial planning, measuring your progress with five simple elements, and improving project profits.

Sound financial management is the basis for a successful practice. One of the dangers small firms face is in allowing a client to approach them with a fixed budget, asking how much design it can get for the price. When faced with this approach, a firm is forced to put together a top-down budget and work plan. Built into this method are several pitfalls:

- *Leaving out profit.* The client's quote includes your profit. Immediately set aside your required profit, then determine your scope of work.
- *Underestimating direct costs.* Under this approach, there may be no reimbursable items. You may need to pay for everything out of your fee. Make sure you allow enough for all your costs.
- *Assuming incorrect consultant fees.* Do not assume you know how much a consultant will charge. Get firm quotes on scope and fee.
- *Trying to "squeeze" into the fee a scope you would want if you were the client.* The fee quoted should determine the project scope. Do not overestimate your abilities to produce and perform. (See "Excess Perfection Syndrome," Fig. 3-7.)
- *Leaving no room to negotiate.* Instead, the client may well expect to negotiate, either to an increased scope or a lower fee.

A far wiser approach is to focus on the bottom line. Regardless of goals for design quality, staff performance, or professional recognition, what counts is a bottom-line strategy that focuses on effective financial performance measured against predetermined goals. Small and large firms alike must realize the importance of the bottom line. W. L. Vanderweil, of R. G. Vanderweil Engineers (Boston), agrees:

> . . . We must run our operation as a sound financial business. One of the things that personally disappoints me in the architecture/engineering business is that attitude that many firms have that makes profit secondary to the quality of design. In fact, they should be equal, as they go hand in hand. To get our share of work, our fees must be competitive, but we try hard not to lowball the client. We stress to our staff that they must run their projects like a business, which is sometimes difficult because many people in our field do not always approach things in a businesslike fashion. By making good profits, we find we are able to pay our people what they deserve, give them the motivation to serve our clients well, invest the money we need for our business to grow, and keep our top people in what is a tightly held business.

In a top-down budgeting method, firms are in danger of unconsciously giving away too much. There is too much room for the client to win and for the firm to lose. It is imperative that the firm assess its overall strategy relative to the scope of work being provided on the set fee that has been determined by a client.

Design firms typically have great difficulty reducing their scope of services from the "standard" suggested by professional societies or by our traditional way of doing business. The successful firms have found a way to cut scope (when the client has a budget) without cutting quality, thereby allowing for an equal level of profit margin on a small project as on a big one. Be certain you focus on the issues of margin and retain the same percentage of profit on a project even if the client's fee to be paid to you seems low in relation to fees received for other similar projects in a market.

Finally, *simplify*. Financial planning need not be complicated. In the smaller firm it is a simplified process to monitor:

- Utilization of staff resources.
- Billing and collections of receivables.
- Negotiating the details of a contract.

SIMPLIFIED FINANCIAL PLANNING

Most design professionals recognize the need to plan the operations of individual projects—to develop time schedules, programs of work to be accomplished, staffing plans, and budgets. But most firms fail to devote enough attention to planning and monitoring the financial results of the firm as a whole. In many firms, the focus of firmwide financial management is merely on cash management and maintaining good borrowing relationships, often the by-products of mediocre financial results. You must develop and monitor a financial and operating plan that is simple and straightforward and that frees architects and engineers to focus on architecture and engineering first and finances second. Financial planning begins with formulating the statement of goals: profit goals and other key financial measures. Using these goals as a guide, the next step is to calculate an annual budget, to be turned into a pro forma annual budget. The final step is to formulate a reporting system to measure progress toward your financial goals—basically the goal for your bottom-line profit (set in the strategic planning process, Chapter 1).

BUDGETING

Design firms have two ways of setting their annual budget: the contracts method or the size of staff method, also known as realization budgeting. Here you will see that the second is the better method of the two.

Contracts Method

A common budgeting method is to anticipate the contracts a firm will get in the coming year as the basis of the financial plan. This is very difficult to calculate because it assumes that current contracts will carry a firm for three to six months, but the remainder of the year's work is unknown. When you don't know what contracts your firm will procure six to eight months from now, you can only guess at their profitability, scope, and schedule. Therefore, when attempting to estimate the number of contracts that will materialize in a year, you can only base it on what you have in your "pipeline." Such a pipeline bears many uncertainties, a market can change, and a "sure thing" project may or may not materialize, depending on the whims of the client. The immediate contracts probably account for only one-quarter to one-third of a year. Thus, to estimate for the entire year, you would multiply the project costs of the first three months by four:

$$3 \text{ months (all projects, all costs)} \times 4 = \text{annual plan}$$

This is an inaccurate, unpredictable method of estimating an annual budget, and very small firms, in particular, commonly use this method because they are unaware of alternatives.

Size of Staff Method

A more stable planning factor is realization budgeting, based on staff size. The number of employees and their ability generally do not change dramatically in one year. Consequently, financial planning using achievable billing capacity per employee is a much sounder basis for planning accuracy.

Realization budgeting is a conservative method strongly recommended for the small firm (and for any firm) because it does not include extra profit that might be made on one current project but not another, future one. It also does not "count on" overtime efforts, making overtime an entirely "extra" income producer.

The following steps for realization budgeting correspond with the column numbers on the form shown in Figure 6-1:

1. List the people in your firm.

2. Write each staff member's annual pay rate next to their name.

3. Figure each employee's target utilization rate. What percentage of total time will each person spend on billable projects? Total time includes technical time, vacation, sick days, fringe benefits time, administrative time, and so on. In the example (Fig. 6-1), the firm consists of 10 people and the median average utilization ratio is 68 percent according to financial statistics from the *Professional Services Management Journal*. The utilization ratio here are set goals to achieve a slightly higher ratio than the average for each position they represent. (If your firm has a lower average utilization ratio than 68 percent, find out why. Take into account your type of business and your profit margin. For instance, interiors firms tend to have lower utilization ratio, in the 50 percent range, but higher hourly billing rates. They thus have a higher profit margin—32 percent, as compared to the 9 percent average.)

4. Determine available hours per year. A standard work year is 2080 hours (40 hours × 52 weeks). Multiply it by each person's target utilization ratio to achieve the billable chargeable hours for each person.

Standard work year × utilization ratio for each person = billable chargeable hours per person

For example, if your typical work year is 2080 hours and your person works at a 75 percent utilization ratio (person #10 in Fig. 6-1), they will generate 1560 hours of time over the next year that is billable to your clients.

5. Determine a targeted hourly billing rate. This can be complicated if you are using a multiplier or a variety of billing rates per individual. It is best to standardize these billing rates—for example, simply charge $100/hour for everyone. At least simplify your process and charge in whole numbers ending in fives or zeros. You must decide on an appropriate and

1. Staff	2. Pay Rate	3. Target Utilization Rate (U.R.)	4. Avail.* Hrs. / yr.	5. Targeted Billing Rate	6. Fees Generated for Year	7. Avail-ability	8. Totals
1. Timmons	$100,000/yr	35%	728	100/hr	$ 72,800	100%	72,800
2. Smith	80,000	52%	1082	100	108,200		108,200
3. Parker	80,000	52%	1082	100	108,200		108,200
4. Browne	60,000	69%	1435	100	143,500		143,500
5. Wilson	45,000	69%	1435	100	143,500		143,500
6. Polson	45,000	69%	1435	100	143,500		143,500
7. Wender	45,000	69%	1435	100	143,500		143,500
8. Bolson	35,000	85%	1768	100	176,800		176,800
9. Lakey	35,000	85%	1768	100	176,800		176,800
10. Power	20,000	75%	1560	100	156,000		156,000
	$545,000						$1,372,800

9. Total $ 1,372,800

10. 5% Writeoffs and bad debts   -   68,640

11. Total available revenue $ 1,304,160

* (2080 * U. R.)

Figure 6-1   Example of realization budgeting.

simple billing rate for your firm. In the example, person #10, with 1560 hours and a 75 percent utilization ratio, has a billing rate of $100 per hour. This person, if in your employ for the entire year, will generate $156,000 in fees.

6. Write the total fees generated for the year based on availability in the next column.

7. Availability. If a person is available for 100 percent of the year, he or she will generate 100 percent of the total billable rate. Give these individuals 100 percent billable ratings. If, however, you are planning to add three persons six months into the year, they will have a billable rating of 50 percent. Multiply the total revenue generated amount ($156,000 in the example for person #10) by the availability rate (100 percent).

8–9. Add together each employee's individual revenue amount for all the firm's employees' total available revenue generated. In the example, that is $1,372,800. This is the total amount of money your staff can generate based on your target utilization ratios (explained further in the upcoming section entitled "Key Financial Measures"), which can be easily measured using a time card.

10. Remember two added factors:

(a) *Write-offs.* There is a certain percentage of time (hours charged on the time cards) you may not get paid for. This ratio should be calculated and subtracted from the total generated revenue amount at this point. Look back over last year's time cards and determine the percentage of hours you had to write off. In the example, the percentage is 2 percent.

(b) *Bad Debts.* Look over last year's books and determine the percentage of debts you had to write off. For the example, there are 3 percent bad debts.

Add the write-off percentage to the bad debts allowance. In the example:

$$2\% \text{ write-offs} + 3\% \text{ bad debts} = 5\%$$

Subtract the write-offs from the total amount of revenue generated (TRG). In the example that would be:

$$\text{TRG} - 5\% = \text{total available revenue}$$

11. Total available revenue. In the example, 5% is $68,640:

$$\$1,372,800 - \$68,640 = \$1,304,160$$

The Pro Forma Annual Statement

Now you are ready to develop a pro forma annual statement using the revenue figures and subtracting all allocable expenses from the total revenue generated (see Fig. 6-2):

1. Salaries from column #2 in Figure 6-1.
2. Benefits such as bonuses, overhead, raises, and other expenses associated with salaries.
3. Rent.
4. Heat.
5. Light and utilities.

Pro Forma Annual Statement

Total Annual Revenue: $1,304,160
Total Budget Expenses: $ 978,120

1. Salaries	$545,000
2. Benefits and salary-related expenses	$ 50,000
3. Rent	$ 40,000
4. Heat	$ 6,000
5. Light and utilities	$ 15,000
6. Reimbursables	$ 20,000
7. Consultants, part-timers, outside personnel, and other services	$302,120
Total Annual Budget	$978,120

Expected Profit = $326,040 (25% of total annual revenue)

Note: This budget is greatly simplified for explanatory purposes only.

Figure 6-2

6. Reimbursables (add income you'll get if you mark up your reimbursables by say 15 percent).

7. Consultants, part-timers, outside personnel, and other services.

Having done all this, you now have an annual financial plan (budget) based on an estimate of firm staff size. With only staff size as a variable, adjusting your plan becomes much more simple than trying to anticipate the probability of future contracts.

Realization budgeting is a simple and rapid planning method. If your firm consists of 10 employees, as in the example, developing your financial plan should take no more than 30 minutes. Figure 6-3a–c is a more realistic, more complex budget for a larger firm.

If you have a personal computer, you can use a spreadsheet program to make your financial planning flexible. You can change the utilization ratios, the standard year, or any other factors to determine variations of your financial plan.

Currently clients' selection criteria for choosing design firms includes price competition or bidding. With an accurate budget, you will know exactly what your costs are and where to set your bid. Without a reliable budget, it is difficult to plan for bonuses and other important expenses throughout the year.

Banking Relationships

One good reason to develop an accurate budget is to maintain banking relationships. Without an effective financial plan, bankers will not understand your business. Most will request to see your annual budget or financial plan. Design professionals are different from most businesses bankers deal with. They have no inventories, they have "work-in-process." They have projects that take at minimum many months to complete, not including construction time. They must meet a payroll every two weeks, whether or not the client pays its bill. A financial plan built around your staff count provides a solid tool to demonstrate control over your finances.

KEY FINANCIAL MEASURES

Armed with an annual financial plan (the budget) for the firm, you can begin setting financial goals and take steps to imple-

TYPICAL FISCAL YEAR UTILIZATION REVENUE PROJECTION

(2088 HRS = 100%)

Staff #	Name	Billing Rate	Budget % Chargeable	Chargeable Hours		Fiscal Availability		Revenue Production
1	Jones	$55.00	55	1144		100		$ 62,920
2	Smith	55.00	70	1456		100		80,080
3	Walker	32.50	85	1768		50		28,730
4	Curtis	28.75	5	104		100		2,990
		(1) Rate	X	(2) Hours	X	(3) Available	=	(4) Revenue
15	Burton	27.25	75	1560		100		42,510
16	Taylor	23.00	65	1352		100		31,096
17	Leonard	20.00	85	1768		10		3,536
8	Russell	18.50	90	1872		25		8,658
	Firm Totals		72%	77,640				

Total Chargeable	$1,338,057
Total Billable (88%)	1,177,490
Total Collectable (85%)	1,137,348

(*a*)

TYPICAL FISCAL STAFF UTILIZATION BUDGET

1 YEAR = 2080 Hrs

NAME	TARGET BUDGET CHARGEABLE	CHARGEABLE HOURS	NON CHARGEABLE HOURS	BREAKDOWN				
				SICK	VAC	HOL	MKTG	G.O.
Jones	55%	1144	936	60	160	80	520	116
Smith	70%	1456	624	60	160	80	200	124
Walker	85%	1768	312	40	120	80	50	22
Curtis	5%	104	1976	40	120	80	136	1600
Burton	75%	1560	520	30	80	80	30	300
Taylor	65%	1352	728	30	80	80	138	400
Leonard	85%	1768	312	30	80	80	0	122
Russell	90%	1872	208	30	80	80	0	18
Totals	72%	77640	23249	3500	6000	4000	6720	3029

(*b*)

Figure 6-3 An example of a complex budget.

PROFESSIONAL DESIGN FIRM REALIZATION BUDGET

ACCOUNT NO.	TITLE	ORIGINAL ANNUAL BUDGET	BUDGET PER MONTH
3000.00	Income		
3100.00	Professional Fees	$1,137,348.	$94,779.
3200.00	Expense Realization	40,000.	3,333.
3300.00	Other Income		
3300.01	Bad Debts Recovered	-0-	-0-
3300.05	Interest Income	3,000.	250.
	Total Income	$1,180,348.	$98,362.
4000.00 to 7000.00	Expense (100%)		
4100.01	Professional Salaries and Wages (58%)	568,522.	47,376.
4200.01	Management Salaries and Wages (7%)	66,804.	5,567.
5100.00	Management Expense (25%)		
5100.01	Rent and Utilities	75,000.	6,250.
5100.05	Equipment Rental & Repair	10,500.	875.
5100.10	E. & O. Insurance	40,000.	3,333.
5100.90	Photography	485.	40.
5100.92	Meals and Lodging	2,500.	208.
5100.94	Postage and Freight	3,500.	291.
5100.95	Miscellaneous Expenses	2,500.	208.
5100.96	Office Mgmt. Travel	4,200.	350.
6100.00	Marketing Salaries and Wages (3%)	27,375.	2,281.
7100.00	Marketing Expense (7%)		
7100.01	Cost of Projects not Obtained	29,026.	2,418.
7100.05	Graphics	25,000.	2,083.
7100.06	Publications	1,200.	100.
7100.10	Conventions	3,000.	250.
7100.15	Travel Expenses	7,000.	583.
7100.20	Public Relations	2,000.	166.
7100.25	Miscellaneous	500.	41.
	Total Expense	$ 975,922.	$ 81,326.
Profit (Loss)		$ 204,425.	$ 17,035.

(*c*)

Figure 6-3 (Continued)

ment those goals. To set goals, first look at your firm's present financial picture and assess the key financial measures of your firm. Then compare your firm's actual performance with the targeted performance on a monthly basis using a brief (one-page) report.

To obtain an up-to-date financial picture the smaller architectural or engineering firm should use five key financial measures to evaluate its operations and profitability:

- Utilization ratio.
- Ratio of accounts receivables turnover.
- Work-in-process turnover.
- Accrual profit and loss.
- Project profitability.

These measures were identified by Moritz Bergmeyer, whose firm was described in Figure 1-3. Calculate each ratio once a month and compile a brief (one-page) report containing the results of each ratio. Figure 6-4 shows a typical monthly report/profit and loss statement prepared by Bergmeyer Associates; this one is from November 1986. If your firm is divided into profit centers or project teams, you can request a similar report from each division leader.

Utilization Ratio

The utilization ratio is the proportion of staff time that is chargeable to specific projects compared to the total time employed by the firm. In most cases, the utilization ratio must be 65 to 75 percent for the firm to maintain profitability. According to the *Professional Services Management Journal* statistics surveys, the median utilization for 1986 to 1989 was 68.9 percent. When a firm's utilization ratio goes below this figure, profitability becomes difficult and the firm struggles financially. Although the median ratio for design firms is 68.9 percent, the average for the top 25 most profitable firms (size, 18 to 25 people) was 78 percent, or 10 percent higher than the average.

The utilization ratio for the entire firm is a mix of ratios for each individual position. Some target ratios for each key position are

Project Managers	63%
Draftsmen	83%

BERGMEYER ASSOCIATES, INC. - MONTHLY SUMMARY

NOVEMBER 1986 - 4 WEEKS

INCOME STATEMENT	CURRENT MONTH BUDGET	ACTUAL	YEAR TO DATE	JOE P.C. 1	ILKKA P.C. 2	DAVID P.C. 3	LEWIS P.C. 7	NICK P.C. 8
INCOME STREAM								
Gross Fee Income		$159,613	$1,381,822	$38,380	$22,159	$53,998	$15,191	$27,253
Net Fee Income	$152,876	$139,056	$1,177,795	$35,652	$17,248	$44,720	$13,273	$26,218
Work in Process		$6,489	$28,989	($1,008)	$2,632	$3,497	$983	$0
EXPENSES								
Reimbursables		$24,056	$189,144	$10,733	$2,140	$9,193	$1,049	$941
Dir. Labor - Overtime		$0	$0	$0	$0	$0	$0	$0
Direct Labor	$51,272	$42,778	$367,900	$8,761	$7,709	$13,714	$2,841	$7,043
Other P/C Labor		$18,488	$106,004	$1,075	$2,290	$2,212	$1,059	$1,319
Corp. Overhead		$57,587	$476,339	$0	$0	$0	$0	$0
P/C Overhead		$0	$0	$1,174	$2,426	$2,153	$856	$863
P/C O/H Transfer		$0	$0	$865	($1,366)	$811	($1,139)	($250)
CADD Transfer		$0	$0	$1,843	$1,554	$2,690	$578	$1,529
Int@10%/Over 60 Recvs		$0	$0	$157	$1,000	$787	$364	$272
Corp. O/H Transfer		$0	$0	$11,476	$9,678	$16,753	$3,603	$9,523
TOT O/H (EXCL REIMB)		$118,853	$950,243	$25,352	$23,291	$39,120	$8,162	$20,299
PROFIT								
Gross Profit		$16,704	$242,435	$15,772	$8,960	$25,915	$10,525	$17,337
Profit	$15,784	$16,704	$242,435	$2,296	($3,272)	$5,685	$5,980	$6,013
P/C YTD PROFIT			$242,435	$21,858	$44,513	$106,360	$47,063	$22,641
P/C % - TOT YTD PROF			100.0%	9.0%	18.4%	43.9%	19.4%	9.3%
ANALYSIS								
Net Profit on Net	10.3%	12.0%	20.6%	6.4%	-19.0%	12.7%	45.1%	22.9%
Net Profit on Gross	0.0%	10.5%	17.5%	6.0%	-14.8%	10.5%	39.4%	22.1%
Current Multiplier	2.98	3.25	3.20	4.07	2.24	3.26	4.67	3.72
Breakeven Multiplier	2.67	2.86	2.54	3.81	2.66	2.85	2.57	2.87
Breakeven + 15%	3.07	3.29	2.92	4.38	3.06	3.27	2.95	3.30
Overhead Rate	160%	178%	158%	189%	202%	185%	187%	188%
Avg. Billing Rate	$42	$50	—	$57	$33	$47	$75	$54
Bill/Charge @$42/HR	129.8%	118.0%	--	135.4%	79.3%	111.6%	177.5%	127.4%
Direct Labor %	33.5%	30.8%	31.2%	24.6%	44.7%	30.7%	21.4%	26.9%

Figure 6-4 A typical monthly report from Bergmeyer Associates (for November 1986). Used with permission.

Managing partner, owner, or CEO	23% (This means that some firm CEOs are 0% chargeable and others resemble project managers and are chargeable as high as 75%.)
Principals	52%

BERGMEYER ASSOCIATES, INC. - MONTHLY SUMMARY - PAGE 2

STAFFING								
Backlog (Manweeks)								
Backlog Tech. Staff								
Tech. Staff	22			3	6	6	3	4
Total Staff	28							
Weeks In Month	4							

EFFICIENCY	GOALS	%	HOURS					
Total Hours ·	--	--	4586					
Chg Hrs/Tech Staff/Wk	--	31.88	--					
Chg Hrs/Tech Hrs	90.0%	91.9%	3053					
Chg Hrs/Total Hrs	70.0%	61.2%	2805	627	518	954	178	490
Staff O-H Hrs/Tot Hrs	6.0%	5.4%	248					
Admin Hrs/Total Hrs	18.0%	16.6%	761					
HVS Hours/Total Hours	10.0%	11.3%	520					
Promo Hours/Tot Hrs	3.0%	2.9%	131					
CADD Hours/Tot Hrs	2.0%	2.7%	122					

BALANCE SHEET	CURR MONTH	PREV MONTH	GOALS					
Cash	$104,558	$70,236	$41,717					
Accounts Receivable	$649,180	$658,719	$347,640	$69,444	$166,760	$214,266	$77,452	$97,307
Total Assets	$829,591	$820,051	$861,053					
Accounts Payable	$69,713	$73,092	--					
Total Liabilities ·	$345,865	$353,028	--					
Net Worth	$483,726	$467,023	--					

ACCOUNTS RECEIVABLE								
Accts Rec 0-60	$319,658	$350,261		$50,475	$46,261	$119,461	$33,618	$64,555
	49.2%	53.2%		72.7%	27.7%	55.8%	43.4%	66.3%
Accts Rec Over 60	$329,523	$308,458		$18,969	$120,499	$94,805	$43,834	$32,753
	50.8%	46.8%		27.3%	72.3%	44.2%	56.6%	33.7%
Avg Coll Period	111	110		68	153	101	110	113

Figure 6-4 Typical monthly report. *(continued)*

These ratios will differ for each firm. A principal may also be a project manager or marketing director. With that in mind, compare these ratios with those of your firm's utilization goals to see if they are realistic.

Here are some ways to increase utilization ratios:

1. Get more work. You'll have more available hours on which the employee may charge time against a project.
2. Cut back on overhead time and overhead staff. This means reducing the amount of time spent on marketing, general office activities, or office education and training,

in relation to the productive hours charged against the project.

3. Eliminate overhead staff entirely, that is, all accounting, secretarial, and other nonchargeable personnel.

4. Shorten schedules. Condense the amount of hours worked on a particular project. Have more people working more hours on the project to increase schedule performance. Doing so stimulates people to work in a greater capacity per hour.

5. Get principals involved in the projects. When the principal becomes entangled in overhead tasks, the utilization ratio can be very low.

6. Get your overhead staff to charge their time to a project. For example, when a secretary works on a set of meeting minutes, time should be charged to the project, instead of to the general office overhead.

7. Bring in some of the outside subcontract work. For instance, if your firm is an engineering firm that subcontracts survey work to others on an independent-contract basis, you may find the utilization rate of your staff can increase if you hire your own survey crews and keep them busy, with your engineers as supervisors of the survey crews.

8. Reduce the total number of hours being charged by all staff. Cut back from a five-day week to a four-day week, requiring staff to charge a bigger percentage of their time directly to projects. This is not an advisable way to cut back on overhead or increase utilization. It can decrease morale and cause some of the better people in your firm to leave.

Measure your staff utilization ratio with their cards, as shown in Figure 6-5.

Ratio of Accounts Receivable Turnover

The accounts receivable turnover formula measures the number of days from the time an invoice is sent to a client to the time it is paid. The average for design firms has, for years, hovered around 64 days from the time the invoice is received to the time it is paid. (See Fig. 6-6.) To determine this figure, total the accounts receivable turnover time for each invoice

---

Controlling Utilization Ratios through Time Cards

Use time cards to measure utilization ratios weekly or biweekly. It might be helpful to design your time cards with a *percentage-chargeable* entry in the lower right-hand corner. Explain to employees the formula for determining this ratio:

$$\frac{\text{Chargeable hours}}{\text{total hours}} = \text{utilization ratio}$$

Inform your employees of the target utilization ratio. Ask employees to be sure that a certain percentage of hours on the time cards are not only chargeable, but also billable. Communicate the utilization ratios to each staff member and negotiate them each year so each person knows their target ratio. This way you can control the salary expense of your firm, your biggest expense item.

The following page shows the time card of Pat Whitaker, principal of Interiors, Inc.:

Figure 6-5 (continued on next page)

and then find the average by dividing that figure by the number of invoices generated for that month. To determine an annual accounts receivable turnover rate, total the monthly accounts receivable averages and then divide by 12.

To reduce accounts receivable turnover, try collecting a portion of your fees in advance. This lowers your accounts receivable turnover, thus in effect "reducing" the number of days between the time you send out, and get paid for, an invoice. Some firms request a 10 percent retainer up front, to be applied to the last invoice. Still others, for small enough projects, request a substantial portion, if not the total fee, up front.

Another way to reduce accounts receivable is to adopt rigid collection procedures. Stop work when a client is in arrears. While this practice may seem harsh, it is the one way for the small firm to guarantee prompt payment. Obviously, judgment must be used on a project-by-project basis before stopping work, to assure that factors such as lost checks are not reasons for nonpayment.

Work-in-process Turnover

Unlike accounts receivables turnover, this is the measure of the number of days between when the work is done and when an

ISI
Interior Space Inc.

PHASES / PROJECT TYPE AND FUNCTION

I — INTERIORS
MO — OVERHEAD
1 — INITIAL ADMIN.
2 — PROGRAMMING
3 — SCHEMATIC DESIGN
4 — DESIGN DEVELOPMENT
5 — CONTRACT DOCUMENTS
6 — FURNITURE CONTRACT DOC.
7 — BIDDING
8 — CONTRACT ADMIN.
9 — CLOSE-OUT/FOLLOW-UP

NON-BILLABLE NUMBERS

GEN. OFFICE	00001	FAC. MGMT.	00007
VACATION	00002	ACCT.	00008
SICK TIME	00003	LIBRARY	00009
HOLIDAY	00004		
MARKETING	00005		
PROF. DEV.	00006		

NAME Whitmboe
NUMBER 01
PAY PERIOD 1st (1-15)

SEMI-MONTHLY TIME RECORD

6633 DELMAR
ST. LOUIS, MO. 63130

Figure 6-5 (continued)

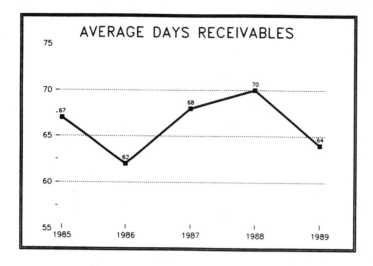

AVERAGE DAYS RECEIVABLES

Average collection periods have fluctuated between 60 and 70 days.

AVERAGE COLLECTION PERIOD (DAYS)

This key measure of a design firm's ability to turn project effort into cash continues to show that firms still suffer from slow collections. The median days of accounts receivable outstanding is currently 64. The current 64 day level is within the 60 to 70 day range found in all five years.

Figure 6-6   Average days receivables chart from the *PSMJ 1989 Financial Statistics Survey.*[1]

invoice is sent to a client. Aim for a work-in-process turnover of 10 days. This means that every 10 days invoices should be generated. To reduce the turnover to less than 10 days, your firm must be paid money in advance on all contracts. One firm has even achieved a negative work-in-process balance—by collecting fees in advance, it actually owes it clients money.

Accrual Profit and Loss

To determine accrual profit and loss, look at the amount of revenue generated versus the expenses generated. This differs from looking at the amount of revenue received versus expense paid, or the cash-basis profit. The basic difference with accrual and cash accounting is one of timing. The accrual basis measures money earned in a specific period; the cash basis measures fees collected.

Measuring profit/loss on a cash basis can be very inaccurate, since a design firm may plan to pay a bill one month, but postpone payment until two months later, thereby affecting the cash-basis profit simply by the timing of its payment of invoices. A firm can also accelerate or postpone the receipt of

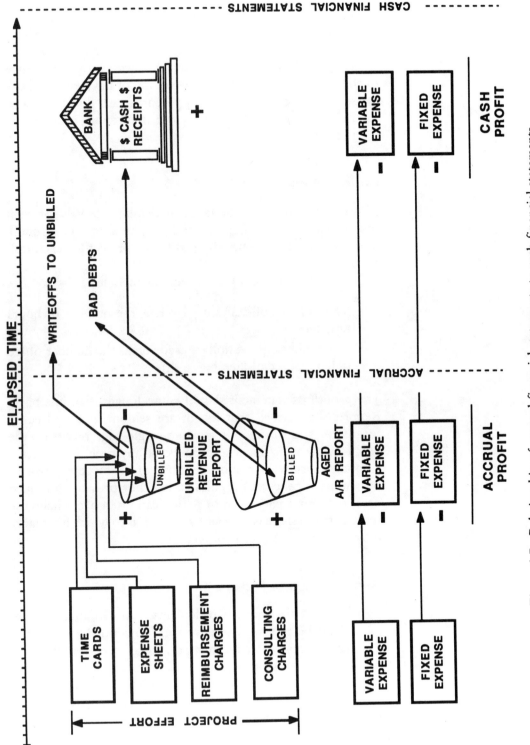

Figure 6-7 Relationship of accrual financial statements to cash financial statements.

195

funds from clients, pushing clients to pay or backing off. Accordingly, the accrual basis is more accurate in measuring the firm's actual performance. Figure 6-7 shows the relationship of accrual financial statements to the cash financial statements.

The accrual profit and loss statement shows the performance of the company regardless of the timing of payments and expenses. It is an early indicator of potential cash-flow problems. Figure 6-4, the monthly financial measures report, is calculated on an accrual basis.

Project Profitability

This key measure must be taken at regular intervals for each project. Analyze project profit and loss, looking very carefully at the specific man-hours charged to the project for each task at each phase of the job.

Simplified profit and loss statements include:

- The number of hours used versus the number of hours targeted.
- The number of fee dollars used versus the number of fee dollars targeted. (See Fig. 6-4.)

The profit/loss statement should be no longer than one page. Reports that exceed that length are seldom read and easily forgotten. You can readily attach a single-page report on the wall to view your financial progress at any time. If you use a computer format, remember that one of the biggest criticisms of computer-generated reports is that they provide too much data; page after page of information can often overwhelm the recipient, and there is frequently no clue as to which figures are most important. Keep it simple.

Get a Complete Picture

By measuring the above five elements, you will attain a complete financial picture that allows you to control your firm in the fastest, most effective manner. Bergmeyer found that a simplified one-page-per-month financial report consisting of these five key ratios, in addition to reading the best and worst of the project reports, was enough to help him manage the firm's operations. (See Fig. 6-4 for the sample monthly finance report.)

By looking at the key indicators, you can then ask critical questions about follow-up financial reporting. The next section further explains how to improve profitability.

PROFIT IS EVERYTHING

The yardstick of success in any operation is its profitability. Most of the 40 design firms examined for this book have a healthy respect for bottom-line profits. Clear, high-profit goals are the key to financial success.

Successful firms do not sacrifice profits to improve design. They build a profit ratio into the design budget. This section explains how to set profit goals and suggests ways to monitor and improve profits.

Goal setting for profit is twofold: the company's annual profit goal and the individual project profit goal.

Preparing the Company Profit Plan

Preparation of the profit plan begins at the annual planning meeting. As suggested in Chapter 1, you should hold a strategic planning meeting at least once a year, usually near the end of the fiscal year. Discuss economic forecasts and the general business climate. Establish guidelines for the principals to use in preparing the annual business plan. For example, you might set a profit goal of 20 percent pretax overall, with specific percentages for individual market segments.

The main point to remember is to *set profit goals high*, so your firm must stretch itself to reach them. As stated in Chapter 1, if you set your goal at 30 percent profit, and only achieve 22 percent, you are still producing more than twice the profit of the marginal firm which sets its profit at 9 percent (the average).

Other factors affecting your company profit are:

1. *Capital Expenditures (Rent Versus Buy Decisions).* It is generally less expensive for the small firm to rent equipment or other capital items. A small firm is typically stretched for capital, and buying a piece of real estate or even computer equipment requires an expenditure of funds that many small firms don't have. Furthermore, buying ties a firm to a particular direction, whereas rent-

ing or leasing allows a firm total flexibility, and thus adaptability to the marketplace.

2. *Investment in Other Ventures.* When a firm invests in another firm, it ties up resources that it could put into the development of its own resources, thus affecting profit. Therefore, the decision to invest in another venture—whether related or unrelated (i.e., real estate)—is a very important one.

3. *Estate Settlements with Deceased Owners.* Many small firms are strapped with heavy payments to the estates of the founders of a particular firm. The impact on profit can be significant; hence the way in which the buy/sell agreement is established is a critical factor as to the longevity and liability that the second set of owners will have to the initial founders of a particular company.

4. *Lease/Purchase Equipment.* Purchasing equipment ties up funds that might be better utilized to "grow" the firm; for example, the moneys might be spent on marketing and/or the pursuit of new projects. By leasing, you can avoid tie-up of funds and build in flexibility.

5. *Market Diversity.* When a market or firm is very diverse, it must expend funds in several different directions simultaneously. Accordingly, a firm focused on a niche or particular service has an advantage over the diverse firm.

6. *Economic Climate.* This greatly influences a firm's profitability. Some firms succeed in spite of themselves just by being in the "right place at the right time." Others fail even though well managed.

7. *Merger Versus Acquisitions.* A merger or acquisition can often enhance a firm's ability to market itself to a different group of clients, thereby improving profitability.

8. *Staff Turnover.* There are both positive and negative factors relating to staff turnover. A certain percentage of staff should turn over each year, allowing the elimination of people who are not performing to standard. Beware, though—too much staff turnover is negative. This may suggest that the firm cannot retain staff or perhaps that its employment policies are not in line with those of the competition. An average turnover of five to eight percent is acceptable.

9. *Branch Office Philosophy.* For firms with branch offices, branch office management will greatly affect profitabil-

ity. Firms that operate branch offices as profit centers (explained later in the text) generally make more profit than those that operate on a cost-center basis. This decision, however, must be made in light of the firm's culture; if a firm wishes to have a single company image in all its branches, then perhaps the cost-center method is best. If the firm, on the other hand, wishes to maintain multiple offices in competition with each other, then perhaps profit-center arrangement is more appropriate.

Once prepared, incorporate the profit goals into the strategic plan (see Chapter 1). Review profit goals at least monthly to measure your firm's financial standing. Compare budget to actual performance (found on the one-page key financial measures report, Fig. 6-4) and investigate variances.

Project Profit

Project profit, in general, is a reflection of your firm's overall profit plan. Goals are typically set by the principals. Decisions on whether to accept a greater or lesser profit goal are generally outside the jurisdiction of the project manager because he or she is often not a principal. The profit goal for a project is set in the negotiation stage and carries over into the budget.

At the negotiating stage, many decisions are made that impact how a project will be carried out. For example, if only $10,000 is allocated to a project, then the budget must reflect the fact that only $10,000 worth of team time is allocated. Many firms do not relate the budget to the actual fee negotiated in the project contract, thereby creating a problem before a project even starts. The project manager must match the scope of services, the budget, and the actual fee generated for each portion of the project. Otherwise, it is almost impossible to achieve the project's targeted profit goal.

Profitable projects result from several factors:

1. *The Right Market.* Some projects a firm should shun. The style of operation it takes to conduct the project profitably may be in direct conflict with the firm's style. For example, not all firms are able to produce government work profitably, even if the job is won.

2. *The Right Client.* Even within your company's natural market, some clients can lead to losses. Clients with too

large a project, too small a project, or unreasonable expectations are problems for firms seeking profits.

3. *The Right Price.* Through negotiation, a price must be
secured from clients that permits the firm to achieve its
profit goal and cover all costs. Specialty firms with limited markets typically must secure high margins.

4. *Control.* Control your projects so resources committed
are in line with the price you secure. Control means
planning and budgeting so that each scope task is assigned specific time guidelines, thus allowing for easy
measurement of actual versus planned results.

5. *Collection.* No project is profitable until fees are collected. Up to that time, profits are theoretical rather than
actual.

Overall, it takes a good project manager to implement each of
these.

IDENTIFY UNPROFITABLE PROJECTS

Reject projects that represent unacceptable risk. Here are reasons to turn down a project:

1. *The Project Is Too Small.* Every firm has its fee floor for
profitability. A fee floor is generally determined by calculating the firm's liability exposure versus the amount
of fee to be collected. Below this floor, the firm by its
nature cannot produce profits, as it will automatically
invest too many resources. Turn these projects over to
even smaller firms that will not compete with you on
larger projects from that client.

2. *The Project Is Too Large.* Any project that represents
more than 25 percent of a firm's annual gross is too risky.
Ask yourself whether, if that project is a failure, the
whole firm risks failing. Instead, consider participating in
a joint venture.

3. *The Project Is from the Wrong Client.* Don't accept work
from a client who is wrong for you, whether the reasons
involve financial instability, litigiousness, unreasonable
expectations, or personality conflict.

4. *The Project Involves Professional Liability Risk.* Certain
types of projects are high-risk. Asbestos-connected, haz-

ardous waste, rehab, and condominium projects may all carry high liability potential. Evaluate your risk before accepting such work by estimating your firm's capacity to defend a destructive lawsuit under each category of project being considered.

5. *The Project Calls for Expertise You Do Not Have.* Do not accept such work. You may be unable to meet your client's expectations and will probably subject yourself to unexpected costs, such as for research and payments to consultants.

IMPROVE PROJECT PROFITABILITY

Since your average 60 to 70 percent of a design firm's total payroll goes into project labor, how well each project is managed is the major determinant of a firm's profitability. Therefore, successful firms need to control, at least semimonthly, the man-hours needed to complete the work. And they need to assess continually the chances of overruns in time to prevent them. This section shows you how to measure profit by analyzing certain trends of the ratios presented in the previous section, "Key Financial Measures."

Note first that utilization is *not* the key to profitability. Each man-hour you charge to a client is not necessarily profitable just because of the multiplier used to establish billing rates. That man-hour, if it is in *excess* of the time that the project *should* have taken, encroaches on "the bottom line"—the contribution to overhead and profit of that project. So, in effect, that man-hour and its costs constitute a *loss*.

If that single man-hour overrun is, mistakenly, included in direct charges to projects, it distorts utilization. You will then agonize about how profitability could be so low when everyone is so busy working on projects.

Next look at the net effective multiplier and, rather than assume your profit problems are the fault of the competitiveness of the market or the reluctance of clients to pay enough for your services, look at the three most prominent red flags of project financial failure:

High work-in-process (i.e., not invoicing clients fast enough).

Low receivable turnover.

Low effective multipliers.

Work-in-process is a common hiding-place for overruns. It postpones the point at which the project manager discovers the project is incurring more man-hours than planned. It claims that an overrun, usually at billable rates, is an asset and not a loss because charged amounts are not yet written off, since invoicing has not occurred.

Low receivable turnover is the result of too much "work-in-process" and lax follow-up on collections. It is a symptom that the client is holding up payment on invoices that bill man-hours spent on project work performed so long ago that the client cannot remember the details. The invoice becomes suspect and you lose time proving it valid.

An *effective multiplier* is a multiple of direct labor salary paid to an individual which creates a fee per hour chargeable to a client. In general, the multiples charged for architects/engineers are in the range of 2.5 times the direct personnel expense. This is the amount paid per hour to the draftsman or designer, plus the cost of the fringe benefits paid to that person. This amount, combined with overhead and profit factors, equals the total multiplier or billing rate chargeable to the client. For example:

$$1.3 \text{ (pay rate + fringe)} \times 1.51 \text{ (overhead)} \times 1.22 \text{ (profit)}$$
$$= 2.4 \text{ (total multiplier)}$$

A low effective multiplier reveals these problems:

- The man-hour budget was established *after* the fee was agreed to.
- The man-hours needed were established as a percentage of the fee and ignored the time needed to get the work done.
- The work was planned before the fee was agreed, but the project manager failed to compute the average base man-hour cost of the project team or failed to use the firm's net effective multiplier goal when negotiating the fee. (In general, a project manager figures an average rate for the people on a given team and applies that average rate to the total number of hours to be performed on a job, thereby eliminating the necessity to produce a finite estimate of the cost involved.) This creates an acceptable effective average multiplier. If the project manager fails to compute to the correct average man-hour multiplier, this can reflect problems in project profitability.

- The project manager considered the man-hour budget padded, so he/she artificially cut the budget as a basis for fee negotiation. This was wrong—the budget was, if anything, set tight to get the job and improve the backlog.
- The principals felt the project important enough to obtain regardless of the man-hour budget.
- The project manager, with the fee already set, failed to assess the degree to which the working budget could be reduced to attain the net effective multiplier target.
- The project manager failed to provide, either to consultants or the client, a clear understanding of the scope needed to meet the client's expectations for the project.

All the above problems result in projects heading for a substandard net effective multiplier before the work is even begun. Overruns are unavoidable from the outset.

To avoid these problems, check the net effective multiplier on each project at least once a month. This helps focus principals' attention promptly on problem projects so they can be corrected. Such a review can reveal a host of other problems:

- Poor productivity.
- Untrained project team members who are not clear about the scope of work they are to perform or the work plan intended when the man-hour budget was established.
- Use of more highly paid people than needed or planned for.
- Failure to agree on the man-hour budget with those assigned to the work.
- Tendency to "goldplate"; that is, doing more than the standard of quality the client actually expects and agreed to in the contract. (See "Excess Perfection Syndrome" Fig. 3-7.)
- Internal rework to meet quality standards.
- Work performed gratuitously beyond the scope agreed to with the client.
- Rework caused when client or firm change their minds about the design or design criteria. The added work is then performed free or for a meager fee that lowers the net effective multiplier.
- An unrealistic semimonthly estimate of man-hours to complete the work.

- Failure to rebudget work packages or tasks included in the project as soon as the budget must be modified for any reason (in such cases, clearly document the reason for such budget changes).
- Too much staff on project teams or excess overtime when agreed schedules are in jeopardy.

High utilization and low overhead rates, though good indicators, will not guarantee high profitability. High overruns, on the other hand, assure poor profitability, and distort the accuracy of the other two measures of effectiveness because utilization looks good while bottom-line performance is being eroded.

Profit Analysis by Market

As mentioned earlier in this chapter (under "Key Financial Measures"), firms that operate in different markets should consider breaking down their profitability analysis into separate markets. For example, an architectural firm may design schools, industrial facilities, and office buildings. It makes sense to measure a firm's profitability in each area.

Do this by measuring the year's profit on each project. Subtotaling the profit for each market and comparing these subtotals to the firm's total profit can demonstrate each market's importance to the company. Relating each market's profit to the gross revenue from that market will, in addition, reveal its relative profit margin. (See Fig. 6-8.)

Measure your firm's profitability from different perspectives. With this kind of management information, firms can decide on their investment in marketing and future areas with growth potential.

These markets can be turned into separate profit centers and managed as such, by developing a monthly key financial measures report for each center. From the example in Figure 6-8, it is clear that housing versus office buildings have different measures of profitability. You can also break down market profits into more finite measures for each project:

Utilization rate,
Cost factors, and
Market share firm.

Relative Importance of a Market to the Firm								
	Office Bldgs.		Housing		Health Care		Total	
	Target	Actual	Targ.	Act.	Targ	Act.	Targ.	Act.
Revenue	$1.2M	$.9M	$.8M	$2.1M	$.5M	$.6M	$2.5M	$3.6M
Profit margin	$.4M	$.09M	$.2M	$1.05M	$.1M	$.2M	$.7M	$1.16M
Profit margin by %	33%	10%	25%	50%	20%	33%	29%	33%

Note that office buildings were targeted for the largest percentage of profitability (margin) at 33%, with housing only targeted for 25%, but that housing actually achieved a 50% margin. More importantly, housing generated more than two-thirds of the firm's total dollar amount of profits at $1.05M. Thus, while office buildings were originally planned to be more important to the firm, the yearly results revealed housing to be a more significant market.

Figure 6-8

This gives you an idea of how the firm is doing in each market, not just how the overall firm is doing. For instance, if you have three markets, two performing at 25 percent margin on gross, and one achieving only 5 percent margin on gross, you must define exactly why you stay in the lesser market when other markets are achieving better performance for you. Many small firms remain in lesser markets for long periods, dragging down their overall profitability, at the expense of entering other key markets in which bigger dollars might be earned.

One 27-person firm is organized into profit centers by building type. These profit centers are like small businesses and are fairly autonomous. They are responsible for managing themselves, negotiating contracts, hiring and firing their personnel, and making a profit. The umbrella firm is there to provide the overall goals, information to run the profit centers, marketing support, and other administrative functions.

This is a very effective approach as long as the principals make certain that the overall firmwide goals are being accomplished. Profit-center managers must not be allowed to get into situations where their individual goals or competition with other profit centers interferes with the firm's best interest. For example, preference should be given to sharing available work among profit centers when that is best for the firm as a whole, even if certain tasks might be accomplished outside at lower cost.

Resolution of this problem requires a balance between competition and collaboration. Part of this is accomplished through the compensation policy. The firm in Figure 6-8 believes in sharing profits (when there are profits) with all employees. At present, half of the profit is kept by the firm and the other half is distributed. The bonus distribution not only takes into account profit-center performance, but also recognition for achieving firmwide goals.

The firm in Figure 6-8 is moving toward an incentive management system where more and more of a person's salary is tied to performance and their value to the firm. They are looking for the incentives that motivate people, that can be measured, and that are correct for the firm. Such incentives might include rewards for being profitable in a profit center at the time profit is billed, recognition for design work when published, advancement based on client satisfaction, and prizes for innovative ideas.

NO-PAPER REPORTING

In the future, many firms will avoid paper entirely and instead use computer-interacted processing for all of their financial reporting. For example, CT Male & Associates of Albany, N.Y., already uses a completely interactive project management system that allows all employees to enter their time directly onto a computer time-card screen. As soon as each time card is complete, the computer updates all projects instantly, enabling management to generate an up-to-date time accounting status on each project. Such a system enhances the timing of invoicing, the reporting of information on the project, and the updating of that information for clients or the project team. If you are now planning to implement a computer-based time accounting system, plan to make it interactive instead of output-based and avoid all of the hassles associated with mountains of paper printouts. Figure 6-9 is another example of a firm that employs no-paper reporting.

No-paper systems eliminate the need for summarizing financial information at one accounting period every 30 days, which takes a significant amount of time and can cause delays and errors in project performance.

The potential for project profitability is higher in a no-paper environment than in a paper-medium environment because all aspects of financial reporting, invoice preparation, and project control are accelerated for the bimonthly time-card "cycle" to an instantaneous update process. For profitable firms of the 1990s, no-paper reporting will be the norm.

Example of Firm with No-paper Financial Reporting

Firm: Harris , Fritz, & Associates, Inc., Architects
Staff: 15
Specialty: Architecture, interiors
Address: 1850 Parkway Place
                 Suite 300
                 Marietta, Ga. 30667

According to firm principal Tony Fritz, the firm had a difficult problem managing the billing process. A switch to computerized project control software has reduced billing time by two-thirds while enhancing the payroll and project tracking functions.

The firm initially prepared its billing on a manual basis. All employees kept their time on bimonthly time sheets that were turned in for payroll as well as project-tracking purposes. These hours were calculated and manually multiplied by each person's billing rate. In addition, reimbursable expenses were kept manually. When the company was very small, this procedure worked well. As it grew and the number of projects increased, the firm had immediate problems.

Harris, Fritz, & Associates now operates its project control with a software package by the Harper Shuman Company. The package also offers a billing software that works with the project management control. The billing software was implemented during the second year of business. Fritz says the first few months were trying, but after that found it reduced billing time to one-third of the time it took with the manual system. In addition, reimbursable expenses are easier to track and the overall efficiency of the billing cycle has increased dramatically.

The measures this firm used to facilitate billing included:

1. Computerized billing.
2. Changing the billing cycle.
3. Use of standardized billing rates.
4. Use of three-part invoice format.
5. Strict deadlines for time sheets from employees.

Figure 6-9

SHARING FINANCIAL INFORMATION

Sharing financial information with staff improves morale and, indirectly, project control and cost control. This practice was encouraged in Chapter 1 and is reviewed here to stress its importance. Here are four suggestions for sharing financial information with employees:

1. *Publish a simple annual report* for employees that highlights the key financial results of the firm. This financial report need not show all of the detailed accounting and the general ledger, but should include general results of the operations.

2. *Make sure financial reporting is done on a regular basis* using the method explained earlier in this chapter, under "Key Financial Measures." Share these measures in a one-page report at least monthly with key persons in the firm. This ensures that all information is current and that all are abreast of the status of overhead, salaries, and project results. With this information, company managers can better adjust activities to actual financial circumstances. (See Fig. 6-4 for a sample monthly financial report.)

3. *Note that financial reporting does not normally include payroll reporting.* Payroll should be confidential.

4. You should *share with employees* such necessary information as project profitability, firmwide profitability, and overhead expense. (See Fig. 6-10 for the Henderson Group's position on information sharing.)

SUMMARY

Many operating managers in small firms see financial management as a great mystery. One reason is the trend of separating management into different functions as a business expands. The individual entrepreneur deals with the basic tools of financial management largely by instinct. But as the business expands, such a division of responsibility tends to obscure the financial overview.

Another problem is communication—some professional financial managers have wrapped themselves in the routines

---

Information Sharing Policy

Firm: The Henderson Group
Staff: 25
Specialty: Speculative properties and other diverse services
Address: 100 South Brentwood Boulevard
           St. Louis, Mo. 63105

Paul J. Henderson, principal of the Henderson Group, says open communication with employees is one of the hallmarks of his firm's success: "Information on contracts and project finances is available to everyone working on each project. They know what the budget is and are constantly updated on the status. In this way, profit responsibility starts 'in the trenches.'"

"In addition, company goals, problems, and opportunities, successes and occasional failures are shared so that everyone understands and appreciates his or her individual role in the firm's performance."

Figure 6-10

and language of accounting and failed to respond to the demands of a changing business. Small firm owners must arm themselves with a plan for financial action and must have a thorough understanding of how that plan can work for them, focusing their attention on each project's profitability while never losing sight of the entire firm's goal.

SUCCESS CHALLENGES

1. Look at your present financial reporting system. How long are the reports? How readable?
2. Review your current budgeting method—are you calculating your firm's revenue based on expected income or on staff size? If you are using a revenue approach, draw up a plan using a staff-size approach and compare the two.
3. Write up a one-sheet view of your firm's financial status—what are the key financial measures you use? Do you use such measures correctly?
4. Review your firm's time-card reporting system—could you benefit from a no-paper reporting system?

5. When was the last time you shared financial information with your staff? Set a date today to dispense financial information.

6. Does your firm view profit as the most important bottom line? How could you divide your firm into profit centers?

REFERENCES

1. Practice Management Associates, Ltd., 1989. *PSMJ 1989 Financial Statistics Survey*. Newton, Mass.

BIBLIOGRAPHY

Gordon G. Allen, September 1987. "Improving Project Profitability." *Professional Services Management Journal*, Vol. 14, No. 9.

Practice Management Associates, Ltd., 1986. *Financial Management Seminar Workbook*. Newton, Mass.

Frank Stasiowski, March 1987. "Profitable Projects." *Professional Services Management Journal*.

Frank Stasiowski, March 1987. "Wrong Projects." *Professional Services Management Journal*.

7 DO'S AND DON'TS OF SUCCESS

This chapter abstracts from the preceding material certain essential recommendations. These are presented in the form of a set of do's and don'ts. However, a strong word of caution applies. There are sometimes good reasons for *not* observing a "do," and for ignoring a "don't." These are clearly stated in each case, and it is up to the reader and his/her unique circumstances to make a reasonable decision.

There are some normally accepted "extras" (fancy offices, cars, etc.) that, contrary to popular belief, don't really affect your success or profitability as a design firm. You may rationalize that these items are the norm in design practice, but firms that follow the norm don't generally achieve success.

Most design firms in the marketplace are traditional firms doing traditional work. They have traditional marketing plans, follow traditional advice from books and seminars on the industry, achieve lower-than-normal profits, struggle with ownership transition, achieve mediocre levels of design, employ small numbers of lower-paid professionals, and struggle for years to maintain profitability, size, and a smooth flow of transition. The firms that stand out, however, reject the status quo; this is what distinguishes them from the mainstream. Later on, under the section called "Don'ts," this chapter lists and explains some of the traditionally, normally accepted "extras" that do not enhance business and, in fact, may work against you.

DO'S

I. Hire a Top Accountant

A good accountant is geared to improving your net worth and your bottom line, and is one of your most valuable resources in the marketplace. Each small firm entrepreneur needs someone with whom they can discuss and devise strategies to improve business performance. See Figure 7-1 for tips on hiring a good accountant and utilizing his or her services effectively. Figure 7-2 shows you how to evaluate your present accountant.

Obtaining and Utilizing a Good Accountant

1. Hire an accountant (or accounting firm) who understands the design business (a list can be obtained from the *Professional Services Management Journal*[1]), including its contracts and procedures, and who has worked for four or five other design businesses.

2. If you choose an accountant firm, choose one from which you can obtain principal involvement on your work. Just as your clients prefer you, as a principal, to be involved in their projects, you should request the same of your accountant firm.

3. Hire an accountant who is knowledgeable in both tax and business strategy. Don't hire an accountant who can only fill out your forms; hire someone who can be an advisor to you on business decisions so that he/she can act as a consultant to you.

4. The accountant should understand your tax situation and banking relationships within the local area. Most importantly, an accountant should be from your geographical region, and understand the nuances of specific banking regulations in your area.

5. Hire an accountant whose business is located nearby. If your accountant is one to two hours away, you won't seek their advice as often as you should.

6. The accountant should be willing to visit your firm at least once per quarter; this will help in gaining a true understanding of your project management procedures.

7. Make friends with your accountant. Having a personal relationship helps ensure that they are more concerned about the progress of your business. You don't want to be viewed as just another client.

8. Make sure the accountant/accounting firm is not overburdened with work to the extent that you get short shrift. Be certain their staff is competent, that they can handle your work expeditiously, and that they respond swiftly when you call.

Figure 7-1

Evaluating Your Present Accountant

Accountant's financial reports are not always effective. The following are some common problems:

- Expenses are listed in alphabetical order on the income statement instead of being categorized to provide organized statistical information.
- The accountant is not specific enough. An example of this is an expense listed as "Officer's Salaries," that is not broken down into direct and indirect components. By not being specific, your accountant may be revealing that he or she is not familiar with the A/E business.
- Bonuses are not separated from salaries. They are shown "below the line" as a non-operating expense. This makes bottom line profits meaningless as a measure of firmwide performance.
- Date is not organized into a format to enable you to differentiate between direct project cost and overhead, and to evaluate the effectiveness of project profits.

The reason for these problems is simple. Your accounting firm is using a "basic" format instead of one specifically suited to design firm accounting. In using this "basic" format, you may save a few dollars, but the results will not be effective in comparing with other firms in your profession.

One other way we can spot poor accounting firm performance is when the accountant assures us, "this method will absolutely keep us from an audit." While we do not recommend over aggressiveness in tax matters, using an audit-proof method is generally too conservative. Tax laws are subject to interpretation and/or multiple methods of reporting. Your accountant should be taking the most favorable action to save tax dollars, not just to avoid an audit.

Discuss your firm's individual needs with your present accountants. If they cannot meet your needs, seek other accountants. Remember, you pay them for meaningful information, tailored to your specific needs as a design firm.

Figure 7-2 Source: "Need A New Accountant?" *Professional Services Management Journal*, December 1984.

2. Hire the Best Staff

When you look at your employees, you may find a proportion who are less capable than yourself, who follow you, rather than leaders that inspire you to greatness. Learn from successful entrepreneurs such as Harvey McKay or Mark McCormack, read what they say, and look at the people they hire. They hire the best and put them in positions where they can excel. (See Chapter 4 on how to hire the best.)

3. Get Good Quality-control Advice

Don't allow disputes, lawsuits, or other items to sidetrack you or your firm from performing at top levels. By getting good quality-control advice, you can handle mistakes before they occur, instead of letting them get out of hand. See the section in Chapter 3 entitled "How to Set Up a Quality-control (QC) Program for the Small Design Office."

Start quality-control management in the initial formulation of the scope of services. Be certain quality control is thought of when writing/signing contracts so that everyone in the company understands the terms and the meanings of each contract item. Good quality control starts with project planning, including:

1. Clearly defining the scope of services.
2. Contracting so that the budget and schedule are integral parts of the contracts, clearly understandable to both the client and your team.

"Missing the boat" on quality control at the beginning of a project cannot be made up for in quality-control checking at the end of the project. Have a quality-control plan for technical aspects of the job: have standard details and procedures for putting together drawings in a similar and consistent manner. Use standards whenever possible. (See Chapter 3.)

4. Develop Your Own Contract

Many successful firms develop their own contracts. If you use a standard association contract, go through it clause by clause (for each project) with your legal counsel to make sure it reflects your project goals and echoes your business standards. Figure 7-3 contains an example of a customized contract. Standard contracts do include much necessary detail, but they are best used as guidelines to tailor your own contract. See Figure 7-4[2] for a delineation of profitable contract terms. However, many small firms do not have the resources to develop their own contracts. If you use standard association contracts, realize it takes each association 7 to 10 years to develop its own contract. Over this period of time, circumstances in the market are changing. While standard association contracts are not (and have not been for the last five years) used by the top 25

ARIZONA ENGINEERING CO.

CIVIL ENGINEERING · LAND SURVEYING · PLANNING

CHARLES WYATT DRYDEN, P. E. AND L.S. PRESIDENT
419 NORTH SAN FRANCISCO ST.· P. O. BOX 999
FLAGSTAFF, ARIZONA 86002 · (602) 774-7179

CLIENT:

_____   DATE: _____

_____   PROJECT NUMBER: _____

_____   OPEN FOR ACCEPTANCE UNTIL:

_____   _____

_____

Identification of Project:

_____

_____

_____

Scope of Services:

_____

_____

_____

_____

Payment for Basic Services:

_____

_____

Retainer Amount: _____

Payment for Additional Services:

_____

_____

Special Conditions:

_____

_____

_____

The terms and conditions on the reverse of this form are a part of this Agreement.

Submitted by: ARIZONA ENGINEERING COMPANY   Accepted for: _____

_____   Accepted by: _____
Charles W. Dryden, President   Please Type or Print Your Name

                                               Signature: _____

                                               Date: _____

CLIENT COPY

Figure 7-3 An example of a customized contract, from Arizona Engineering Company. Used with permisssion. *(Continued on next page)*

TERMS AND CONDITIONS

The Client agrees to furnish Arizona Engineering Company (the Firm) with full information as to the Client's requirements, including any special or extraordinary considerations for the Project. The Client agrees to inform the Firm of any special services which the Client needs and which the Client wants the Firm to perform. The Client agrees to make available to the Firm all pertinent existing data known to the Client.

It is the Client's responsibility to assure that the Firm will have access to the Project site for activities necessary for the performance of the services. The Firm will take precautions to minimize damage due to these activities, but the fee does not include the cost of restoration of any resulting damage.

The Client acknowledges that the Firm's opinion as to probable construction costs, if offered, does not guarantee that actual bids will not exceed the estimate.

If the fee arrangement is to be on an hourly basis, the rates shall be those that prevail at the time services are rendered. 1990 rates are as follows:

Principal	$125.00
Engineer (P.E.)	$ 65.00
Engineer (E.I.T.)	$ 55.00
Engineering Technician	$ 42.50
Clerical Services	$ 42.50
Survey Manager	$ 60.00
Survey Crew Chief	$ 50.00
Survey Technician	$ 30.00
2 Person Survey Crew	$ 80.00
3 Person Survey Crew	$110.00

Assignment of personnel to project tasks shall be at the discretion of the Firm. The Firm will charge time portal to portal for work done away from the Firm's office. If the Firm is asked to work outside normal business hours, the Firm will charge for such work at 1.5 times the scheduled rate. Services related to litigation or arbitration will be charged at 2.0 times the scheduled rate.

Reimbursable expenses are as follows:

Travel	$ .50/mile
Meals and Lodging	Actual Cost
Toll Telephone Charges	Actual Cost
Expedited Shipping	Actual Cost
Printing - Small Copies	$1.00/Sheet
- Large Copies	$2.50/Sheet

The Firm will bill the Client for services and reimbursable expenses, at the Firm's option, either upon completion of such services or on a monthly basis. It is mutually agreed that backup documentation will not be required for professional services or for reimbursable expenses. Retainers shall be credited on the final invoice. Payment is due and payable on presentation of invoices. The Client agreed to pay the Firm promptly upon receiving invoices for all services rendered under this agreement.

If the Firm has not received the Client's payment within 30 days of the invoice date the Firm may, without further notice to the Client, without waiving any claim or right against the Client, and without liability whatsoever to the Client, suspend services until the Firm has been paid in full all amounts due the Firm for services and expenses, including interest.

No interest will be charged if the Firm receives payment within 30 days after the Client is invoiced. Interest of 1.5% per month, compounded monthly, will begin accruing on the 31st day after the Client is invoiced. The amount of any payments received from the Client will be applied first to interest owed to the Firm, then to principal. The Client agrees to pay all interest charges which result from late payment of fees as additional charges not subject to any other fee limitations contained in this agreement.

The Client shall indemnify and hold harmless the Firm and all of the Firm's personnel from and against any and all claims, damages, losses and expenses (including reasonable attorney's fees) arising out of or resulting from the performance of these services, provided that any such claim, damage, loss or expense is caused in whole or in part by the negligent act, omission, and/or strict liability of the Client, anyone directly or indirectly employed by the Client (except this Firm), or anyone for whose acts any of them may be liable.

In recognition of the relative risks, rewards and benefits of the Project to both the Client and to the Firm, the risks have been allocated such that the Client agrees that, to the fullest extent permitted by law, the Firm's total liability to the Client for any and all injuries, claims, losses, expenses, damages or claim expenses arising out of this agreement from any cause or causes, shall not exceed ten times the fee or $50,000, whichever is less. Such causes include, but are not limited to the Firm's negligence, errors, omissions, strict liability, breach of contract or breach of warranty.

In the event that either party to this agreement institutes action to enforce the terms of this agreement, it is mutually agreed that the prevailing party shall be entitled to reasonable attorney's fees and expenses, in addition to any other awards pursuant to such action.

The Client acknowledges that all maps or plats, drawings, specifications, and other documents, prepared by the Firm in the course of the Firm's work under this agreement are instruments of professional service in respect of the Project. The Client agrees to hold harmless and indemnify the Firm against all damages, claims, and losses, including defense costs, arising out of any reuse of such documents without the Firm's written authorization.

The Firm makes no warranties to, third parties. Any person or party relying on documents prepared pursuant to this agreement without the written consent of the Firm does so at its own risk and without liability of the Firm.

The Firm's services will be performed in accordance with generally accepted engineering and surveying principles and practices. This warranty is in lieu of all other warranties, either express or implied.

The obligation to provide further services under this agreement may be terminated by either the Client or the Firm upon seven days' written notice in the event of substantial failure by the other party to perform in accordance with the terms of this agreement through no fault of the terminating party. This agreement may be terminated by the Client upon at least seven days' written notice to the Firm in the event that the Project is permanently abandoned. In the event of termination, the Client shall pay the Firm for all services rendered to the date of termination, including termination expenses.

This agreement constitutes the entire understanding between the Client and the Firm, and may only be modified by a written instrument signed by both the Client and the Firm. The effective date of the Firm's agreement with the Client will be the date the Firm receives a signed copy of this agreement. The Firm will accept the signed agreement as Notice to Proceed with the work.

Figure 7-3 A customized contract. *(continued)*

PSMJ

Professional Services Management Journal ■ Ten Midland Avenue ■ Newton, MA 02158

29 Terms To Include In A/E/P Contracts

OVER THE PAST 15 YEARS PSMJ PUBLISHERS HAVE observed design firms using various terms to improve their contracts with clients. While we do not provide legal services or advice, we share with you below, as an exclusive PSMJ subscriber benefit, 29 contract term ideas. Study these suggested terms and rewrite them to meet your own firm's specific circumstances. You may not get every one into your next contract, but each new one you add will improve your firm's approach to the "business of design." As always, check with your attorney before finalizing any contractual change.

1) Prepayment: "Upon acceptance of this contract by the client to provide professional design services, a prepayment of $___ will be required to initialize the project."

> *Explanation: Cover working capital obligation on the project. If the project will take three months or less to complete, request 100% of the fee up-front. If it will last longer, request a lesser percentage of the fee up-front, etc.*

2) Fee in Escrow: "Upon acceptance of this contract by the client to provide professional services, a deposit of $___ will be placed in an interest-bearing escrow account in the name of XYZ Associates. These funds, including interest, will be released to XYZ on _____, 1989, or upon completion of 75% of the work on this contract, whichever occurs first."

> *Explanation: Use this clause if you fail to get prepayment. It allows you to earn interest on funds which will eventually be paid.*

3) Job Cancellation Fee: "Because of potentially significant revenues from other projects foregone by XYZ Associates to take on this project, if this project is can-celled within X days of starting by the client, a cancellation fee of $___ will be immediately due and payable according to the following schedule: 0 to 30 days, $___; 31 to 60 days, $___, etc."

> *Explanation: In the event the project is cancelled, get the client's commitment to pay you for opportunities you lost by committing to work on his project. This cancellation fee will decrease the longer the project has run, as you should have earned a greater portion of expected revenues.*

4) Project Restart Fee: "Because of substantial costs incurred by XYZ Associates to stop and restart a project once it is under way, should this project's progress be halted at any time for 30 or more days by the client, for any reason, a project restart fee of $___ or 10% of the total fee earned to date, whichever is greater, will be due and payable immediately."

> *Explanation: The longer you work on a project, the longer it takes to get back up to speed after a stop. The longer the stoppage, the more potential for changes. Seek some compensation for events beyond your control.*

5) Construction Contingency: "A contingency fund of ___% [usually 3% to 5%] of the total estimated construction cost of this project will be established by the client. The purpose of this fund will be to pay for any ➤

Figure 7-4 Profitable contract terms, from *Professional Services Management Journal.*[2] *(continued on next page)*

unanticipated changes that occur during the course of the design and construction of the project."

Explanation: Insist the client secure extra funds in his initial financing to cover contingencies that may not be anticipated at the beginning of the project. The funds to cover these contingencies may not be easily secured down the road.

6) Automatic Escalator: "After ____, 1989, all fees and hourly rates quoted within this contract may increase by ___%, at the determination of the design firm, and may increase by ___% annually thereafter."

Explanation: Most firms put a clause in their contracts stating that after some date, "all fees will be subject to renegotiation." This is not the same as specifying a specific percentage increase. "Renegotiation" could result in decreased fees to the design firm.

7) Limit of Liability: "It is understood that any and all professional liabilities incurred by XYZ Associates throughout the course of rendering professional services on this project shall be limited to a maximum of the net fee received by XYZ Associates, not including reimbursable expenses and subconsultants, for all services rendered on the project."

Explanation: This is simply a more reasonable limit of liability than that of the total fee.

8) Late Penalty Schedule: "All invoices not paid promptly will be subject to an additional administrative fee according to the following schedule: 30 to 59 days overdue, $500.00; 60 to 89 days overdue, $750.00; etc."

Explanation: This clause will help you get paid faster. It may also bypass usury laws by not being referred to as an interest penalty.

9) Sample Invoice Format: "All invoices will be formatted as in the attached example provided in Appendix A."

Explanation: Define the invoicing procedure according to what is best for you as opposed to the client. This sets the stage for additional fees should the client want to vary from the "standard."

10) Certification Indemnification: "XYZ Associates will be totally indemnified on all certifications which are required to be signed on behalf of the client during the course of the project."

Explanation: Discourage requests for signing of certifications with their associated liability.

11) Certification Fees: "Understanding the significant liabilities incurred by XYZ Associates when signing certifications, a certification fee of $5,000 will be due and payable for the first certification required on this project, $4,000 for the second certification required, etc."

Explanation: If you must sign certifications, get compensated for the associated risk. The per-certification fee should decline with each additional certification required.

12) Limitation on Design Alternatives: "XYZ Associates will... [use one of the following 1. ...limit the number of design alternatives provided under this contract to three, 2. ...limit to ___ hours the time expended in design, or 3. ...stop developing project design...] by ____, 1989, upon which design will be considered complete."

Explanation: Make sure you're not designing all the way through the project, or if you do, get paid for the effort.

13) Premium for Client Team Member Reorientation: "There will be a client team member reorientation fee of $10,000 paid for each project team member from the client who is added or replaced prior to 25% completion of the project, $20,000 for each team member added or replaced prior to 50% completion, etc."

Explanation: New project team members in the client's office cost you time and money. Prepare for such a likelihood (and discourage when avoidable) by passing the cost to the client. The obvious downside to this clause is that the client may want you also to sign off rights to change team members.

14) Job Site Signage: "Because of its standing as a professional firm, XYZ Associates has complete authority over all content, graphics, and placement of all job site signs with the exception of those required

Figure 7-4 Profitable contract terms. *(continued)*

in the interest of maintaining worker safety and the security of the facility."

Explanation: *It is in your best interests to maintain control over project signs from the standpoint of maximizing marketing opportunities and maintaining your professional identity.*

15) Graphics Control: "Because of its standing as a professional design firm, XYZ Associates has complete control over the graphic content and presentation of all studies, reports, and other documents produced under this agreement."

Explanation: *Same as #14 above.*

16) Lien Provisions: "The client acknowledges that it has secured legal rights to the property upon which the project will be built or that such right will be secured by ____, 1989. The client further acknowledges that non-payment of fees owed under this agreement will result in a mechanics lien being placed on the property upon which the project is/will be located."

Explanation: *Even though most state statutes allow you to do this anyway, it never hurts to have it clearly spelled out in the contract.*

17) No Back-up for Reimbursables: "No back-up data or copies of bills will be provided for reimbursable expenses invoiced under this agreement. Should back-up data be requested, it will be provided for an administrative fee of $100 per monthly invoice requiring verification, plus $1.00 per copy of back-up data supplied."

Explanation: *Supplying back-up for reimbursable expenses takes time. The typical A/E/P firm doesn't have staff resources to squander on non-billable activities.*

18) No Exact Reimbursables: "The client will pay 15% of each total monthly invoice for professional services submitted by XYZ Associates as a reimbursable fee to cover all typical reimbursable expenses."

Explanation: *This clause greatly simplifies your accounting and saves money. It also eliminates the need to keep track of mountains of detailed back-up.*

19) Client Signatures at Various Stages in the Project: "Beginning with the date of project initiation, all drawings produced under this agreement will be signed by an authorized representative of the client each 60 days during the project."

Explanation: *Document any design changes mandated by the client. You will minimize future misunderstandings on client wants and needs. Notice that the above clause was written to provide signatures at a date, not a phase or percentage of completion. It's too easy to end up in an argument with your client over what defines or constitutes completion of a phase. Hence, PSMJ recommends never tying payment of fees to "phase completion."*

20) Ownership and Copyright of Documents: "All drawings and documents produced under the terms of this agreement are the property of XYZ Associates, and cannot be used for any reason other than to bid and construct the above-named project."

Explanation: *Documents used for other than their original purpose may result in liability to the original design professional.*

21) Fee for Prints After Five Years: "After five years from the date of project completion, or on ____, 1990, a document reproduction fee of $___ [typically $500 to $1000] per sheet will be charged."

Explanation: *The minute you bill the client for anything, it may have extended the applicable statute of limitations along with your potential liability. Seek compensation for this risk. Furthermore, unless a firm physically surveys a project on which it provides prints, it does not know what physical changes have been made after construction, rendering prints obsolete.*

22) Higher Fees Paid For Changes: "Any changes requested in the attached scope of services provided under this agreement will be billed at a multiplier of 1.25 times customary hourly billing rates."

Explanation: *Project changes mean a costly remobilization, a greater potential for errors and omissions, and disruption of other project schedules. Seek compensation at higher rates than normal.*

Figure 7-4 (continued on next page)

23) Stamp Only After Payment: "XYZ Associates will not stamp drawings produced for any phase of this project under the terms of this agreement until all invoices billed up to that point in the project have been paid in full."

Explanation: This is one more attempt to get paid expeditiously.

24) Stamp on Drawings: "XYZ Associates accepts no liability for any plans or specifications produced under this agreement until such drawings are stamped as approved by all relevant building department officials."

Explanation: This clause is used to help limit liability.

25) Contract Validity: "This contract is valid only if signed on or before ____, 1989, unless officially extended by both parties."

Explanation: Don't make open-ended commitments that you may not want or be able to live up to in the future. This clause also helps to define the time of project completion.

26) Free Publicity: "XYZ Associates has the right to photograph the above-named project and to use the photos in the promotion of the professional practice through advertising, public relations, brochures or other marketing materials. Should additional photos be needed in the future, the client agrees to provide reasonable access to the facility. The client also agrees to cite the name of XYZ Associates as the _____ designer in all publicity, presentations, and public relations activities which mention the name of the facility."

Explanation: This doesn't cost your client anything, yet can mean a great deal to you.

27) Third Party Legal Defense After a Specified Period of Time: "After September 1, 1995, any legal costs arising to defend third party claims made against the XYZ Associates in connection with the above-named project will be paid for in full by the client."

Explanation: If you are at fault, your errors would certainly have been discovered in five years of operating the facility, so why should you be bothered with third party claims that you obviously weren't responsible for?

28) Royalty Clause: "Acknowledging that XYZ Associates has significantly contributed to the long-term real value of the above-named project and property through the rendering of unique design services, a term will be added to the legal deed on the property by the client at time of closing providing XYZ Associates a royalty of $___ each and every time the property is sold subsequent to the initial closing for a period of 99 years."

Explanation: Since you create real value, you may be entitled to a share of the project's profits as it changes hands in future years. This must be written into the first deed on the property by the client at closing.

29) Hazardous Waste: "Any hazardous waste or asbestos required to be removed, encapsulated or otherwise contained during the course of this project will result in compensation to XYZ Associates equalling 3.0 times above normal customary hourly billing rates for any plans, specifications, or construction observation services provided. XYZ Associates will additionally be indemnified from any and all liability associated with the removal, encapsulation or containment of hazardous waste or asbestos."

Explanation: Discourage involvement with hazardous waste and asbestos, but get paid well if it is required by the client.

Figure 7-4 Profitable contract terms. *(continued)*

most profitable firms in the *PSMJ 1989 Financial Statistics Survey*[3] there are many instances in which using the standard association contract is better than using your own. To decide which type of contract is appropriate for you, consider the following:

1. If you cannot afford an attorney to review your contract, then use the standard association contract.

2. If your clients insist on standard association contracts, or require you to spend exorbitant amounts of time negotiating nonstandard items on your own contracts, then perhaps you should use the standard versions.

3. If your firm's primary goal is not profitability, and not liability protection, then perhaps it may be more equitable for you to use a standard association contract which is coordinated with all other aspects of the contract, including general conditions and other items.

4. If you cannot write your own contract terms or don't desire change, then by all means stay with the standard association contracts.

5. Although standard association contracts have a good history, are well recommended by liability companies, and serve a valid purpose in the marketplace, the most profitable firms have found that it is better to use standard association contracts as a *foundation* upon which to build, the goal being to create their own, better contract.

6. The standard association contract is a "vanilla pudding" contract because it must cover such a wide variety of circumstances; therefore, it cannot possibly relate to a particular firm as well as a customized contract.

7. If you are crossing out more than 20 percent of the paragraphs in a standard contract, then it may be time for you to consider developing your own contract.

5. Teach Selling to Every Project Manager

Make sales an integral part of your project managers' duties. Do not retain project managers who cannot bring in clients. Teach project managers selling tips for presentations. Some advice you can offer them follows:

1. Remain natural. Don't "dress up" extraordinarily for a presentation. Dress naturally and comfortably in a businesslike manner. A regular suit and tie is fine—don't go overboard and buy a special presentation suit.

2. Learn to "talk on your feet." Successful project managers practice public speaking. They go out into the community and become involved in the local chamber of commerce, business clubs, and so forth.

3. Learn to use the tools of presentation—flip charts or slides. Practice.

4. Don't overdo presentations by having too many people performing the actual presentation of material. A maximum of three other people should be involved. Bringing more people to the presentation requires tremendous coordination that can undermine the project manager's confidence level.

5. Collect as much data and research on a presentation as possible. Confidence is the key to selling and if a project manager collects all the data himself, he'll have more confidence in the use of that data in the presentation.

6. Focus on Service

Service is *the* key to success.

Clients remember bad service as well as good. Bad service can undermine any strategy you take in a professional design firm. See Chapter 3 for more detail.

7. Be Distinctively Different

Position your firm in a way that gives you a distinctive difference in the marketplace. See Chapter 3 for details.

8. Call Clients Regularly

Most successful firms have regular, established relationships with their clients. They are friends with them, and remember them after the project is done. Project managers should get very friendly with clients, to the point where they can genuinely call them friends. Obviously, a business relationship differs from a personal one. It's very seldom that a client friend is as close as a personal friend. However, the idea is to build very professional, yet personal friendships, open and honest relationships that will encourage or obligate the client to choose you as their design professional.

Build relationships with clients—there is no downside to getting too friendly.

9. Listen, Read, and *Think*

Successful design professionals listen carefully, read widely, and are infinitely curious about things outside of their environment and how they apply to the firm. For instance, many people only read the magazines directly related to their profession. Very successful design CEOs read novels and other publications totally unrelated to the design environment. For example, read books on leadership, such as *Iacocca*, or read about the new opportunities being created in Europe for U.S. firms, or the rise and fall of companies such as Drexel Burnham Lambert. Although such subjects are outside the architectural/engineering professions, they may prompt a CEO or successful firm owner to think about how his or her firm may react to various circumstances.

10. Welcome Change

"If it ain't broke, fix it." This is contrary to what most of us believe, but successful firms tend to fix things *before* they break. Most firms wait until after the fact. Successful firms, however, never accept the status quo. For example, if a set of slides or a particular contract has worked for three clients, most firms would decide to use them for the next three presentations; the successful firm would improve or change them.

11. Challenge the Norm—Relinquish Tradition

When everything seems normal, go outside the norm and challenge it in the marketplace. As in the example above involving the slides/contract, the successful firm challenges its strategy. Rethink *your* strategies to ensure that they keep your firm ahead of the rest. Welcome change, don't just create standard operating procedures. The asbestos market is a good example. When most people ran away out of the fear of liability, those that stayed analyzed the asbestos market, challenged traditional approaches, developed strategies, and dove in, looking at the positive side—the opportunity to be nearly alone in a niche.

12. Respect and Praise your Staff

Treat your staff as superiors or at least as equals, because they are important in building your small firm's reputation. See Chapter 5 for tips on how to motivate your staff.

DON'TS

1. Don't Have Partners

Many firms have partners. Partners are accepted as the norm in the design industry. However, some firms argue against partners. Their arguments include the point that a single partner drives the firm, keeping total control of the entity. This allows the firm to react and move quickly to capture new opportunities, instead of wasting time arguing about whether to pursue such a direction.

Most successful small firms have a limited number of partners. One small (35-person) interior firm in St. Louis had four partners requiring equal amounts of compensation and had struggled for years dealing with the four-partner environment; there were partner meetings every week, conflict between the partners, factions within the firm, and nonproductiveness that drove down the partnership earnings and the resulting profitability of the firm. Only when they eliminated two of the partners did the firm achieve its current level of 33 percent net profit.

This firm learned from experience that it needs only limited people to manage and make decisions. Too many opinions inevitably cause problems. Choose fewer partners and choose them wisely.

Figure 7-5 presents the disadvantages of partnerships. If you do have a partnership, see what you can do to improve it. Some tips to improve your partnership appear in Figure 7-6.

The Disadvantages of Partnerships

Regardless of their formal structure, as a single proprietorship, partnership, or corporation, most professional service firms operate internally as a partnership. Here are some limitations to this form of organization:

1. Because partnerships are a voluntary association of individuals, participants are likely to become oversolicitous of the feelings of their associates. Areas of disagreement are covered over rather than resolved. Unresolved issues can cause frustration to the point where one or more partners leave.

2. Partners may end up creating their own independent operations that may not work in unison or even harmony. Truly strong partnerships are not just an amalgamation of individual professional practices but a unified effort.

3. Because partnership relations are complex, there is a natural reluctance to admit new partners if that will result in complicating the ownership/operations environment: key employees may be lost if they see that final recognition of their value—partnership—is not open to them.

4. The partnership organization can lead to indecisive management. Partners are reluctant to act without complete consultation or even without unanimous agreement. Even minor policy decisions may be delayed unreasonably. The organization gives the appearance of either being indecisive or unaware of problems.

Given the drawbacks of a partnership-style organization, your firm can follow these steps to avoid its pitfalls:

1. Establish a strategic planning process that ensures that all partners are committed to the same goals and objectives. Emphasis is placed on resolving issues and disagreements by means of a common vision of your firm's future and each individual's participation in its achievement.

2. Management functions should be assigned to one individual with specific authority to act. He/she would make all but major policy-setting decisions, and thus allow the firm to take fast decisive action when necessary, without elaborate consultation requirements.

3. Income derived from partnership should be separated from income earned as an employee. Partners receive a fair and appropriate return on their investment as owners. They also receive, separately, compensation as a result of individual performance as employees. Partnership percentages are separate from job responsibility and titles.

4. When appropriate include those outside the partnership in decision making. Professionalize the management of the organization. For example, the board of directors in a corporate format can include those who can provide special expertise and flow of new ideas, without the major shareholders losing control of the organization.

5. Commit the partnership to making new partners as soon as they are recognized as capable and key to the success of the firm. Most professionals see equity positions as the final recognition of their achievements.

6. Provide a way for partners to phase out their participation as they approach retirement, or as they redirect their attention to other areas of endeavor.

The partnership style in the professions will survive for a considerable time. Recognize the weakness of that format and take steps necessary to ensure the organizations's survival.

Figure 7-5

Improve Your Partnership

Most design firm principals, like most married couples, never seek outside help to improve the way they work with each other. Even when they do not seek help, it's usually too late, but most often they never get help, even when their relationship is a major source of dissatisfaction.

Ask yourself if this quote could be from one of your partners:

> "I've got a fairly good idea about how to deal with problem employees, but that's not my biggest concern. What I'm wondering about is me and my partners. We hardly ever talk frankly about our own performance. Or even about how we're getting along with each other. We're not unhappy, but we're not happy either. We're successful, but we're not happy. And I don't think we're alone either. What can we do to deal with this kind of problem and maybe even improve the quality of our partnership?"

Let's say that you, like the person who posed this question, want to improve the quality of your relationship with your partners. What can you do? Here are some immediate suggestions:

1. Make the improvement of your relationship with your partners a top priority. Like a marriage, a partnership is a relationship between people. If any relationship is going to succeed, it takes work. Too many partners say they're going to improve relations, but never do. Like gardeners who plant the seeds but forget to tend the garden, they get out of it what they put into it: not very much.

What does "making a commitment to improve our partnership" really mean? Time, effort, and energy. It also means:

- accepting your partners as having a right to be different from you and not trying to make them be more like you
- being willing to sit down periodically and talk openly about your relationship with each other
- being able to listen to the other person's point of view, especially when it's different from your own thoughts and feelings, especially when there are problems
- taking responsibility for the contribution you're making to problems in the relationship, rather than blaming it all on the others
- being willing to look for solutions to problems that everyone can live with rather than trying to have it all your own way

Although the above sounds good in theory, almost everyone knows how hard it is to put into practice. That's why it's important to make a strong personal commitment right up front.

2. Personally reflect on your relationship with your partners. Each should think independently about the quality of the relationship between the partners, any problems that exist, and develop suggestions for making it a less frustrating and more satisfying partnership for everyone. Each should make these suggestions in writing so that important thoughts can be captured for later discussion. Use these questions to stimulate your thinking:

- What do you value in your partners?
- How have they helped the firm and enriched your life?
- What frustrates you about them?

Figure 7-6 *Source:* "Improve Your Partnership," by Marty Grothe and Peter Wylie, *Professional Services Management Journal,* Vol. 9, No. 11, November 1982.

- Have these frustrations gotten in the way of the firm's growth or your personal satisfaction?
- How has your relationship with your partners evolved over the years?
- How are problems between you and your partners dealt with—out in the open, too openly, under the table, or swept under the rug?
- What are some of the sensitive touchy subjects that should be talked about but never get mentioned?
- What topics have you ducked?
- What do you suppose your partners haven't mentioned to you?
- How are you and your partners viewed by other key people, like clients, junior partners (including those who have left the firm), and employees?

3. Get together with the partners to talk about improving the relationships. Spend at least one day in a quiet, secluded spot where there are no telephones and other distractions. Bring a flip chart to record main points.

Start by asking each person to focus some thought-provoking questions, like: "On a day to day basis, how satisfied or dissatisfied are you with your relationship with each of your partners?" "What are the major sources of frustration and dissatisfaction?" "What could we—your partners—do to make your life less frustrating and more satisfying?"

To ensure each person gets an opportunity to respond fully, apply the following ground rules:

- When the first person starts talking, everybody else should listen *attentively*. Particularly avoid such ineffective gestures as interrupting, rolling your eyes, or disregarding the ideas of the person who's talking.
- When the first person finishes talking, the rest should encourage him or her to say a little more, asking "What else would you like to add?" or "What you're saying is very interesting. Keep talking."
- When the first person finishes building on original remarks, the next person should be formally invited to begin speaking.

After each partner has responded to the first question, move on to the next question and go through the above process again.

4. By the time everyone responds to all of the questions, the group will have amassed an enormous amount of information. The important next step is to start working on a few things everyone can agree to even if they don't seem to be the most important things to you. Don't worry at this point if "touchy" subjects have not surfaced, or what to do about areas of disagreement. Get the group started working on joint efforts. More difficult projects can be tackled later, and some will even take care of themselves.
5. Ask for help if you need it. If you can't do what was suggested or you try and find that you couldn't do it on your own, don't be afraid to ask for outside help. Rather than see it as a failure, asking for help when it's needed is a sign of maturity and effectiveness.

There are many reasons to improve the quality of your relationship with partners, some of which have to do with things like productivity and profits. However, the most important reason is that you will get more satisfaction and fulfillment out of your working life, and speaking very personally as partners for many years, that's what it's all about.

Figure 7-6 *(continued)*

2. Don't Employ Family Members

Hire employees on the basis of ability, not relationships, especially familial ones. There is simply no room for this kind of special accommodation in a successful firm. The only exception to this axiom is when a family member has worked for 10 to 15 years outside the family business and returns with recognizable capability to take over the firm.

3. Don't Count on Working Only Forty Hours per Week

The principals of successful firms work an average of 65 hours per week according to the *Professional Services Management Journal*'s salary survey data.[1] Late hours, in most instances, is the way to push your profitability up and keep it there.

4. Don't Be Afraid of Liability

There was a dramatic upswing in liability insurance premiums in 1985–1986, and exorbitant rates have remained a problem for most design firms. In a continual search to avoid liability and reduce premiums, design professionals are eroding their level of control on many (if not all) design projects. The list of what we "don't do, don't supervise, don't inspect" is now longer than the list of what we really *do* for our clients.

Design professionals today are shackled with liability, but the fear of liability is creating more of a problem. In fact, most design professionals today are giving up control over projects out of fear of liability. For example, most do not "supervise," but "observe"; rather than "approve," they "review"; rather than "review," they "observe." All of these choice words presented by liability companies have backed design professionals into a position of fear, making them feel that anything they do is fraught with liability that could eradicate a small firm's resources in one fell swoop.

This mindset is so detrimental to design professionals that many are missing out on certain market segments. The "doors" to these markets are those left "open" to that minority of firms that are not so fearful of liability. In fact, successful firms have an almost innate lack of fear of liability. They pursue markets aggressively with a reasonably realistic view of their liability, but their decisions are neither shackled nor controlled by liability.

Two outstanding examples of firms that provide services outside the normal range of liability are The Scott Companies Architects Interiors Engineers, Inc. which guaranteed schedule and budget (Fig. 1-8), and the LEA Group (discussed near the end of Chapter 3), which guarantees its roofs will not leak for five years. Both firms are proactive with regard to the fear of liability. They suppress their fear in favor of obtaining a bigger market share.

Reexamine your firm's real value to clients, and grasp hold of those areas clients want you to control. Don't allow construction managers, program managers, contractors, attorneys, or other consultants to get paid for work you have become afraid to do, while you are held hostage by the real "cancer" of liability—your own fear of a claim.

Many successful firms challenge the current liability philosophy of avoiding high-risk work; they venture outside of the norm, and do things many firms may consider too chancy. There is a relationship between risk and profit, and the greater the risk, generally the greater the profitability. Seek to reduce liability through effective project management and contract terms. See the section on quality control in Chapter 3 for a program to reduce liability. To minimize liability through contract terms, one firm, Meehan Associates Architects (New Hampshire), made money providing nontraditional consulting, such as expert witness testimony. The firm agreed to give expert testimony only if the contract completely indemnified them of all liability. Figure 7-7 is a summary of liability exclusions.

5. Don't Develop a Bureaucracy/Keep "SOP" to a Minimum

Abhor procedures. Get away from paperwork and outlines. Find simple, straightforward ways to do things. Try to:

1. Develop performance standards.
2. Eliminate "office procedures."
3. Do away with written documentation, inter-office memos.
4. Call directly rather than send memos.

Summary of Liability Exclusions

Professional liability insurance policies don't cover every situation a design professional encounters; exclusions are always included. Always be aware of exclusions before signing your policy. Exclusions appear in insurance policies for two basic reasons:

- **They clarify that certain exposures are more appropriately covered under other types of policies.** Because of the broad language used in a professional liability policy, coverage found in worker's compensation and auto policies, for example, must be specifically excluded.
- **They exclude coverage for certain exposures that the underwriter doesn't intend to provide because:** it may be against public policy to do so; such coverage may require an additional premium; or the insurer may not be able to provide such coverage.

Some exclusions are negotiable, such as exclusions against joint ventures and design/build projects, but almost all others are not. So, even if you have insurance, you must know how to manage the risk created by exclusions. There are basically three ways to manage the risk:

1. Negotiate the client contract so that it's insurable.
2. Avoid the risk by walking away from the job.
3. Make adjustments to assume the cost of the risk yourself. For example, if you choose to participate in an uninsurable job, get a limitation of liability agreement.

Following are exclusions that are typically found in a professional liability policy:

- **Liability assumed by the A/E in a client agreement.** The intent of a professional liability policy is to cover liability arising from negligence, which is a uniform and relatively predictable type of liability exposure. Liability arising from contractual agreements, however, can be diverse and unpredictable.
- **Liability arising from services not customary to a design professional.** Premiums and coverages found in professional liability policies evolved in response to the familiar "bundle" of services performed by A/Es. Non-customary services can create significant claims not anticipated by the premiums charged.
- **Pollution and Asbestos.** These are major social and political problems confronting the entire nation, which result in an unstable situation for insurance underwriters who can't quantify and price the risks they represent.
- **Joint Ventures.** These risks vary widely as to the degree of professional liability hazard they pose, but can be added to a policy when adequate information is provided.
- **Design/Build.** Like joint ventures, these can vary widely in the hazards they pose, but coverage is usually available when underwriters receive specific information.

Be aware of these exclusions when you're reviewing your policy; this could save you a lot of time and money later.

Figure 7-7   Source: "Beware of Liability Exclusions," by James Atkins, *Professional Services Management Journal*, Vol. 16, No. 5, May 1989.

Minimize written standard operating procedures (SOP) to avoid overhead time being spent developing elaborate manuals that often are never used. Instead, replace them with performance standards that allow your staff to be totally creative in accomplishing what must be done. Performance-related standards are better than task- or procedure-related standards. They allow individuals to create their own methods to reach the stated result or goal; task-oriented standards are time- and space-consuming, and do not allow for personal creativity (which leads to better personal satisfaction).

Of course, there are certain SOPs that are necessary, such as a quality-control/quality-assurance system (QC/QA). For a QC/QA system, it is good to have standard checklists that set the goals for performance to be achieved, but do not outline the "procedures." Contract language is another area where firm standards should be developed. Such standards save time, assure consistency of approach, and permit people to learn by following the standards. In general, however, successful small firms keep SOP to a minimum.

6. Fire Nonperforming Employees

Have a low tolerance for nonperformance. Identify weak employees and dismiss them. (See the section in Chapter 4 entitled, "Fire Incompetents.") This does not mean that you do not take legal steps to document nonperformance. Put in writing any warnings, poor performance reviews, and the like well in advance of letting an employee go. Periodically assess the staff's performance and do not ignore nonperformance, hoping it will improve itself.

7. Don't Focus on Winning Design Awards

There is one amazing discovery in the *Professional Services Management Journal*'s research of highly successful design firms: *they don't receive many design awards*. Many profitable design firms are not well known for design by their peers. They do not seek peer design awards (some even abhor them), they don't pay for design awards, and they don't fund processes to pursue design awards. However, they do go after design awards given by their clients, such as the Urban Land Institute's Designer of the Year Award. The Institute is a client group of developers. Figure 7-8 contains a listing of some client design awards. Successful firms get many awards from their clients, but few from their peers. Figure 7-9 contains a profile of The Scott Companies Architects Interiors Engineers, Inc. and the opinions of its principal on the relationship of design awards to profitability.

8. Don't Join Only Peer Associations

Fourteen of the top 25 most profitable firms in the *PSMJ 1989 Financial Statistics Survey*[3] did not belong or encourage membership in any of their peer associations. This may seem contrary to the professional ethic, but many top firms simply do not support, belong or reimburse peer association membership. How can they be successful? The answer is simple and straightforward. *Their clients do not belong to the peer associa-*

Client Design Awards

American Association of Museums
American Concrete Institute
American Geological Institute
American Planning Association
American Plywood Association
American Public Works Association
American School and University Magazine
Associated General Contractors of America
Association of American Geographers
Canadian Institute of Mining and Metallurgy
Chain Store Age Executive Magazine
Chargers Publishing (restaurants and institutions)
Department of the Navy
Glass Association
Institute of Residential Marketing
National Association of Home Builders
Pacific Coast Builders Conference
Tocci Building Corporation
Tri-State Real Estate Journal

Figure 7-8

Profitability Versus "Awardability"

Firm: The Ray Scott Companies Architects Interiors Engineers, Inc.
Staff: 35
Specialty: Retail, health care, multiunit housing, educational facilities, and
            government work
Address: 601 S. Lake Destiny Road
            Suite 400
            Maitland, Fla. 32751

The Ray Scott Company traces its beginnings to 1984, when its principal, Ray Scott, left a partnership in Catalyst, a design-oriented firm, to start a service-oriented establishment of his own. Scott says the change of focus from design to service has increased profitability incredibly: "We were trying to design every project as an award-winning project. The result was most projects were over budget and over schedule . . . When you concentrate on design, you tend to eat up the fee. We won a lot of awards, but we didn't make a lot of money on the firm." Scott says clients were unhappy, and contractor relations strained, even adversarial. The bottom line is that Catalyst, after seven years in business, had a business worth of $150,000; it never broke $1 million in gross fees in any year Scott was a partner. The Ray Scott Company broke the $1 million mark their first year, and has increased its gross fees by $1 million every year since 1984. Their business value in 1989 was $2 million. "Service is the reason why" the firm has done so well, according to Scott, not design awards.

Figure 7-9

tions either. A client-dedicated company cares less about peer relationships and more about client relationships. Peer relationships amongst architects and engineers are high on the list of important items for most design professionals, but have little use as a tool to enhance firm profitability. If you are active in your peer associations, at least remember that you are not networking in this milieu. Seek membership in the groups your clients join.

9. Don't Have Fancy Offices

Amazingly, many architects and engineers spend considerable money on elaborate office environments to make sure that their office's image is better than their clients'. Having an office that makes an overwhelming impression on your client is not really necessary. Not surprisingly, the most successful firms have normal offices located in out-of-the-way places, thereby

Necessities Versus Extras

Necessities	Extras
1. Sturdy typewriters	1. Weekly birthday parties
2. Ample office supplies	2. Fresh flowers in conference or
3. Expert drafting services	reception areas
4. Clean environment	3. Catered lunches for principals
5. Proper lighting	4. Expensive parking spaces in
6. Clean restrooms	urban settings for principals
7. Access to private telephones	5. Private elevator in your building
8. Office privacy; doors that shut tight	6. Original artwork on walls
9. Adequate storage facilities: file space; closet space	7. Oriental rugs
10. Mailroom with accurate postage scales	8. Designer furniture
11. Ample packaging supplies	9. Latest contemporary drafting equipment
12. Accurate receiving department	10. Full kitchens
13. Clean, presentable reception area	11. China
	12. Outside coffee service
	13. Candy/vending food service
	14. Daily cleaning services for small tasks such as emptying wastebaskets
	15. Directed lighting where generalized lighting will do
	16. Designer curtains

Figure 7-10

reducing office expenses and cutting an overhead expense that is simply inelastic in poor economic times. Successful small firms have functional, clean offices, but they don't have first-class design-award-winning offices.

A list of an office's functional necessities versus unnecessary extras appears in Figure 7-10.

10. Don't Expect CADD to Improve Productivity by Itself

In many of the small firms, computer-aided drafting and design (CADD) often doesn't exist. They've found that they can hire outside experts, including independent contractors, specializing in CADD in a much faster way than they can by having their own CADD system. As many of us know, some firms have lost multiple thousands of dollars investing in CADD systems that were never used correctly and are now obsolete.

You must choose carefully how to use CADD within your environment. You may choose not to purchase your own equipment, not to have a CADD department, and not to have multiple people using CADD. CADD can in fact produce a higher level of profitability when you hire outside experts, such as contractors or other firms, than when you bring CADD in-house.

If you feel an in-house CADD system is the only way to keep up with recent technological advances, consider buying it for you and your designers, not for your draftsmen. The trend in the industry has been to assume that CADD will improve productivity, but whose? Perhaps its greatest use is at the design level, where its flexibility can lead to more innovative design with more choices for the client, in less time. There are a number of CADD consultants who can assist you in determining your firm's CADD needs. Just be careful not to go "whole hog" and buy an expensive system that no one will use. Take care to evaluate a system for all its advantages and disadvantages—the cheapest system may be outdated next year, but so might be the most expensive. Again, seek consultation from knowledgeable, and neutral, CADD professionals (not CADD salesmen). Consult the latest edition of the *Professional Services Management Journal CADD Application and User Survey*.[1]

11. Don't Impress Clients with Nice Toys

Most wealthy design professionals lead very ordinary lives. In fact, most drive Chevrolets. You won't find many Ferraris, Porches, and other luxury cars in the parking lots of firms achieving great profits. One successful design professional, in fact, tools around in a pickup truck. The point is, don't try to impress your clients with fancy toys; it is much more important to concentrate on cultivating client relationships.

SUMMARY

As a small business owner, you must determine what items are necessary to help your business thrive and must eliminate items that only create the illusion. Separate what you need from what you want. Keep what you need, and closely analyze those items that you want, to see if they are *really* going to help you succeed.

SUCCESS CHALLENGES

1. Are you thinking creatively about every aspect of your practice? Are you challenging each traditional item, or are you just doing it "the way it's always been done"?

2. Are you overspending on unnecessary items? Eliminate some luxuries, the savings from which could make the company more profitable.

3. Is your office location really necessary? Should you be in a less expensive office environment, rather than in the typical prestigious downtown office, trying to impress clients?

4. Are you challenging your staff to innovate and come up with new ways to cut costs? For example, would using CADD help cut costs?

5. Are you utilizing CADD systems in the most effective way by using them not only for drafters but for high-level designers?

6. Is new technology overwhelming you, or are you embracing it to stay ahead of the competition?

7. Are you continually seeking new ways to be more profitable, or do you follow traditional ways?

8. Develop five performance-oriented processes to replace five standard operating procedures.

9. Are you reading material that falls outside of your professional field? Are you listening to thinkers, actors, movers, and shakers in other fields and applying their strategies and tactics to your field?

REFERENCES

1. Published by Practice Management Associates, Ltd., Newton, Mass.
2. "Profitable Contract Terms." *Professional Services Management Journal*, Vol. 8, No. 12, December 1981.

3. Practice Management Associates, Ltd., 1989. *PSMJ 1989 Financial Statistics Survey*. Newton, Mass.

BIBLIOGRAPHY

Marty Grothe and Peter Wylie, November 1982. "Improve Your Partnership." *Professional Services Management Journal*, Vol. 9, No. 11.

"Need New Accountant?" *Professional Services Management Journal*, December 1984.

"Why Partnerships Fail." *Professional Services Management Journal*, December 1984.

8 GROWTH

Too many firms, in mapping out their long-range planning, get trapped into the cliche of growth. Many professionals feel that small firms will not survive if they do not grow. While there are merits to growth, this chapter addresses questions such as when you should grow and how quickly, and also points out the merits of the small organization that you risk losing by deciding to grow.

GROWING TOO FAST

Firms that grow too rapidly encounter difficulties. Growing too fast can wipe out the firm's financial ability because of the cost of financing normal work-in-process and accounts receivable growth. It can hurt compensation policies because lack of cash can cause delays in implementing raises or giving bonuses. Growing too fast can bring about quality-control problems that can eventually prove fatal to the company.

The opportunity for growth comes in every firm's life. The choice of whether to grow or not is critical for the small firm. In many cases, a firm cannot grow because it lacks sufficient resources—capital, people, talent—to attract the types of projects that will enhance its growth. Conversely, other firms grow without control, making it difficult to sustain profitability.

WHEN TO GROW

In considering growth, be sure your firm has the resources to handle expansion, particularly these three important elements:

1. The firm should have enough retained earnings to support growth in accounts receivables without having to borrow more than one-third of the total accounts receivables. If a firm is forced to borrow more than this amount, then the interest charges will detract from its profitability and thereby stymie the growth.
2. The firm should have enough available talent to enable growth. Firms often commit to growth only to find that they don't have enough design professionals to sustain it.
3. You should have a well-developed organizational plan. Growth without a well-defined organizational plan will result in chaos, which will undermine profitability and eventually cause a diminishing of firm size.

WAYS TO GROW

Here a few ideas on growth that go beyond the typical track of diversifying:

1. Grow geographically within a particular service or specialty. It's much easier to spread geographically than to diversify your services.
2. Grow through your clients. Allow clients to take you to different locales by taking on bigger projects further from the home office. Growth via clients allows you to establish a presence in other locales which can yield subsequent work in that area.

GROWTH RATE

Plan any expected growth rate carefully. Generally, growth in excess of 10 percent gross revenue per year will put significant strain on a firm. Growth is best controlled at 5 to 10 percent per year. When you grow more than 25 percent per year, there is significant pressure put upon the overall resources of the firm; capital is required to support receivables growth, new talent is needed, and interoffice relationships and management structure will change. Such significant growth could injure the firm rather than help it. Some firms, in fact, have grown to their detriment, only to find that they are either out of business, or are reducing significantly in size.

DEFINING YOUR GROWTH

Before planning any growth, be sure you understand what kind of growth you are looking for: staff size, dollar volume, or quality. Because of the perception in the past that growth is inevitable, many firms struggle with the issue.

Some firms have decided that growth in size has not been good for them, and have reduced their size while trying to retain or increase dollar volume. Many firms grow only by a percentage margin each year to cover cost-of-living increases for employees. After reading this chapter carefully, consider what is best for your vision and your firm.

STAGES OF GROWTH

Growing design firms pass through several stages. Each stage can be characterized by the activities of the firm's owner, principals, and managers. Determine where you are according to the following stages.

Stage 1

Most firms are started by one or two people who have secured a project. All the firm's energy is centered around the promotion of a single design service. The organization is an informal one in which all employees tend to be "jacks-of-all-trades" rather than specialists. The owner/founders are involved in design and carry out most of the activities within the firm, resulting in an intensive work effort to produce good service for the client.

Decisions are made quickly, and are based on an intimate knowledge of the firm and its people. There is little complexity because there are few projects, and clients are served well because there is time to meet their needs.

Stage 2

Because of the energy and enthusiasm displayed by the owner/founders, the firm begins to grow. Word of mouth sparks interest among other clients. A more structured organization and control procedures become necessary to keep track of operations. Specialized business expertise, such as financial and marketing management, becomes necessary.

When the firm reaches 20 to 30 people, the owner/founders are not able to be involved in the day-to-day supervision of each employee. When the staff grows to 40 members, business managers are brought in and tasks become specialized, with lines of communication formalized by monthly management procedures and reporting. Overhead starts to increase.

Stage 3

To maintain growth, authority must be shared with lower-level management. Project management systems are developed to encourage lower-level employees to become involved in the authority/responsibility chain and to take on client responsibilities.

At this stage, many design firm CEOs are unhappy as managers because they are removed from day-to-day work "on the boards" and are in professional management positions for which they are untrained. In this stage, increased specialization leads to further penetration of markets and the beginning of a defined image for the firm.

Stage 4

Strong departments are developed along with a project management system. Many managers lose sight of company goals, instead focusing on personal and departmental ambitions. Because the firm's corporate management is still "young" and has not fully "matured," the interpersonal relationships among managers are not dealt with expeditiously, resulting in lower morale. Consultants are hired to improve operations, personnel, and marketing management.

This stage is often the most traumatic because the CEO must decide whether professional, outside management is needed to help the firm grow.

Stage 5

Formalized long-range planning and budget procedures become the cornerstone of a design firm at this stage. The firm's future depends on a coordinated plan/direction, which requires input from a management team to achieve well-thought-out goals. There is a desire by many in top management to recreate an environment similar to that in Stage 1. Typical activities at this stage include the aforementioned long-range planning as well as market and financial planning.

As a design firm moves through the five growth stages, it can undergo a tremendous amount of stress, financial and otherwise; the firm's product—design—may suffer in the process. Many firms have gone bankrupt because they have grown too fast, while others have gone out of business because of the benefits that are lost with growth.

BENEFITS OF SMALL FIRMS

Take the following benefits of small firms into account when deciding whether or not to grow:

Flexibility. The larger a firm is, the more it is weighted down with high overhead and more rigid operating procedures. These procedures reduce the firm's ability to respond quickly to changing markets and technology. The classic example is a firm that forms a committee to study a decision that could have been made in a small firm in a matter of days, and it takes the committee several months.

Motivated Employees. Employees of small firms can see the relationship between the firm's success and their own contributions toward it. Every day they are directly involved: they work on projects, meet clients, and see the results of their efforts in the built environment. As a firm grows, however, employees may lose sight of the fact that their work contributes to the overall project. If this happens, employees lose personal interest in the success of the firm.

Creativity. Small firms are innovative in meeting market demands because of the close contact between marketing, design, and management personnel. As the firm grows, this contact is lost and with it goes much of the company's competitive, creative edge. When was the last time your firm had a design review in which the entire team was present to critique a project?

Ease of Decision Making. Growth dictates that top management becomes more and more removed from day-to-day operations "on the boards." Information must be formalized through reports and procedures, and channels of communication become cluttered with paper. As top management becomes less familiar with many of the firm's activities, it is less able to interpret information that is received. Thus, decisions may not be made quickly or correctly. As a result, the perception of those in the marketplace may be that the quality of your work is slipping.

Effective Management. Young, aggressive design professionals who start up new firms are able to manage one or two projects effectively. However, as a firm grows, demands for improved sophistication in management capability increase exponentially. Design professionals are not equipped in most cases to meet the demands of high-level management placed upon them by the growth of their own practices.

SUMMARY

As a firm grows, most entrepreneurial managers may not really wish to create a large organization. Since large organizations have bureaucratic environments, aggressive, independent design professionals may look back wistfully at their once-small, intimate firm that let them express their creativity.

If your firm struggles with the issue of growth, consider the five stages outlined above and learn from other firms' mistakes. Long-range, financial, and marketing planning are not the exclusive domains of large firms. Even small firms should structure a long-range plan that includes effective marketing and financial strategies. (See Chapter 1.)

Nowhere is it written that you must grow if you have a long-range plan; however, it is written here that you will *not* grow appropriately without one. Choose how you want to grow, and then formulate a long-range plan to accommodate a 10 percent growth rate per year. This will ensure slow, steady growth in size, gross revenue, or quality.

SUCCESS CHALLENGES

1. Consider your company size. How big (or small) would you like your firm to be? Set up a planning meeting to discuss how to reach and maintain that goal.

2. Can your staff be motivated to perform more work, work more hours, or use time more efficiently to increase firm profits? Consider sharing profits with employees to motivate them toward higher productivity and revenue growth without a growth in firm size.

3. Make a list of the reasons why you started (or joined) your small firm. If the firm grows, how many of these attributes will be lost?

4. Could you expand your services to a larger geographical area? Consult marketing professionals and references that will help you put together a geographic expansion plan. Set a date today to discuss these plans with key people.

BIBLIOGRAPHY

"Staying Small Successfully." Insert to the *Professional Services Management Journal*, 1988.

9 THE PSYCHOLOGY OF WINNING

When analyzing professional sports, there are easily identifiable traits of winning coaches and players. In football, consider Mike Ditka's fiery stance on the field of play, his drive toward winning at every opportunity, and his intolerance for lack of performance. One can easily identify the "psychology of winning" in the sports arena. Design firm principals must also have such a desire to win. They must have an internal focus bent on challenging each and every competitor in the marketplace and on succeeding at all costs. This psychology is identified in all successful small firms. There is inevitably this difference between those principals headed toward success and those doomed to failure or mediocrity.

Successful firm principals often disdain generalizations on how to approach the design practice. Instead, they focus on a winning attitude and position their firms such that they wipe out all competitors.

A *Professional Services Management Journal*[1] survey of 25 firm principals, all of them successful small business entrepreneurs in first-generation firms, showed that a critical trait was the entrepreneur's struggle between *self* and *company*. In a successful firm, that struggle translates into the principal's conflict between his/her role as guru and the role of chief. This seemingly small concern is in fact a key ingredient of the successful organizations which were examined in doing the research for this book. In the star-focused firms, the principal passes up the traditional management organization in favor of becoming a star, with every part of the firm supporting the march to stardom.

Principals of fledgling firms often have not yet decided whether to build a managed organization or be the star. This is the worst possible scenario. When the chief vacillates between building an organization with multiple partners on one hand, and becoming a guru on the other, there are constant changes in policy and operations. Choose one or the other.

Both types of firms can be successful. Also, there are some variations; for example, the principal does not have to be the guru; he/she might position two or three project managers in such roles and instead control the design firm's day-to-day operations. On the other hand, star-focused firms have one high profile star, with day-to-day management handled by others.

If you are a small firm entrepreneur, examine your role within your firm. Check off a yes or no answer to these questions. Have you decided that:

You don't want any partners?
Yours will be the name on the door?
The organization will always be under your control?
You must be involved in every design?
Your financial system must be under your own control?
Your presence in every client presentation is essential?

If you have answered yes to these questions, then you are clearly the control-directed guru in your small firm. If, however, you have decided that:

You want your firm to have many partners,
You will develop operational procedures,
You want detailed multipage contracts, and
You want well-trained project managers,

then your focus is on management of your internal operation.

Guru firms are externally focused—on their clients. Operationally centered firms are internally focused on their management procedures. This is revealing when it comes to measuring success. A small, focused guru-centered firm has a better chance of success than a small internally focused firm. For the small firm that wishes to stay small, adding partners and striving for an internal organization tend to take the place of a client-directed organization. The drawback of guru firms, of course, is that they usually have no transition plan. Internally focused firms can be relatively successful and have great transition plans.

OWNERSHIP TRANSITION

Design professionals tend to burden themselves by dwelling on the fact that they must transfer ownership to someone else, often over a 15-year period. Normal design firms overplan transitions, and the years of planning and commitment of finances that go into planning ownership transition yield little actual transition relative to their cost.

Firms that are highly successful concentrate on the leader in the firm, and the leader does not engage in transition planning. As stated in Chapter 1, it is important to determine whether to have a leadership transition plan, or not. Do not waste years and money struggling with this decision. Perhaps you'll decide to make the decision in 10 year's time—even that's a decision. Whatever your preference, come to terms with it immediately. Doing so allows you to refocus your energy on performing better for clients rather than wasting it on this potentially overwhelming distraction.

COMPETING WITH YOUR PEERS

Several traits stand out among successful small firm entrepreneurs. One of the most important is knowing how to compete with peers. Here are six ways that will help you do this:

1. *Demand Excellence.* There is no substitute for doing a good job and the time that it requires. Establish a standard of excellence by implementing a comprehensive quality-control system. Be sure communication is clear at the start of a project to ensure that both your firm and the client understand the scope of work they'll be getting for the agreed price.

2. *Ignore Jealousy.* Jealousy can be an undermining force for the successful entrepreneur. Focus on achieving project success, not on just "doing it better" than competitors.

3. *Watch Your Back.* When you get to the top, others try to knock you down. Watch out so you are sure that your

staff, marketplace, ideas, or processes are not being stolen (or even in the case of the last two, cheapened) by a competitor.

4. *Think Ahead.* Think of the product life cycle, strive for new ways to satisfy your clients, and be one step ahead.

5. *Share.* Be a professional. Share nonproprietary information with your peers, and they will do the same, to the benefit of both of you.

6. *Pride.* In interacting with your peers, strength does not necessarily mean being hostile, it simply means having pride in your worth.

A FINAL WORD

Much of the advice on success in this book may have appeared to be bold and sweeping. Obviously, no one firm is going to fit the exact profile this book suggests. Suggestions for success were taken from many diverse firms and should be understood in that light. Remember, however, that these concepts, if applied, will make the difference in your firm. A firm needs to have a directed leader, focused on a vision, who puts his or her energy into seeing that visions come true.

The small firm of such a driven leader, who steers its focus toward a particular market, has a higher probability of succeeding than the typical small firm, which is struggling to forge a reputation and is accepting any and all types of projects, at varied pricing arrangements and contract terms.

This book has attempted to establish some criteria against which to measure your firm's success. Profitability is the one criteria that is most readily understood and that is why it is amply used. Profitable firms are directed, focused, and driven by creative leaders. Examine your own firm's strategies and compare them to the strategies suggested here. Consider the success challenges at the end of each chapter to assess whether or not you have the leadership you need to go forward and make the changes necessary for your firm to succeed. Obviously, there is no guarantee for sustained success in any firm. Outside factors, such as market changes or leadership transitions, can undermine the success of any firm.

Do not let this book's definition be the only definition of success. Your small firm can be considered successful if it measures up to your own criteria for success. You can increase the probability of your success by sitting down and starting with the first suggestion in this book. Write out a one-sentence vision upon which to build your strategic plan. Armed with a mission, you need only summon up the passion—the psychology of success—to carry it out.

SUCCESS CHALLENGES

1. Is your staff sharing information among themselves in a consistent, focused direction?
2. Is your firm strong enough to turn away work that does not coincide with its market and strategic business plans?
3. Have you decided whether to have a leadership transition plan or not? Does everyone in the firm know your criteria for "becoming a leader"?
4. Is your firm's purpose clearly understood by all parties in the firm? Are you reinforcing that purpose daily with your actions?
5. Are you becoming a better leader through continued training?
6. Are you going to, with the help of the first chapter, write your small firm strategic plan?

REFERENCE

1. Published by Practice Management Associates, Ltd. Newton, Mass.

A MANAGEMENT AND MARKETING CONSULTANT LIST

Each year since 1975 we have compiled a list of management and marketing consultants who specialize in serving architects, consulting engineers, planners, and other design professionals. To make the list, a firm must demonstrate to us that they have broad experience in solving the unique management problems of these "non-widget-making" firms.

The list is divided into All Phases of Management, Comprehensive Marketing, Public Relations/Marketing Communications, Financial Management, Human Resources, Executive Recruiting and Quality Management/QA/QC Services.

If you need a management consultant, we recommend that you approach only those few who will be able to help solve your problem. You should not send a canned letter to everyone on the list—that wastes your time and theirs.

If you need recommendations, contact PSMJ and A/E Marketing Journal Publisher Frank Stasiowski, Ten Midland Ave., Newton, MA 02158, 617/965-0055.

A. ALL PHASES OF MANAGEMENT

A/E RESOURCES–develops and implements practical solutions in the areas of operations management, project financial management, firmwide financial management, ownership expansion and transition acquisitions and mergers. Contact Richard D. Pipkin, A/E Resources, 116 New Montgomery Street, Suite 506, San Francisco, CA 94105, 415/957-1956.

THE ARCHINOMICS GROUP–is a management consulting firm offering real estate, project management and development advisory services to the corporate real estate and construction industries, and their related professional and financial service firms. Our clients include Fortune 500, law firms, public entities, and developers, both nationally and internationally. Our expertise is development-related problem-solving. Contact F.R. Rick Duran, The Archinomics Group, Inc., 342 Forest Street, Suite 300, Winnetka, IL 60093, 312/446-5328.

AUTOMATION INTEGRATORS–technical and management consulting firm assisting professionals in the A/E industry with planning, selection, organization, programming, personnel, and optimization of minis, micros and CADD. Contact Timothy C. O'Connor, P.E., Automation Integrators, 30100 Telegraph Road, Suite 478, Birmingham, MI 48010, 313/644-8870.

LLOYD BAKAN CONSULTANTS–internationally recognized organization provides marketing, management and public relations services, including planning, programming and implementation strategies specifically orientated to the singular needs of each client. Contact Lloyd Bakan, Lloyd Bakan Consultants, 13400 Maxella Avenue, Suite F-250, Marina Del Rey, CA 90292, 213/822-0681.

BARLOW ASSOCIATES, INC.–20 years consulting exclusively to design professionals. More than 500 clients in North America. Services include: seminars, organizational studies, profit improvement, financial/project management, mergers/acquisitions, ownership transfer, etc. Contact Ken Barlow, Barlow Associates, Inc., 701 Evans Ave., 4th Floor, Etobicoke, ON, Canada M9C 1A3, 416/626-8000 or FAX 416/626-0876.

BARNES AND BRANDT, INC.–believes in a balance between creativity and effective business practice in the design community and seeks to assist in the areas of Marketing, Management and Executive Search. We are results-oriented and offer consulting services with the goals of improved communication, expanded markets, higher visibility, greater efficiency, and increased profitability for our clients. Contact Diane Barnes, Barnes and Brandt, Inc., 53rd at Third, 885 Third Avenue, New York, NY 10022-4802, 212/230-3235.

C. WAYNE BEACHUM & ASSOCIATES–18 years serving design professionals exclusively. Practice includes: ownership transition, marketing, comprehensive management audits, profit improvement, organizational development, project management systems, financial planning, budgeting and incentive compensation plans. Contact Wayne Beachum, C. Wayne Beachum & Associates, P.O. Box 25723, Charlotte, NC 28212, 704/567-1116.

CAMERON ASSOCIATES–evaluates strengths/weaknesses, analyzes options and develops strategies, including mergers or acquisitions, restructuring, recruitment. Leads strategic and operational planning sessions. Acts as intermediary with merger partners. Contact Mark A. Cameron, Cameron Associates, 55 New Montgomery Street, Suite 800, San Francisco, CA 94105, 415/543-8980.

THE CONSULTANT COLLABORATIVE–specializes in ownership and senior management: teambuilding; goal setting; ownership transition; business development; strategy; organizational planning; management retreats; control systems; structure; compensation; and professional motivation and development. Contact Chip Clitheroe, The Consultant Collaborative, 18862 Arbutus Street, Fountain Valley, CA 92708, 714/964-2117.

CONSULTANT MANAGEMENT SERVICES, INC.–advice in the areas of strategic planning, marketing, pricing, human resources management and development, organization design and structure, employee attitude surveys, in-house management training, market research, ownership transition, merger/acquisition analysis. Consults strictly to A/E firms of all sizes. Contact Nora Lea Reefe, Consultant Management Services, Inc., 5445 Mariner St., Suite 210, Tampa, FL 33609, 813/286-0859.

THE COXE GROUP–comprehensive firm that has served design professionals for over 20 years. Eleven principal consultants specialize in general management, marketing, ownership transition, merger and acquisition, financial planning, organization and development, CADD, and executive search. Contact Nina Hartung, The Coxe Group, 2 Mellon Bank Center, Philadelphia, PA 19102, 215/561-2020.

EDGAR, DUNN & CONOVER, INC.–provides general management consultant assistance in the areas of organization, business planning, profits improvement, marketing, finance/accounting, compensation and merger/acquisitions. Contact James M. Edgar, Edgar, Dunn & Conover, Inc., 847 Sansome St., San Francisco, CA 94111, 415/397-5858.

EDWARD DAVIS & COMPANY–provides assistance in broad spectrum of A/E management issues. Twenty-nine years experience in actual practice in ENR top 100 firm, five as Chief Operating Officer. Contact Edward Davis, Edward Davis & Company, 1003 Wirt Road, Suite 112, Houston, TX 77055, 713/973-2535.

ENION ASSOCIATES, INC.–30 years serving design professionals; comprehensive management studies include: organization structure, project management, personnel assessment, financial systems, compensation, marketing, ownership transition, strategic planning, and executive recruiting. Contact Dick Enion, Enion Associates, Inc., P.O. Box 185, Swarthmore, PA 19081, 215/566-7550.

FLYNN-HEAPES CONSULTING–specializing in strategic planning for A/Es. Serves firms seeking greater control, including those in accelerated growth modes, tough economies, and ownership transition. Planning covers five strategic arenas and emphasizes action. Contact Ellen Flynn-Heapes, Flynn-Heapes Consulting, 37 E. Linden Street, Alexandria, VA 22301, 703/549-4019.

GAIO–(includes Bids, Inc., G.A.L., and The C.G. Evergreen Co.) provides comprehensive specialized services staffed by related experienced professionals. Focus groups: management/financial, marketing/sales, communications, training, development, research/analysis. Assistance provided 2000 A-E-P-I-C firms since 1970. Contact Raymond L. Gaio, AIA, President/CEO, GAIO, 530 S. Hauser Blvd., Los Angeles, CA 90036, 213/934-4525.

HALL & COMPANY–has worked with over 100 A/E firms nationwide in implementing ownership transfer plans, self-insurance plans, mergers and acquisitions and accounting systems installations. Contact Michael Hall, Hall & Company,

1910 Fairview Avenue East, Seattle, WA 98102, 206/726-1500.

HENSEY ASSOCIATES–Mel and Carol Hensey have been serving engineering and technical firms and agencies since 1974, with problem-solving in: effectiveness, organization, profitability, planning, management and people. Contact Carol Hensey, Hensey Associates, 8776 Long Lane, Cincinnati, OH 45231, 513/931-0414.

HOYLES ASSOCIATES, INC.–national practice exclusively serving A/E/Ps since 1976: strategic planning, organizational structure, ownership transition, business plan development, finance/accounting, marketing plans/surveys, technical operations/project management. Contact Bud Hoyles, Hoyles Associates, Inc., 810 Peace Portal Way, Suite 175, P.O. Box F-195, Blaine, WA 98230, 604/538-2326.

IMPACT-MANAGEMENT SYSTEMS, INC.–provides consulting and training services including team building, corporate planning, goal setting and management development primary focus in the Denver metropolitan area. Contact David L. Feasby, 2150 W. 29th Avenue, Suite 500, Denver, CO 80211, 303/458-5022.

ARTHUR D. LITTLE, INC.–international management and technology consulting firm established in 1886. Assistance in all aspects of design firm management strategy, acquisition/divestiture, marketing, finance, ownership transition, and organizational issues. Contact Marc Rubin, Arthur D. Little, Inc., 20 Acorn Park, Cambridge, MA 02140, 617/864-5770.

WILLIAM J. MAGER, CERTIFIED MANAGEMENT CONSULTANT–26 years experience serving the design and consulting professions. Practice limited to top management problems of planning, ownership transition, acquisitions and mergers, valuations, executive effectiveness. Contact Bill Mager, 205 Security Building, 203 East Fourth Ave., Olympia, WA 98501, 206/357-8555.

MANAGEMENT DESIGN–19 years experience servicing over 400 A/E/D/P firms in all phases of general management, including analysis of financial, marketing, and human resources functions as they contribute to a strategic business plan; ownership transition planning; organizational structuring and management retreats. Contact George L. Schrohe, Management Design, 100 Bush Street, Suite 650, San Francisco, CA 94104, 415/989-4338.

MARTIN-SIMONDS ASSOCIATES, INC.–is a management consulting firm specializing in strategic planning, human resources, training and related services to architectural and engineering firms in the United States and abroad. Contact John M. Simonds, Martin-Simonds Associates, Inc., 3100 Smith Tower, Seattle, WA 98104-2361, 206/623-2562.

McCONOCHIE CONSULTING–strategic planning, goal-setting, retreats and major meetings, training, seminars, individual principal-level counseling. Contact Carol McConochie Rauch, McConochie Consulting, 620 W. Gatehouse Lane, Philadelphia, PA 19118, 215/247-5128.

SRI INTERNATIONAL–SRI International's environmental Business Program is a dedicated management consulting practice addressing technical, marketing, regulatory and business issues for a variety of private clients. Contact Raymond J. Carlisle, SRI International, 333 Ravenswood Avenue, Menlo Park, CA 94025, 415/859-5925.

TECHNICAL MANAGEMENT CONSULTANTS, INC.–assists design firms with long-range planning, business development, profit improvement, manpower evaluation, ownership transition, organizational development, sales and leadership training and board of director effectiveness. Contact Bill Peck, Technical Management Consultants, Inc., 1925 Century Boulevard NE, Suite 4, Atlanta, GA 30345, 404/321-4852.

TENNEY CONSULTING–specializing in all phases of management of the building industry business including the 7 P's of the professional design services mix-pricing, New Products/Services Development, Promotion, Personnel, Process Management Systems, Distribution and Physical Facility Presentation. 20 years building experience nationwide, track record. Member, National Bureau of Professional Management Consultants Advisory Council. Contact S.M. Tenney, 54 South 9th Street, #318, Minneapolis, MN 55402, 612/340-0071.

DON THOMPSON ASSOCIATES–services include retreat facilitation, strategic planning, management audits, ownership transition, organizational development, human resource training in communications and other in-house seminars. Contact Don Thompson, Don Thompson Associates, 3247 Embry Hills Dr., Atlanta, GA 30341, 404/455-8414.

EVERETT S. THOMPSON ASSOCIATES–consultant exclusively to management of architectural and consulting engineering firms. Organization studies, long-range planning, human resources management, training programs and acquisition searches. Contact Everett S. Thompson, Everett S. Thompson Associates, 1501 Briarcliff Dr. SE, Grand Rapids, MI 49546, 616/949-1309.

WARNER RABOY ASSOCIATES–specializes in consulting with A/E/P firms on competitive strategic planning; marketing professional services; written/verbal communication techniques financial management; and project management information systems. Contact Suzanne Warner Raboy, Partner, Warner Raboy Associates, 521 Fifth Ave., Suite 1740, New York, NY 10175, 212/732-9666.

B. COMPREHENSIVE MARKETING

LLOYD BAKAN CONSULTANTS–see listing under "A. All Phases of Management."

BARNES AND BRANDT, INC.–see listing under "A. All Phases of Management."

BREUER CONSULTING GROUP–helps design firms identify and penetrate new markets and strengthen their presence in existing markets. Makes specific recommendations for business development and coaches staff during implementation. Offers client surveys, planning promotions, and sales strategies and training. Develops lively programs to motivate technical staff. Contact Mary Breuer, President; Breuer Consulting Group, 405 Francisco Street, San Francisco, CA 94133, 415/296-9600.

BUILDING DEVELOPMENT COUNSEL, INC.–provides professional services for A/E firms nationwide in pursuit of

Federal Government Design awards. Identify projects, agency contacts, 254/255 critiques and contract negotiating assistance. Contact Mark Price, Building Development Counsel, Inc., 1825 I Street, N.W., Suite 400, Washington, DC 20006, 202/429-2069.

CAMERON ASSOCIATES–analyzes market demand, predicts emerging markets, researches position in the marketplace, develops competitive strategies, formalizes marketing plan, introduces firms to potential clients, organizes presentations, conducts debriefings. Contact Mark Cameron, Cameron Associates, 55 New Montgomery Street, Suite 800, San Francisco, CA 94105, 415/543-8980.

CATALYST MARKETING GROUP, INC.–provides strategic marketing planning, training and implementation services, including proposal writing, presentation assistance and marketing data base development. Directs marketing communication programs including brochures, newsletters, public relations and direct mail. Contact Louis E. Grzesiek or David Dretzka, Catalyst Marketing Group, Inc., 1720 E. Garry Avenue, Suite 221, Santa Ana, CA 92705, 714/250-5566.

CONSULTANT MANAGEMENT SERVICES, INC.–see listing under "A. All Phases of Management."

THE COXE GROUP–provides comprehensive marketing services from planning through implementation. Specialists in strategic marketing. Consultants have authored several books addressing marketing issues unique to the design professions. Contact Nina Hartung, The Coxe Group, 2 Mellon Bank Center, Philadelphia, PA 19102, 215/561-2020.

COYNE ASSOCIATES–national firm since 1975, consults in evaluating/organizing marketing and PR programs, marketing plans, workshops/sales training, presentation interviews, staff evaluation, corporate identity. Contact John Coyne, Coyne Associates, 4010 E. Lake Street, Minneapolis, MN 55406, 612/724-1188.

FEATHERS CONSULTING SERVICES, INC.–provides marketing assistance in the field of planning, implementation of the plan and day-to-day updating of leads and opportunities. Contact Sally Feathers, Feathers Consulting Services, Inc., 4164 Tarrybrae Terrace, Tarzana, CA 91356, 213/345-8762.

FLYNN-HEAPES CONSULTING–comprehensive services in the four quarters of successful A/E marketing: planning, market research, sales, and communications. Counsel, production, and in-house training. Contact Ellen Flynn-Heapes, Flynn-Heapes Consulting, 37 E. Linden Street, Alexandria, VA 22301, 703/549-4019.

GAIO–see listing under "A. All Phases of Management."

HOYLES ASSOCIATES–nationally serving clients in all phases of Marketing/Sales - Strategic Market Planning - Marketing Surveys - Identifying New Markets/New Services - Marketing Manager versus Principals/Staff Relationships/Accountability. Contact Bud Hoyles, Hoyles Associates, Inc., 810 Peace Portal Way, Suite 175, P.O. Box F-195, Blaine, WA 98230, 640/538-2362.

RICHARD G. JACQUES CONSULTING MARKETING & STRATEGIC PLANNING–provides diversified services enhancing clients' understanding of market dynamics and developing strategies for realizing their full potential within increasingly competitive environment. Over 20 years experience. Contact Richard G. Jacques, Richard G. Jacques Consulting Marketing & Strategic Planning, Six Lemay Street, West Harford, CT 06107, 203/521-9122.

KENNEY AND ASSOCIATES–comprehensive services. Planning through implementation: marketplace positioning, competitive strategies, marketing program evaluation, marketing plans, research, direct client contact, customized training sessions/seminars, proposal preparation, presentation strategy/training, and communications. Contact Carolyn E. Kenney, Kenney and Associates, 4334 Edgewood Avenue, Oakland, CA 94602, 415/531-1297.

K. LENTZ MMA–develop and generate action-oriented marketing plans, public relations programs, marketing databases, and direct mail programs; strategize and produce proposals/creative presentations; conduct seminars and perform marketing management searches. Contact Kay Lentz, 2600

Citadel Plaza Drive, Suite 510, Houston, TX 77008, 713/864-2623.

MANAGEMENT DESIGN–for 10 years, assisted firms in strategic planning, research, sales tactics, client perception surveys, promotions and operations; program implementation and goal attainment. Contact Ken Lerch, Management Design, 100 Bush Street, Suite 650, San Francisco, CA 94104, 415/989-4338.

MARKETING CONCEPTS–provides marketing planning related to business plans and objectives, management skill enhancement training, executive level marketing and sales training, performance appraisal systems. A marketing facilitator. Contact Arthur F. Helf, Marketing Concepts, 623 High Street, Worthington, OH 43085, 614/431-2006.

McCONOCHIE CONSULTING–strategic marketing and planning, proposal and presentation strategies, client development, client relations, staffing and organization, retreats, training, seminars, trouble-shooting. Contact Carol McConochie Rauch, McConochie Consulting, 620 West Gatehouse Lane, Philadelphia, PA 19118, 215/247-5128.

ROBERT L. MILLER ASSOCIATES–works with management to help define firm's services, identify market goals, find ways to reach them. Design firm communication specialists; former Hill & Knowlton account executive. Contact Robert L. Miller, AIA, Robert L. Miller Associates, 2144 California NW, #404, Washington, DC 20008, 202/483-4083, or 153 W. 27, Suite 900, New York, NY 10001, 212/627-9450.

MARKETING RESEARCH CONSULTANTS–MRC provides market research services, including image surveys, market studies, and new office location surveys; recently merged with advertising agency to provide full-service marketing communications. Contact Tina McGerk Rible, Marketing Consultants, 10200 Riverside Drive, #200, Toluca Lake, CA 91602, 818/760-1230.

MS ASSOCIATES–over 12 years experience marketing for A/E firms and over 60 clients; from planning through communications (brochures, proposals, presentations). Specialists in successful presentation training. Contact Margaret Spaulding, MS

Associates, 944 Market St., Suite 705, San Francisco, CA 94102, 415/398-7088.

PEEL & THOMAS–provides comprehensive marketing management and communications consulting services. Our principals are architects and engineers with over 35 years experience in marketing professional design services. Contact William L. Peel, Jr., Peel & Thomas, 1300 Post Oak Boulevard, Suite 1220, Houston, TX 77056, 713/621-1556.

ROSENZWEIG PROFESSIONAL SERVICES MARKETING–provides strategic plans, market planning and public relations including: budgets, direct mail, advertising, special events, staffing, newsletters, speakers bureaus, press programs, design and copywriting for brochures. Contact Patricia Rosenzweig, Rosenzweig Professional Services Marketing, 53 West Jackson Blvd., Suite 523, Chicago, IL 60604, 312/987-9541.

FRANK H. SMITH III, AIA–provides assistance in overall market program evaluation, market plan development, new client/market identification, qualification statement/presentation preparation, client maintenance, image studies and brochure development. Contact Frank Smith, 4222 Conway Valley Rd. NW, Atlanta, GA 30327, 404/237-7750.

TENNEY CONSULTING–see listing under "A. All Phases of Management."

C. PUBLIC RELATIONS/ MARKETING COMMUNICATIONS

BA COMMUNICATIONS–(formerly Boemer Associates) specializes in media placement for architectural, engineering, interior design, and construction firms, as well as related associations and societies. We strategize, analyze and publicize. Contact Lois E. Boemer, BA Communications, 12 Mt. Ida Terrace, Newton, MA 02158, 617/527-2080.

LLOYD BAKAN CONSULTANTS–see listing under "A. All Phases of Management."

BISHOFF SOLOMON COMMUNICATIONS–provides marketing, communications, and public relations services including effective marketing strategies and programs, media coverage and relations, collateral materials, and special events. Contact Janey Bishoff, Bishoff Soloman Communications, 214 Lincoln Street, Suite 204, Boston, MA 02134, 617/782-0207.

BREUER CONSULTING GROUP–develops promotions programs with a sound foundation in marketing. Affiliated with a national, award-winning graphic design group specializing in A/E firms. We are fast writers of compelling copy with strong concept capability. We develop direct mail, brochures, newsletters, seminars, and other tools to get your message heard. Contact Mary Breuer, President; Breuer Consulting Group, 405 Francisco Street, San Francisco, CA 94133, 415/296-9600.

CAMERON ASSOCIATES–analyzes existing collateral, plans and budget comprehensive communication programs, creates and writes communications or PR pieces. Experienced in publications, mailings, advertising, generic and specialized brochures, trade shows, and exhibits. Contact Mark A. Cameron, Cameron Associates, 55 New Montgomery Street, Suite 800, San Francisco, CA 94105, 415/543-8980.

CAPELIN COMMUNICATIONS, INC.–quite simply, the standard of measure for writing, publicity, speaking, audits, events, crisis management, strategy, counsel. National clientele (only professional firms), 10-person staff, PRSA-accredited. Contact Joan L. Capelin, Capelin Communications, Inc., 257 Park Avenue S., New York, NY 10010-7304, 212/353-8800.

CATALYST MARKETING GROUP–see listing under "B–Comprehensive Marketing."

CHANNELS ADVERTISING AND PUBLIC RELATIONS–Channels provides complete marketing communications services for the real estate industry and other professional industries. Contact Elissa Morrash, Channels Advertising And Public Relations, 340 Townsend Street, Suite 426, San Francisco, CA 94107, 415/543-3334.

CORBIN DESIGN–designs and implements identity programs and marketing materials for design professional firms across the nation. Instructor for nine years at Harvard GSD's summer marketing program. Contact Jeffry Corbin, Corbin Design,

109 East Front, Suite 304, Traverse City, MI 49684, 616/947-1236.

COYNE ASSOCIATES–see listing under "B–Comprehensive Marketing."

FLYNN-HEAPES CONSULTING–award-winning planning, design, and production of communications materials, events, and publicity for A/Es. Strong support service for your speaking and writing goals. Contact Ellen Flynn-Heapes, Flynn-Heapes Consulting, 37 E. Linden Street, Alexandria, VA 22301, 703/549-4019.

FUESSLER SCHWARTZ, INC.–has developed marketing, communications, and public relations programs for over 40 firms since 1984. We are a full-service agency emphasizing strategic planning, positioning, and market research to develop targeted advertising, direct mail, collateral material, and media campaigns. Contact Rolf Fuessler, Fuessler Schwartz, Inc., 324 Shawmut Ave., Boston, MA 02118, 617/262-3964 or 617/266-1068 (FAX).

GAIO–see listing under "A–All Phases of Management."

HARDEMAN COMMUNICATIONS–public relations programs, public information consultation, publications (concept, writing, graphics). Specialists in professional service firms. New York State-certified Women's Business Enterprise. Contact Ann Hardeman, Hardeman Communications, 70A Greenwich Avenue-285, New York, NY 10011, 212/620-3028.

JOHN IRVINE & ASSOCIATES–experienced in public relations/marketing communications for the building and design industry, including publicity, presentations, newsletters, brochures, direct mail, community relations, marketing support materials, etc. Contact John Irvine, President, John Irvine & Associates, 200 N. Tustin Ave., Suite 100, Santa Ana, CA 92705, 714/953-9449.

KENNEY AND ASSOCIATES–planning through production and implementation of communications materials for the design professional. Writing and presentation training seminars, special events, brochures, newsletters, articles, and direct mail.

Contact Carolyn E. Kenney, Kenney and Associates, 4334 Edgewood Avenue, Oakland, CA 94602, 415/531-1297.

JOHN R. KUBASEK & ASSOCIATES, INC.–serves construction industry clients exclusively; development of total marketing strategies and implementation of plan(s); full public relations and in-house graphics services; accredited advertising agency. Contact John Kubasek, John R. Kubasek & Associates, Inc., 407 Manor Rd., Staten Island, NY 10314, 718/727-4366.

K. LENTZ MMA–see listing under "B–Comprehensive Marketing."

MANAGEMENT DESIGN–assists firms in establishing programs and plans to strengthen image, reputation and position. Areas include advertising, events, media management, new identities, direct mail programs, publishing and PR programs. Contact Ken Lerch, Management Design, 100 Bush Street, Suite 650, San Francisco, CA 94104, 415/989-4338.

MARKETING RESEARCH CONSULTANTS–see listing under "B–Comprehensive Marketing."

ROBERT L. MILLER ASSOCIATES–works to define firm's message, identify targets, find (or create) ways to reach them. Design firm public relations specialists; former Hill & Knowlton account executive. Contact Robert L. Miller, AIA, Robert L. Miller Associates, 2144 California NW, #404, Washington, DC 20008, 202/483-4083, or 153 W. 27, Suite 900, New York, NY 10001, 212/627-9450.

MS ASSOCIATES–specialists in cost-effective promotion; backgrounds in journalism and A/E marketing; from planning through implementation (direct mail, advertising, getting published in your clients' media). Contact Joan van Duyl, MS Associates, 944 Market Street, Suite 705, San Francisco, CA 94102, 415/398-7088.

PB COMMUNICATIONS–quick turnaround of targeted PR/marketing materials by division of major A/E/P firm. Concept/design/production of brochures, newsletters, special events, presentation boards, slides and graphics. Contact Rose Reichman, c/o PB Communications, One Penn Plaza, New York, NY 10119, 212/465-5048.

JUDY PASCOE, WRITER–broad experience in conceptualizing and writing marketing materials including brochures, newsletters, and articles for design professionals. Emphasis on fresh, creative approach. Contact Judy Pascoe, 430 1/2 E. Front Street, Traverse City, MI 49684, 616/947-0922.

PEEL & THOMAS–see listing under "B–Comprehensive Marketing."

ROSENZWEIG PROFESSIONAL SERVICES MARKETING–see listing under "B–Comprehensive Marketing."

TENNEY ASSOCIATES–see listing under "A–All Phases of Management."

D. FINANCIAL MANAGEMENT

ARTHUR ANDERSEN & CO.–provides assistance in government contract procurement, financial matters, taxes and consulting. Has served over 100 architect-engineering firms in recent years. Contact Edwin P. James, Arthur Andersen & Co., 33 West Monroe St., Chicago, IL 60603, 312/580-0033.

C. WAYNE BEACHUM & ASSOCIATES–see listing under "A–All Phases of Management."

THE COXE GROUP–offers both general and specialized financial management services to all types of design firms. Services include: ownership transition, firm valuation, merger/acquisition, and long-term financial planning. Contact Nina Hartung, The Coxe Group, 2 Mellon Bank Center, Philadelphia, PA 19102, 215/561-2020.

DESIGN MANAGEMENT CONSULTING, INC.–comprehensive advice on financial issues, including firm valuation, ownership transition, incentive compensation, profit planning, government regulations and financial reporting systems. Contact Bill Fanning, Design Management Consulting, Inc., 271 Cross Gate Dr., Marietta, GA 30068, 404/971-7586.

LOWELL V. GETZ, CPA–advises on financial and tax matters for ownership transition planning, mergers/acquisitions. Tested and certified in business valuations by the American

Society of Appraisers. Contact Lowell V. Getz, 820 Gessner, Suite 265, Houston, TX 77024, 713/461-8061.

HALL & COMPANY–see listing under "A–All Phases of Management."

HOYLES ASSOCIATES, INC.–nationally serving clients in all phases of financial/accounting-valuations-ownership structuring-ESOP design-profitability improvement-computer based integrated accounting/project cost control/project management. Contact Doug Irving, Hoyles Associates, Inc., 810 Peace Portal Way, Suite 175, P.O. Box F-195, Blaine, WA 98230, 604/538-2326.

THE JANUS COMPANY–assistance with financial planning, profit improvement, accounting and project control systems, management reporting, hiring and training financial staff, and personnel issues in small, medium, and large firms. Contact Joan Lautenschleger, Principal, The Janus Company, 48 Fayette Street, Boston, MA 02116, 617/426-2789.

MANAGEMENT DESIGN–offers profit planning, budgeting, and forecasting assistance with emphasis on profitability. Broad experience in accounting functions for cash and A/R management and project cost accounting. Contact George L. Schrohe, Management Design, 100 Bush Street, Suite 650, San Francisco, CA 94104, 415/989-4338.

MLT ASSOCIATES–provides financial management on a part-time or consulting basis: financial statements, cash management, budgeting, project profit controls, systems conversions (CFMS or other). Contact Mark Thivierge, MLT Associates, 103 Warren Avenue, Boston, MA 02116, 617/266-7169.

REPOLE ASSOCIATES–part-time controller, financial manager. Specializes in business plans, cash forecasts, and control of profitability. Also does recruiting, company valuations and ownership transitions. Contact Joe Repole, Repole Associates, 15 Gryzboska Circle, Framingham, MA 01701, 508/879-6340.

WARNER RABOY ASSOCIATES–see listing under "A–All Phases of Management."

E. HUMAN RESOURCES

APPEL ASSOCIATES–services include: retreat facilitation, team-building, inter-group conflict management, communications processes, decision-making and problem-solving processes, human relations and human resources management. Contact Boyce Appel, Appel Associates, 86 Allen Rd., Atlanta, GA 30328, 404/255-3200.

BARNES AND BRANDT, INC.–see listing under "A–All Phases of Management."

CONSULTANT MANAGEMENT SERVICES, INC.–see listing under "A–All Phases of Management."

THE COXE GROUP–provides expertise in all area of human resource management, effective employee communications, and executive search. Contact Nina Hartung, The Coxe Group, 2 Mellon Bank Center, Philadelphia, PA 19102, 215/561-2020.

HENSEY ASSOCIATES–see listing under "A–All Phases of Management."

MANAGEMENT DESIGN–conducts salary/benefit surveys and provides human resources consulting, including employee recruiting/retention plans, position descriptions, performance evaluation processes, personnel manuals. Contact Rose Anthony, Management Design, 100 Bush Street, Suite 650, San Francisco, CA 94104, 415/989-4338.

MARTIN-SIMONDS ASSOCIATES, INC.–see listing under "A–All Phases of Management."

CHARLES M. McREYNOLDS–30 years experience in all aspects of human resources as applied to consulting engineers and architects. Author of book *Human Resource Management for Design Firms* published by ACEC. Contact C.M. McReynolds, 19 Suffolk, Suite A, Sierra Madre, CA 91024, 818/798-4287.

F. EXECUTIVE RECRUITING

BARNES AND BRANDT, INC.–see listing under "A–All Phases of Management."

BREUER CONSULTING–identifies, recruits, screens, evaluates and places qualified candidates for technical and non-technical management-level positions exclusively for design firms. Nationwide network and track record. Contact Mary Breuer, President; Breuer Consulting Group, 405 Francisco Street, San Francisco, CA 94133, 415/296-9600.

CAMERON ASSOCIATES–searches for and identifies candidates for management, marketing, and professional/technical positions in architectural and engineering firms. Contact Mark A. Cameron, Cameron Associates, 55 New Montgomery Street, San Francisco, CA 94105, 415/543-8980.

CLAREMONT-BRANAN, INC.–provides professional recruiting and search expertise exclusively to A/E/ID service firms. Specialists in mid to senior level technical and staff positions nationwide. Contact Phil Collins, Claremont-Branan, Inc., 2295 Parklake Dr. NE, Suite 520, Atlanta, GA 30345, 404/491-1292.

THE COXE GROUP–facilitates searches, recruits, evaluates, and recommends qualified candidates for technical, marketing, and financial positions. National network of contacts. Contact Nina Hartung, The Coxe Group, 2 Mellon Bank Center, Philadelphia, PA 19102, 215/561-2020.

THE FULLER GROUP, INC.–specializes in the recruitment and placement of design professionals. Serves the recruitment needs of A/E/P firms nationwide. Conducts both contingency and retained searches. Contact Ruth Fuller, Hon. AIA, or David Fuller, The Fuller Group, Inc., 5252 Westchester, Suite 275, Houston, TX 77005, 713/663-6073.

LARSEN & LEE, INC.–consultants on executive selection to the engineering architectural industry since 1975. Assignments in over 30 states and 10 countries including a major foreign government. Contact Don Larsen, Larsen & Lee, Inc., 7200 Wisconsin Ave. #702, Bethesda, MD 20814, 301/657-1330.

K. LENTZ MMA–see listing under "B–Comprehensive Marketing."

MANAGEMENT DESIGN–as an adjunct to its management and marketing services, facilitates searches for senior technical, financial, operations and marketing staff. Fixed and hourly fees negotiated. Contact: Ken Lerch, Management Design, 100 Bush Street, Suite 650, San Francisco, CA 94104, 415/989-4338.

McNICHOL ASSOCIATES–over 13 years experience as specialists in aiding architectural, engineering and construction firms nationally with executive recruitment services for management-level positions. Contact John McNichol, McNichol Associates, 600 Chestnut Street, Suite 1031, Philadelphia, PA 19106, 215/922-4142.

CHARLES M. McREYNOLDS–we specialize in locating partners, regional office managers, department chiefs and technical gurus. Our searches are conducted on an hourly rate basis with a guaranteed maximum. We don't conduct contingency or advance fee searches. Contact Chuck McReynolds, Charles M. McReynolds, 19 Suffolk, Suite A, Sierra Madre, CA 91024, 818/798-4287.

MARJANNE PEARSON ASSOCIATES–executive search and other recruiting services for architectural and related design firms. Specialists in working with high-profile firms for design, technical, management, and marketing positions. Contact Marjanne Pearson, Marjanne Pearson Associates, 97 Scott Street, San Francisco, CA 94117, 415/553-8780.

POWERS CONSULTING, INC.–serves planning/design firms-architects, consulting engineers, A/E's, interior designers-on a national basis, providing clients with search services on a retained basis. Contact William D. Powers, Powers Consultants, Inc., 2241 A South Brentwood Boulevard, Suite 4, St. Louis, MO 63144, 314/961-8787 or 314/961-8792.

VSI, INC.–is an executive recruitment firm specializing in the design and building industries. We operate nationally with working relationships with European firms. Generalized Human Resources consulting is also available. Contact Donna Gaines, VSI, Inc., 320 Interstate North Parkway, Suite 490, Atlanta, GA 30339, 404/956-1600 or Charles L. Roberson,

VSI, Inc., 645 North Michigan Avenue, Suite 860, Chicago, IL 60611, 312/664-6767.

G. QUALITY MANAGEMENT/QA/QC SERVICES

A/E QUALITY MANAGEMENT ASSOCIATES, INC.–provides cost-effective total quality management planning, organizing and installation for A/E firms, focused on their unique quality management issue. Assess, revitalize or start TQM programs companywide for effective QA/QC results. Contact William M. Hayden Jr., A/E Quality Management Associates, Inc., P.O. Box 56022, Jacksonville, FL 32241-6022, 904/268-2731.

HALL & COMPANY–see listing under "A–All Phases of Management."

THE REDICHECK FIRM–conducts quality assurance training seminars and project peer reviews with the objective of reducing design errors and omissions caused by lack of coordination among disciplines. Contact William T. Nigro, AIA, The Redicheck Firm, 4954 Post Road Pass, Stone Mountain, GA 30088, 404/498-3334.

B SAMPLE MARKETING PLAN

Our company has grown to a medium-size design firm through diligently pursuing several plans. Our principals maintain memberships in professional organizations and attempt to stay active through attendance and company representation. Additionally, we stress that each individual of the company, particularly the engineering staff, is a member of the marketing team. As such, they represent our company's abilities at every function they attend and follow through on potential job opportunities. We do not mind patting ourselves on the back and telling others that we are capable of doing a job—and we attempt to customize each proposal so that it shows our strengths.

Among the steps that we have taken to make our marketing stronger:

a) Hired a marketing coordinator.

b) Hired a technical writer.

c) Regularly read copies of the following publications:

1) *Commerce Business Daily*
2) Los Angeles daily newspapers
3) *Small Business Exchange*
4) *San Diego Transcript*

d) Regularly take out ad space in technical publications.

e) Offer monetary support to social activities of customers.

f) Customize as much as possible individual resumes for each proposal. In addition, we continually update our resumes to show new job experience.

g) Write letters to key companies when NOT responding to an RFP.

h) Maintain a large "Consultant" file where we can go for information concerning potential sub-consultants or teaming. When we are aware of a potential project which may be larger in scope than our company is capable of undertaking, we make phone calls to others in an effort to become part of a team.

i) Enter all company jobs into a database so that they can be easily accessed and used to customize proposals, as well as used to track the types of jobs we have had.

j) Give each proposal a number. Keep track of success record. Note company who receives job (if not us!).

k) Attempt to make as many "shows" as possible, to increase our visibility.

l) Maintain up-to-date, professional brochures.

MARKETING COORDINATION

```
            ┌─────────────────────┐
            │    MASTER GROUP     │
            │                     │
            └─────────────────────┘

┌──────────┐ ┌──────────────┐ ┌─────────────┐ ┌──────────────┐
│   ESI    │ │ GOVERNMENT   │ │ CORPORATE   │ │ DEVELOPERS   │
│          │ │              │ │             │ │              │
│          │ │              │ │             │ │              │
└──────────┘ └──────────────┘ └─────────────┘ └──────────────┘
```

INTRODUCTION

Before a plan is implemented, this process shall be followed:

Conception of idea
↓
Cost/Benefit Ratio, Cost Analysis
↓
Coordination-Discussion of plan with members of master group
↓

Evaluation of plan by master group-analysis, direction, responsibilities and recommendation
↓
Implementation of plan, if feasible

GENERAL CORPORATE MARKETING COSTS

This is a list of general corporate costs for a marketing plan:

1. Staff Cost/Time Commitment

Developers		$100,000
ESI		$ 42,500
Corporate/Institutional		$ 36,100
Nontraditional Computer		$120,400
Traditional		$155,000
	Total	$454,000

2. Seminars/Presentations

Developers		$ 2,000
ESI		$ 26,500
Corporate/Institutional		$ —
Nontraditional computer		$ 10,000
Traditional		$ 20,000
	Total	$ 58,500

3. Advertisements/Printing

Developers		$ 15,000
ESI		$ 3,000
Corporate /Institutional		$ —
Nontraditional computer		$ 10,000
Traditional		$ 2,500
	Total	$ 30,500

4. Educational

Developers		$ 7,500
ESI		$ 7,500
Corporate/Institutional		$ —
Nontraditional computer		$ 10,000
Traditional		$ 20,000
	Total	$ 45,000

TOTAL COST	$588,000

5. Staffing

Developers		$ 40,000
ESI		$ 25,000
Corporate/Institutional		—
Nontraditional computer		$160,000
Traditional		$105,000
	Total	$330,000

6. Equipment/Miscellaneous

Developers		$ 35,000
ESI		$ 7,000
Corporate/Institutional		$ 5,000
Nontraditional computer		$102,000
Traditional		$ 20,000
	Total	$169,000

TOTAL	$1,087,000

MAGNITUDE COSTS 1990

Nontraditional Services
(Includes Government Marketing)

• Market areas
   Entire East Coast

• Market Services
   Desktop Publishing
   Computer Design and Graphics
   GIS/Databases
   Color Plotting
   Mapping
   Software/Hardware Sales

• Budget Projection (Based on 40-hour week)
   Staff Cost/Time Commitment

KRK -50%	$ 50,000
DMW - 50%	$ 23,000
BBK -60%	$ 21,600
EMB - 20%	$ 6,000
VIP - 20%	$ 6,800
GLR -10%	$ 4,750
RAM - 5%	$ 2,750

Additional Graphic -10%		$ 2,500
Desktop -10%		$ 3,000
	Billable Time	$120,400
•Educational—In House Seminars		$ 10,000

TOTAL COST	$130,400

•Staffing (Part-time at 30 hours/week and $5/hr.)

1–3 Months	6 Part time	$ 46,800
3–6 Months	2 Part time	$ 15,600
	1 Full time Database	$ 40,000
6–12 Months	2 Part time	$ 15,600
	1 Full time Database	$ 42,000
		$160,000

•Equipment

Furniture		$ 10,000
Computers	2 Work Stations	$ 50,000
	Maintenance	$ 12,000
	2 Disks	$ 30,000
		$102,000

TOTAL COST	$383,400

1990 NONTRADITIONAL COMPUTER USES

Game Plan

	Projected Cost	Projected Income
1. GIS—RCG, MTM, KRK, EMB To be discussed Meeting	$200,000	$1,000,000
2. GIS Follow-up, 2 hours/week/person DMW, EMB, KRK, BBK	$ 20,000	$ 500,000±
3. Presentations/Publications KRK, DMW, RAM, VIP, GLR, EMB	$ 10,000	$ 100,000
4. Joint Venture–Market Research Legg Mason KRK, DMW, Input Operator	To be determined	To be determined
5. Computer Services Book by	$ 600	—

6.	Capabilities Plan—VIP, KRK by	$ 10,000	—
7.	254/255 Forms Updated		
	EMB, Tracy, DEL, GLR	$ 500	—
8.	Resumes - by 3/10, TN, GLR	$ 500	—
9.	Software Sales—KRK	$ 5,000	$ 25,000
10.	Hardware Sales—KRK	$ 45,000	$ 90,000
	(includes hardware)		
11.	Tax Maps—Baltimore County	$ 18,000	$ 50,000
12.	Petrochemical-Research/		To be
	Invest.	$ 2,500	determined
13.	Misc. Investigations/Follow-ups		
	KRK, DMW, VIP, GLR, FNC, BBK,		
	RAM, Walt, EMB	$ 75,000	$ 500,000
	Total	$387,100	$2,265, 000

C SEMINAR ATTENDEE STATISTICS

STAYING SMALL SUCCESSFULLY
Beaver Creek, Colorado
February 26-28, 1988

QUESTION	HIGH	LOW	AVERAGE	MEDIAN	1987 MEDIAN
1. What % of your total time is currently charged to projects?	120.0%	30.0%	57.0%	57.0%	50.0%
2. What % of your total time is currently spent on marketing?	50.0%	1.0%	15.8%	12.0%	24.8%
3. What is your annual base salary?	$128,000	$37,700	$74,613	$72,800	$55,200
4. What is the average dollar amount of your annual bonus?	$52,000	$0	$18,633	$10,000	$15,000
5. What is the annual amount of your total compensation (salary, dividends, and bonus)?	$225,000	$39,200	$100,179	$90,000	$75,000
6. What is the annual base salary of the second in command in your firm?	$62,600	$27,500	$47,784	$45,000	$53,000
7. What is the annual bonus of the second in command in your firm?	$20,000	$0	$6,567	$7,100	$6,000
8. What is the annual base salary of your marketing director?	$45,000	$45,000	$45,000	$45,000	$36,000
9. What is the annual bonus of your marketing director?	$3,200	$3,200	$3,200	$45,000	*
10. What is the annual base salary of your chief financial person?	$40,000	$14,500	$26,849	$31,200	$28,000
11. What is the annual bonus of your chief financial person?	$10,300	$0	$2,000	$1,200	$2,000
12. What is the annual base salary of a department head in your firm?	$55,584	$33,000	$42,337	$40,000	$42,000

* Insufficient Information

QUESTION	HIGH	LOW	AVERAGE	MEDIAN	1987 MEDIAN
13. What is the annual bonus of a department head?	$6,900	$0	$3,288	$3,300	$5,000
14. What is the annual base salary of a project manager in your firm?	$52,000	$22,880	$35,463	$41,000	$38,500
15. What is the annual bonus of a project manager in your firm?	$6,000	$0	$2,330	$2,700	$3,000
16. What is your firm's % of total staff time charged to projects?	85.0%	64.0%	74.7%	75.0%	69.2%
17. What is your firm's % of total time charged to projects by all technical staff only?	95.0%	80.0%	87.0%	88.0%	82%
18. What % of overtime did your firm work last year?	25.0%	1.0%	8.5%	4.3%	10%
19. What is your firm's annual employee turnover rate?	20.0%	0.0%	8.1%	8.0%	7%
20. What % of annual gross fees are spent on marketing?	10.0%	0.0%	3.0%	2.0%	3.7%
21. What % of annual gross fees are spent on long range planning?	10.0%	0.0%	2.2%	5.0%	1%
22. What % of annual gross fees are spent on all accounting activity?	10.0%	0.5%	3.9%	3.5%	3%
23. What is your total per person cost for your accounting function (bookkeepers, controller, financial manager, business manager, support staff)?	$38,000	$5,460	$23,979	$23,000	$22,000
24. What % of annual gross fees are spent on education and training?	5.0%	0.0%	1.6%	1.0%	1.2%
25. What is your firm's overhead as a % of direct labor charged to project?	163.0%	10.0%	103.8%	112.0%	134%

281

QUESTION	HIGH	LOW	AVERAGE	MEDIAN	1987 MEDIAN
26. What % of annual gross fees are spent on all salaries?	112.0%	27.0%	47.8%	42.0%	48%
27. What % of annual gross fees are spent on tax sheltered compensation?	59.0%	0.0%	8.2%	3.6%	5%
28. What % of direct labor is spent on all employee fringe benefits?	38.0%	0.0%	19.1%	21.0%	19%
29. What is your accounts receivable turnover in days? (Formula is current A/R balance divided by the result of dividing annual billings by 360.)	132	0	52	50	65
30. What is your WIP turnover in days? (Formula is current WIP balance divided by the result of dividing annual billings by 360.)	90	0	27	20	29
31. What was last year's % of pre-tax profit on gross fees before any discretionary disbursements such as profit sharing or bonuses?	86.0%	0.0%	19.8%	11.0%	10%
32. What is your firm's net revenue (not including consultants) per employee (total staff)?	$85,900	$15,000	$49,936	$48,705	$43,602
33. What % of your firm are non-tech overhead people?	32.0%	0.0%	18.2%	20.0%	0%
34. What was your firm's last year actual multiplier on direct labor charged to new clients?	3.48	0.00	2.25	2.50	2.50
35. Do you provide company cars? How many?	10 yes 5	2 no 0	2	3	3

QUESTION	HIGH	LOW	AVERAGE	MEDIAN	1987 MEDIAN
36. Does your firm give Christmas bonuses?	7 yes	4 no	1 N/A		
37. What percentage of your total staff owns shares?	47.0%	0.0%	13.3%	20.0%	16%
38. How many branch offices does your firm have?	1	0	0	N/A	N/A
39. Our firm is ___ A ___ E ___ A/E ___ Planning ___ Other	2 Architects, 2 Planners,	2 Engineers, 2 Architects/Planners, 1 Planner/Landscape Architect	2 Architects/Engineers		
40. Our firm is a ___ Corporation ___ Partnership ___ Other	11 Corporations		1 Partnership		
41. Our firm is in the ___ Northeast ___ Southeast ___ Northwest ___ Southwest ___ Canada ___ Midwest ___ West	3 Southeast 3 Southwest 2 Midwest	1 Northeast 1 Northwest 1 Canada 1 West			
42. Our firm has ___ total staff.	26	6	14	15	18

INDEX

A

Accountant:
  evaluating, 213
  hiring, 212
  obtaining, 212
  utilizing, 212
Accounting plan, for leadership
  transition, 49
Accounts receivable, turnover, ratio
  of, average, 191–192
Accrual, 194, 196
  financial statements, 195
ACEC, 124
  Peer Review Program Manual,
  125
Achievement, atmosphere of, 171
Action plan, 89
  one-year, 90
ADD Inc., 64–65
Administration, corporate, 55
Advancement opportunity, 162
Advertisements, newspaper, 139–
  140
Advisory board, use of, 68
Agreement, mutual, employment,
  165
Ahlberg, Hal, Professional Service
  Industries, 157
Air-handling systems, redesign, 70
American Consulting Engineers
  Council, 124
Analysis, of payroll burden, 158
Annual, profit, 204
Annual budget, 179
Annual financial plan, 185
Annual report, 208

Annual statement, pro forma:
  example, 184
  how to calculate, 184
Appraisal, performance, criteria,
  35
Arizona Engineering Company:
  benefits, 163
  contract, sample, 215–216
Associations, peer, 232
Atmosphere, of achievement, 171
Average collection period, 194
Awards, design, 231–232

B

Backen, Arrigoni, and Ross, selectiveness, 78
Bad debts, 183
Balance of power, 31
Ballast, David Kent, quality control, 111
Banking relationships, 185
Basic organizational types, 25–27
Benefits, 160–162
  offered by design firms, 163
  offering none. Hoskins Engineering, 161
  optional, 162
  package, as motivator, 160
  part-time employees, 162
Bergmeyer, Moritz & Associates,
  188, 196
  financial plan, 23–25
  monthly summary, 189–190
  vision, 9–10
Bidding, 104–105, 123
  communication during, 105

Black & Veetsch, large firm marketing, 19
BOCA code, 129–132
Boilerplate contracts, 131
Bonus(es), 166
  cash vs. stock, 168
  Christmas, 168
  deferred, 169–170
  dollars, 167
  incentive, 167–171
    plan, 167
  as motivation, 157
  payments, small, 170
  plans, 166
  project, 167–168
  quarterly, 169
  stock as, 168–169
Book, publishing, 81
Borrowing, relationships, 179
Bottom line, 201
  managing, 177–210
Branch office, philosophy, 198–199
Brochures, usefulness, 89
Budget, 104, 214
  annual, 179
  control, 116
  fee negotiation, 199
  goals, 105
  marketing, 93
  realization, 187
Budgeting, 71, 180–185
  for bonuses, 167
Budgets, 179
  client, 128
Building:
  code, checklist, 129–132
  departments, contact, list, 110
Bureaucracy, 299
Business:
  -centered practice, 108
  development, sample plan, 57–58
  vs. practice-centered, 108

C

CADD:
  and productivity, 234
  terminal, 128
Candidates, finding for hire, 11
Capital expenditures, rent vs. buy decisions, 197–198

Car, company, as a bonus, 168
Career:
  pathing model, Schmidt Associates Architects, Inc., 172–173
  planning:
    Schmidt Associates Architects, Inc., 171–173
    and training, 35, 38–45
  tracking, 170–174
Carpenter, William, 177
Cash:
  management, 179
  flow, problems, 168
Cavendish Partnership:
  benefits, 163
  employment agreement, 151–155
  mission statement, 18
CEO:
  Customer Profile, 111–116
  role of, 11
Certification:
  fees, 218
  indemnification, 218
CH2M Hill, culture statements, 17, 20–21
Champion:
  checklist for choosing, 12
  defining a, 12
  importance of, 14
Change, 223
Chargeable hours, 192
Checking and approval systems, 117–118
Childcare and work schedules, 46
Christmas bonuses, 168
Circulation/traffic studies, 71
Claims, prevention of, 117
Client(s), 235
  actions, 92
  answers, 98
  calls, 128
  contact memorandum, sample, 101
  contact with, 65
  design awards, 232
  maintenance, 95
  management, 96
  managers, 97
  objections, 98
  perception of your firm, 126
  proposals, 119
  repeat, ways to retain, 64

retaining, suggestions for, 65
right, choosing the, 199–200
selection of planning and design
  firms, factors, 92
services, 55
servicing, 103–135
signatures, 219
surveys, 81
Coaching, 142
Collection, 200
Commerce Business Daily, 273
Communication, during bidding,
  105
Community activities, 66
Company, 247
  car, as a bonus, 168
  profit plan, 197
  quality, standard, 126
Compensation, 157–176
  as incentive, 166–170
  deferred, 169–170
  delaying, 170
  differing from, 106
  firmwide, 170
  in price-competitive marketing,
    170
  rewards/benefits, 46
Computer:
  technology, 1
  time-card screen, 206
  uses, nontraditional, 279
Concepts, 6
Confidence, building, 79
Construction, 105
  administration, 71
  contingency, 217–218
  cost studies, 71
  documents, 123
  management, 71
Consultant:
  fees, 178
  file, 273
Contact(s):
  direct, 97
  face-to-face, 97
Continuing education, in your
  firm, 37
Contract:
  administration, 123
  checklist, 121–123
  developing, 214
  negotiating, 179
  signing, celebration, 131

Contractor(s):
  vs. employees, 146, 148
  independent, 69, 146, 148
  outside, 146
Contracts, 199–210, 217–220
  boilerplate, 131
  employment, 150–155
  method, budgeting, 180
  29 terms to include, 217–220
Control, 200
  of your ego, 139
  of utilization ratios, through
    time cards, 192
Coordination, 117
Corporate administration, 55
Corps of Engineers, 65
Cost(s):
  analysis, 275
  benefit ratio, 275
  magnitude, 278
  marketing, corporate, 277
Coxe Group Management Consultants, 106–108
Creativity, 243
CSI MASTERFORMAT, 46–47
CT Male & Associates, computer
  time-card screen, 206
Culture statements, 13, 15–21
  CH2M Hill, 17, 20–21
  elements of, 15
  sample, 19
Customer, profile, CEO, 111

D

Dating papers, 110
Decision making, ease of, 243
Decisions, go/no go, 79–80
Deferred:
  bonuses, 169–170
  compensation, 169–170
Delays, 119
Delegating:
  flexibility in, 146
  instructions when, 147
  of tasks, 144–148
Dennis Yates Associates,
  market-focused team ap-
  proach, 30
Departmental organizations, 27
  advantages of 28–30
  disadvantages of, 27–28

Departmental organizations (Continued)
illustration, 31
Design, 123
alternatives, limitation on, 218
awards, 231–232
client, 232
as a feature, 103
firms:
benefits offered, 163
categories of, 107
importance of, 103
professionals, motivating, 157–175
with pay raises, 164
sample strategic plan for, 57
vs. service, 106–110
Details, follow up, 108
Dictionaries, 72
Differentiating, 8 ways of, 128
Direct costs, 178
Disciplines, difficulty in adding, 30
Ditka, Mike, winning, 247
Documentation, project activities, 105
Documents:
copyright, 219–220
ownership, 219–220
Do's and don'ts, of success, 211–237
Drafting services, 71
Drawings:
stamp of approval, 220
working, 104
Duffy, Ruble, Mamura, Brygger:
benefits, 163
newsletter, sample, 73–74

E

Earth Technology, focus, 62
Economic:
climate, 198
social factors, effect of, 92
Economic Research Council, publications, 21
Effective multipliers, 201–202
Ego, control, 139
Eley Associates Architects, benefits, 163
Eligibility rules, in selecting an as-

sociate of the company, 48
Emotion, in work performance, 174
Employee:
assistance, 46
turnover, 162
Employees:
encouragement of, 35, 37
vs. independent contractors, 146, 148
motivation, 243
nonperforming, 231
referral, 143
salaries, 164
Employer–employee, relationships, 150
Employment:
agreement, sample, 151–155
contracts, 150–155
offer, making an, 147
probation period for, 149
Energy audits, 70
Entrepreneur, 144, 248
as classic networker, 69
Entrepreneurships:
driving forces, 69
small, 1
Environmental impact studies, 71
Equipment, lease/purchase, 198
Errors, prevention of, 117
Escalator clause, 218
Estate, settlements, 198
Excellence, 249
Excess perfection syndrome, 125–127
illustration of, 127
Exit, requirements, quality control, 130
Expert, building a reputation as, 69
Expertise, in projects, 201
External factors, effect of, 92
Extras, affecting profitability, 211

F

Facilities management, 71
sample plan, 59
for wastewater facilities, 70
Factors, outside, 250
Family members, employment of, 228

Fax:
  machines, 128
  numbers, 110
Fee:
  advance, to reduce accounts re-
    ceivable, 192
  in escrow, 217
  increasing, 77
Finance, sample plan, 56–57
Financial:
  failure of projects, 3 red flags,
    201
  information:
    importance of sharing with
      staff, 25
    sharing, 208
  measures report, 204–206
  plan, 23–25, 71
  employee involvement, 24–25
  importance of, summary, 244
  profit, 25
  planning, 179
    simplify, 179
  report, monthly, sample, 189–
    190
  reporting, 208
    no-paper, example, 207
  standardization, 24
Fire:
  protection, requirements, quality
    control, 129
  resistance, requirements, quality
    control, 129
Firing, incompetents, 149–150
Firms:
  design-focused, 106
  service oriented, 106
Firmwide:
  compensation, 170
  financial management, 179
Fiscal:
  year
    end of, bonus distribution,
      169
    utilization revenue projection,
      example, 186
    staff utilization budget, 186
Five-quarter pool, 169
Flexibility, 243
Flextime and part-time, 46
Focus, 250
  conveying spirit of firm's, 106

effect on profit, 61
narrow, 62
service, 61, 222
ways to, 61
Focusing:
  advantages of, 63
  practice, 61–102
  the practice, advantages of, 62
  steps to, 63
Follow-up, for clients, 91
Functions, supporting, effectiveness
  of, 91

G

Goal-oriented job descriptions, 35
Goals, 144
  budget, 105
  financial, 188
  measurable, 89–90
  profit, 179, 197
  statement, 91
  writing them down, 5
Goldplating, 203
Go/no go decision, 79–80
  criteria, worksheet, 80
  factors influencing, 80–81
Government, actions, effect of, 92
Graphic:
  control, 219
  signage, 70
Gross revenue, 204
Growth, 97, 239–245
  defining, 241
  rate of, 240–241
  sample strategic plan for, 57
  stages of, 241–245
  with teams, 29–30
  too fast, 239
  ways, 240
  when, 239–240
Guru, 139
  firms, 248–249

H

Harley, Ellington, Pierce & Yee
  (HEPY), compensation, 158–
  159
Harris, Fritz, & Associates, Inc.,
  207
Hazardous waste, 220
  audits, 70

Health care:
  planners, 69
  planning, 71
Henderson Group:
  information sharing, 209
  planning process, 53
  selectiveness, 76–77
Hiring, 137–138
  the best, 138
  the ideal candidate, TMOTWH, 141
  marketers, 87
History book, producing, 72
Hoskins Engineers, profile, 160–161
Howard, Needles, Tamend, & Bergendoff (HNTB), 72
Human Resources:
  plan, 33–46
  sample plan, 59
Human Resources Division, organizational chart, 34

I

Incentive:
  bonuses, 167–171
  compensation, 166–170
Incompetents, firing, 149–150
Information sharing, Henderson Group, 209
Innovation, 8, 126
Interior:
  design, movie theaters, 70
  health care architecture, 70
  Space, Inc., networking, 68
Interview:
  attending, 91
  questions, 145–146
Investment, ventures, 198
Invoice, format, 218

J

Jack Johnson Company, newsletter, use of, 75
Jealousy, 249
Job:
  advertising, do's and don'ts, 144
  cancellation fee, 217
  description, performance-
  oriented, 35–37
  positions, 171
  site, signage, 218–219
  swap, twofers, 141

K

Key:
  financial measures, 179, 185
    performance results, 26
  indicators, 197
Kohn Pedersen Fox, vision, 6–8

L

Large firm, marketing plans, 18
Leader, type of, 49
Leadership:
  picking, criteria for, 48–49
  selection, criteria, 47–49
  selection plan, 47–49
  transition:
    accounting plan, 49
    problems of, 47
    stock distribution, 169
  wants and needs, 49
Leads, for projects, 91
LEA Group, 133
Leanness, in organizations, advantages of, 69
Lease/purchase equipment, 198
Legal defense, third party, 220
Letters, quick response to, 108
Liability, 218, 228–229
  avoiding, 105
  crisis, 111
  exclusions, summary of, 230
Lien, provisions, 219
Light and ventilation, requirements, quality control, 130
Listening:
  for achievement, 171
  to employees, 165
Litigation, prevention of, 117
Little things that count big, 106–110
Loss, 194, 196, 201
Low-income housing, financing for, 70
Loyalty, company, in performance, 174

M

McCormack, Mark, hiring, 213
McElroy, Martin, excess perfection, 125
Mackay, Harvey,
  hiring, 213
  Swim With the Sharks Without Being Eaten Alive, 111
Magazines, 72
Magnitude, costs, 278
Mail, direct, 65
Mailing list, 89
Maintenance, 123
Man-hour:
  budget, 202–203
  overrun, 201
Management, 97
  cash, 179
  effective, 243
  financial, firmwide, 179
  marketing, consultant list, 253–272
  style, 3
  system, an incentive, 206
Managers:
  extra insurance coverage, as a benefit, 162
  profit-center, 205–206
Managing:
  the bottom line, 177–210
  meetings, 104
Market(s):
  analyses, 71
  building a reputation in, 8
  choosing a niche, 8
  decisiveness, 8
  diversity, 198
  focus for too many varied, 76
  identification of, 93
  importance of, 205
  low budget, 22
  needs, 61
  niche, 62
  profit analysis, 204–206
  research, 79
  right, 199
  shift, 62
Marketers:
  full time, 81
  when to hire, 87

Market-focused teams, 27
  organization, illustration of, 28
  small firm, 27
Marketing:
  brochures, 89
  call report, sample, 100
  clarification of, 94
  control, 93
  coordination, 275
  costs, corporate, 91, 277
  expense, analysis, 82–85
  hints, 88
  in-house, 96
  and management, consultant list, 253–272
  meaningful, 79–81
  plan, 273–274
    cost and organization, 23
    creating a, 88
    direction, 18–19, 21–23
    elements of, 91
    focus, 23
    large firms, 18
    measurable goals, 22
    small firm, 79
    staff involvement, 22
    writing, 90–91
  program, 92
  reducing dollars spent on, 66
  research, 92
  structuring, 79–81
Matarazzo Design, 14
  motivational leader, 13
Materials, handling and processing, 71
Matrix:
  organization, 31
  disadvantages of, 32
  illustration, 32
  pure, 32
  structure, evolution of, 33
Measurable goals, 89–90
Meehan Architects, vision, 7
Meeting(s):
  managing, 104
  minutes of, 110, 131
Memorandum, client contact, 101
Merger *vs.* acquisitions, 198
Mission statements, 13, 15–18
  Cavendish Partnership, 18

Mission statements *(Continued)*
  Scott Companies Architects, 17
Mission worksheet, 16
Mobility, 164
Money, as motivating factor for leaving a job, 162
Motivating design professionals, 157–175
Motivation, 142
  employees, 243
Movie theaters, interior design of, 70

N

Necessities, *vs.* extras, 234
Negotiate, 178
  profit, 199
Net effective multiplier, what it reveals, 203
Network, 67
  building, 96
Networkers, successful, 69
Networking, 66–69
  example of successful, 67
  Interior Space, Inc., 68
  roundtable discussion, 68
  Summerlin Associates, Inc., 67
Newsletter(s), 72
  characteristics of, 87
  cost-effectiveness of, 75
  enhancing your image through, 86
  publishing, 81, 87
  use of, to break into a market, 75
Newspaper:
  ads, for staff, 33
  advertisements, 139–140
  announcements, 66
Niche:
  exploding a, 69–72
  steps to selecting, 70
No, how to refuse jobs, 76–79
Nonperforming employees, 231
No-paper:
  financial reporting, example, 207
  reporting, 206
Norm, challenging the, 223–224

O

Objections and answers, clients, 98
Occupancy, requirements:
  quality control, 129
  special, 131
Offices, fancy, importance of, 233
Openings, announcing jobs, 143
Operations, 123
  projects, 179
  sample plan, 59
Optional benefits, 162
Organizational plan, 25, 26–33, 240
Overhead:
  expenses, analysis, 159
  rate, profit distribution, 26
  staff, elimination of, 191
Overruns in time, 201
Owners, salaries, 164
Ownership, 162
  transition, 249
  stock distribution, 169

P

Pape–Dawson Consulting Engineers, Inc., 9
Partners, 224–227
Parnterships:
  disadvantages of, 225
  improving, 226–227
Part-time:
  employees, benefits, 162
  and flex time, 46
  workers, 146
Patton, General George, 8
Pay raises:
  as motivation for design professionals, 164
  timing, 164
Payroll, reporting, 208
Peer:
  associations, 232
  competing with, 249
  review, 124
  Review Program Manual, ACEC, 125
Penalty fee, late, 218
People skills, importance of, 142, 143
Perfection, excess, 125

Performance, 104
  appraisal, criteria, 35
  criteria, 149–150
  expectations, 97
  level of, 117
  oriented job descriptions, 35,
    36–37
  review, 38–45, 165
  standards of, 149–150
Performers, top:
  developing from within, 140–
    141
  top, traits, 141–142
Persistence, 65
Personality traits, importance of,
  142
Personnel, 137–156
Pierce, Ralph, Harley, Ellington,
  Pierce & Yee, 158–159
Plan:
  financial, 23–25
  strategic, elements of, 13
Planning:
  financial, 179
  importance of, 5
  leader, picking a, 51
  meeting, conducting a, 49–53
  process, 12–13
    repeating, 53
  session, scheduling, 53
  strategy, 5–60
Pollock, Wilson, 65
Position(s):
  announcing, 143
  planning, 34–35
Postoccupancy evaluation, 124
Postproject services, 71
Practice:
  business-centered, 108
  centered business, 108
  mix, 91
Predesign stage, 118
Prepayment, 217
Preproject approval, 71
Price:
  client objections to, 98
  competitive marketing, 169–170
  right, 200
Pride, 250
Principal(s), 247
  insurance coverage, as a benefit,
  162

  salesman, 94
Probation period, for employment,
  149
Problems, 110
Productivity, 203
  and CADD, 234
Product life cycle, 250
Professional Service Industries,
  motivation, 157
Professional/technical growth,
  162
Profit, 178, 194, 196–197
  analysis, by market, 204–206
  annual, 204
  center, management, 24
  goals, 179
  loss:
    measuring, 194, 196
    statement, 69
      sample, 70
  plan, company, 197
  project, 199–204
  sharing, 168, 206
  typical for firms, 25–26
Profitability, 91, 205
  affected by extras, 211
  vs. awardability, 233
  analysis, 204
  project, 207
    improving, 201
Profit center, 205–206
  managers, 205–206
Pro forma annual statement:
  calculating, 184
  example, 184
Program, planners, 69
Programming, 123
Programs, quality-control, 105
Project(s):
  bonuses, 167–168
  choosing, 8
  delaying, 77
  delivery, tasks, 117
  documentation, 105
  getting principals involved,
    191
  managers, 97
    as salesmen, 95, 221–222
  performance, targeting, 105
  profit, 199–204
  profitability, 196, 207
    improving, 201

Project(s) (*Continued*)
  progress, 105
  services, 71
  team, client objections, 98
Proposals, 119–120
  checklist, 120
  clients, 119
  submitted, 91
Publications, 81
  Economic Research Council, 21
Publicity, 220
Public relations, 89
Publishing:
  advantages of, 66
  book, 81
  newsletter, 81
Pull-through demand techniques, 75
Purpose, importance of defining, 61

Q

Quality:
  assurance system, (QC/QA), 231
  client objections to, 98
  company, standard, 126
  services, sample plan, 56
  standards, 117, 203
Quality control, 28, 111, 117–118
  actual work, 120
  advice, 214
  circles, guidelines for, 125
  current methods, 124
  definition of, 117
  job site, 71
  litigation, 111
  program, 105, 118
    how to set up, 118–119
  staff control, 126
  tips, 128
Quarterly bonuses, 169
Questions, to ask employees, 165

R

Raises, 166
  pay, timing, 164
Ratio, of accounts receivable turnover, average, 191–192
R.C. Byce & Associates:
  benefits, 163

market-focused team approach, 29
Realization budget, 185, 187
  example, 182
Receivables,179
  turnover, 201–202
Recordkeeping, 46
Records, management, 117
Recruitment, attracting good people from competitors, 33
Recycling old buildings, 70
Referrals, 76–77
  employee, 143
Reimbursables, back-up for, 219
Relocation, willingness to, 164
Rent *vs.* buy decisions, capital expenditures, 197–198
Repeat work and clients, 91
Report, marketing call, sample, 100
Reporting:
  financial, 197
  no-paper, 206
Research and development, 96–97
Residential kitchen interiors, 70
Responsiveness 110–111
Restart fee, 217
Revenue:
  gross, 204
  projection, fiscal year, typical, example, 186
Review, peer, 124
Reward, 142
R.G. Vanderweil Engineers, 178
  incentive plans, 166
Roundtable, discussion, for networking, 68
Royalty, clause, 220

S

Salary, 166
  dollars, 167
  employees, 164
  levels, 171
  owners, 164
  seeking new position, 162
  spread between owners and employees, 164
  target, 149
Sales:
  expectations, in writing, 97

face-to-face, 96
skills, 94
telephone, 97
Salesman, qualities of, 96
San Diego Transcript, 273
Schedule, 71, 103–104, 116, 119,
214
client, 128
objections to, 98
project, 105
shortening, 191
Schmidt Associates Architects, 35,
177
career planning:
pathing model, 172–173
tracking, 171–173
hiring, 138
performance review, 38–45
Scope, 178, 203
of work, for employees, 165–
166
Scott Companies Architects, 15,
17, 106, 232
services, 109
Securing finances, 71
Selecting an associate, rules of eligibility, 48
Selectiveness:
Backen, Arrigoni and Ross, 78
Henderson Group, 76–77
Self *vs.* company, 247
Selling:
books on, 95
clarification of, 94
employees, 93–96
nonpressure, 72
particular projects, 91
project manager, 221–222
techniques, 94
Seminars, 81
to spread company name recognition, 86
Toby Nadel, 86
Service, 134
areas, 71
client, 103–135
vs. design, 106–110
exporting, 72
focus on, 222
good *vs.* bad, 103
providing outstanding, 105–106,
110–111

Scott Companies, 109
sells, 103
Services:
client, 55
scope of, 214
Shared values, 19
Sharing:
financial information, 208
profits, 206
Short-staffed, 146
Simplify, financial planning, 179
Sirrine Engineers, 177
Size of staff method, budgeting,
180–185
Skidmore Owings & Merrill, large
firm marketing, 19
Small:
businesses, dealing with portion
of larger project, 69
business persons, 146
definition of, 3
entrepreneurships, 1
firms:
ability to move quickly into
new markets, 62
benefits of, 243–244
Small Business Exchange, 273
Smith, Seckman, and Reed, 29–30
SOP, 229
Specialist, dangers of presenting,
119
Staff:
fiscal, utilization budget, 186
hiring, 213
involvement, in marketing plan,
22
overhead, 191
quality control, 126
resources, 179
respect, 224
turnover, 198
Staffing:
plans, 179
recruitment, 33–34
Standards, of performance, 149–
159
Standing out, 126
Stanley engineers, dictionaries, 72
Star:
driven firms, 47
focused firms, 247–248
Start-up, 123

Statistics, seminar attendee, 281–285

Staying Small Successfully, seminar attendee statistics, 282–285

Stock, as a bonus, 168–169

Stop work, to collect payment, 192

Strategic market position, assessment, 6

Strategic plan, 251
  adding departments, effect on focus, 30
  concepts of, 6
  meeting, conducting a, 49–53
  outlining, 6
  sample, 55–59
  six elements of, 50
  typical, 53–59

Strategies, 250

Strategy and planning, 5–60

Strong:
  delivery (procedure) firms, 107
  idea (brains) firms, 107
  service (gray hair) firms, 107

Structural, requirements, quality control, 130

Student and team employment, 46

Subcontract, 191

Substitutions, 123

Success:
  definition of, 3, 250–251
  do's and don'ts, 211–237
  ensuring, 251
  motivators for, 5

Summerlin Associates, Inc., networking, 67

Surveys, 81

Swim With the Sharks Without Being Eaten Alive, H. Mackay, 111

T

Talent, 240

Targeting clients, not projects, 64

Tasks, delegation of, 144–148

Team:
  client objections to, 98
  member, reorientation, 218
  student employment, 46

Technical people, as salespeople, 94–95

Telephone:
  car, 110
  contacts, how to prepare for, 99
  numbers, 110
  portable, 128
  sales calls, schedule for making, 98
  service, 108
  skills, 97

Textbook, 72

Thomas Wirth:
  Landscape Architects, focus, 62
  profile, 63

Time:
  management, 92
  record, sample, 193
  schedules, 179

TMOTWH, 141

Top down, budgeting method, 178–179

Top performers:
  bonus as, 168
  developing from within, 140–141
  how to meet top competitors, 140
  traits, 141–142

Tracking, career, 170–174

Tradition, relinquishing, 223–224

Traditional:
  practices, going beyond, 164
  work, 211

Training, and career planning, 35

Transition, ownership, 249

Trends of the ratios, 201

Turner, Ted, Vision, 6

Twofers, job swap, 141

U

UNIFORMAT, 46

Unprofitable projects, 200

Upfront services, 71

Usefulness selling, 72–76
  campaign, building of, 75

Utilization ratio, 188–191
  controlling, through time cards, 192
  increasing, 190

V

Vacation time, as a bonus, 168
Value engineering programs, 71
Vanderweil Engineers, hiring, 137
Visibility, 66
Vision, 250
    Bergmeyer, Moritz, 9–10
    defining your own, 8
    emulating a model, 10
    Kohn, Pedersen, Fox, 6–8
    Meehan Architects, 7
    need for, 6–12
    one sentence, 251
    statements, sample, 15
    Turner, Ted, 6
    written, 12–13
Volunteer, 66

W

Waterproofing, 133

Whitaker, Patricia, 68
Winning, the psychology of, 247–250
Work:
    ethic, in performance, 174
    in-process, 201–202
        turnover, 10 days, 194
    schedules and childcare, 46
    traditional, 211
Working drawings, 104
Write-offs, 183

Y

Yacht design, 70
Yellow pages, 88

Z

Zilm, Frank, newsletter, 72
Zoning ordinance, checklist, 132